The Greek
Political Experience

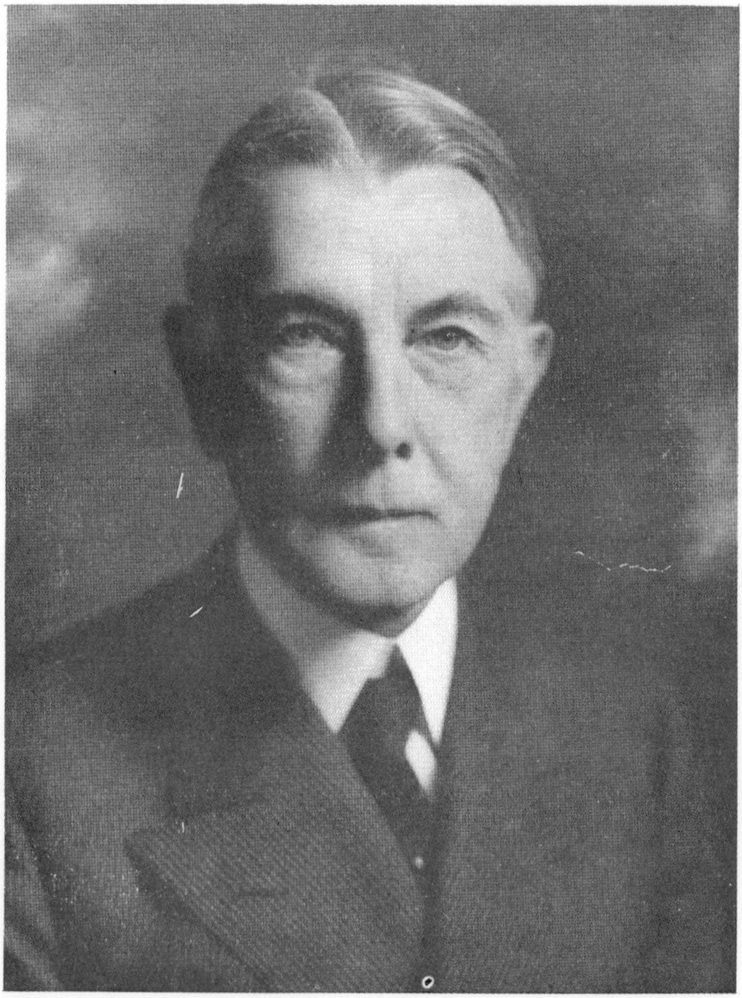

The Greek Political Experience

*Studies in Honor of
William Kelly Prentice*

NEW YORK / RUSSELL & RUSSELL

COPYRIGHT, 1941, BY PRINCETON UNIVERSITY PRESS
REISSUED, 1969, BY RUSSELL & RUSSELL
A DIVISION OF ATHENEUM PUBLISHERS, INC.
BY ARRANGEMENT WITH PRINCETON UNIVERSITY PRESS
L. C. CATALOG CARD NO: 68-27081
PRINTED IN THE UNITED STATES OF AMERICA

199859

GVILIELMO KELLY PRENTICE
INVESTIGATORI RERVM GRAECARVM DOCTISSIMO
NATALEM AGENTI SEPTVAGESIMVM
HOC OPVSCVLVM
AMICI ATQVE ALVMNI
D.D.D.

DIE XXVIII MENSIS OCTOBRIS ANNI MCMXLI

PREFACE

In presenting this volume to William Kelly Prentice, Ewing Professor of Greek Languages and Literature, Emeritus, in Princeton University, we thank his friends and classmates who generously supported this undertaking and his students and associates for their scholarly collaboration.

The former Director of Princeton University Press, Joseph A. Brandt, contributed the suggestion that this *Festschrift* would have greater value if the individual studies were planned about a central theme. To him and to his staff we express our appreciation of their unfailing courtesy throughout the progress of this work.

A.C.J.
N.T.P., JR.
P.R.C-N.

CONTENTS

I. The People and the Value of Their Experience
NORMAN T. PRATT, JR.
page 3

II. From Kingship to Democracy
J. PENROSE HARLAND
page 14

III. Democracy at Athens
GEORGE M. HARPER, JR.
page 36

IV. Athens and the Delian League
B. D. MERITT
page 50

V. Socialism at Sparta
P. R. COLEMAN-NORTON
page 61

VI. Tyranny
MALCOLM MAC LAREN, JR.
page 78

VII. Federal Unions
CHARLES ALEXANDER ROBINSON, JR.
page 93

VIII. Alexander and the World-State
O. W. REINMUTH
page 109

IX. The Antigonids
JOHN V. A. FINE
page 125

X. Ptolemaic Egypt: A Planned Economy
SHERMAN LEROY WALLACE
page 147

CONTENTS

XI. The Seleucids: The Theory of Monarchy
GLANVILLE DOWNEY
page 162

XII. The Political Status of the Independent Cities of Asia Minor in the Hellenistic Period
DAVID MAGIE
page 173

XIII. The Ideal States of Plato and Aristotle
WHITNEY J. OATES
page 187

XIV. Epilogue
ALLAN CHESTER JOHNSON
page 214

Bibliography
page 225

Index
HOLMES V. M. DENNIS, III
page 237

LIST OF MAPS

Greece
after page 60

The Hellenistic Kingdoms
after page 108

Asia Minor
after page 172

The Greek
Political Experience

I. THE PEOPLE AND THE VALUE OF THEIR EXPERIENCE

BY NORMAN T. PRATT, JR.

THE political experience of the Greeks was prodigious. It embraced the origins of most of the forms of government yet devised, many political experiments and programs, many failures and many successes; these all can be observed in a continuous development over a long period of time. It therefore affords rich material in which to analyze and appraise social efforts. Furthermore, wherever evidence is sufficient for ascertaining the relevant facts, fundamental issues emerge clearly because of the intensity with which the Greeks acted and the directness of their historical records. Phenomena are rendered the more observable by the relatively small scale of the political stage. However, within the limit of this smaller scale of activity the complication was great: the geographical compactness of the Mediterranean basin made the international relations complex; to these another set of "international" relations was added because every Greek city was essentially an independent nation in respect to both internal composition and foreign policy.

For full understanding and appreciation of this complexity it is imperative to consider briefly the Greek land and its people or, more precisely, the various ancient peoples who occupied the Balkan peninsula in prehistorical and historical times. These matters are noteworthy not merely because they illuminate the understanding of historical phenomena in Greece: they also bear no little significance in themselves and, in larger reference, constitute a means of penetrating more deeply the distinctive value inherent in what the Greeks thought and did politically.

The historical Greeks were exceedingly conscious and proud of being Greeks, of their relative community of race, language, religion and manners. Even stronger, however, and symptomatic of the diversity and particularity of these peoples was the consciousness of their individual "nationalities," of their homogeneity within the individual city-states. This feeling was sometimes embodied in the notion of autochthony, the belief that the historical occupants of a territory were indigenous, were, in the literal meaning of the Greek word, "sprung from the land itself." The ancient literature, chiefly of Athenian provenience, has associated this conception particularly with that people. One of the more nationalistic minds of Athens, the orator Isocrates, has expressed it in a most extreme and chauvinistic form (*Panathenaicus*, 124-5): "For our ancestors regulated both their own affairs and those of the city as piously and nobly as befitted those who were born from the gods, who first inhabited a city and adopted laws and who always practised reverence toward the gods and justice toward men, being neither of diverse origin nor immigrant, but alone of the Greeks autochthonous. . . ." Noteworthy in this quotation is the fusion of race-theory and religion, especially in the modern era when, in despite of extensive knowledge concerning race-diffusion, etc., such as ancients like the Athenians never enjoyed, men continue to invest theories of race with a faith which resembles and often supplants or perverts religious faith.[1] Whatever the facts may be concerning the origin of the Athenians and the other historical Greeks—and very much still remains to be established—it is abundantly clear at least that the Athenian view expressed by Isocrates typifies the inaccuracy, if not the conscious misrepresentation, which is characteristic of most such nationalistic claims.

In the half-light of present knowledge it is possible to say with virtual certainty only that the historical Greeks were an amalgam of several racial strains. There is some agreement among scholars that the strains were three in number, but it is really impossible to speak so specifically. There are, in fact, no decisive ethnographic criteria extant from prehistoric antiquity; even where differences of culture and language are discernible, these do not necessarily involve racial differences. It is possible, however, from the available

---

[1] On this point the following sentence is written by A. J. Toynbee, *A Study of History* (2nd ed.; Oxford, 1935), vol. I, p. 216: "The most popular of the idols that have been set up by this rather priggish and pedantic school of superstition is 'Nordic Man': the xanthotrichous, glaucopian, dolichocephalic variety of *Homo Leucodermaticus* whose pet name (given him by Nietzsche) is 'the Blond Beast'."

THE PEOPLE AND THEIR EXPERIENCE

evidence to delineate the main course of development with a fair degree of probability.

In the Neolithic Period, which may be regarded generally as terminating early in the third millennium before Christ, the Greek mainland, a large part of Asia Minor and the islands were occupied by pre-Hellenic, non-Greek-speaking peoples. There is some slight linguistic evidence that these Neolithic folk, whom the Greeks later called "Pelasgians," may have been related in language, but it is impossible to determine their racial affinities. Probably racial purity disappeared from among them long before the earliest period of pre-history of which cultural traces have survived. From this primitive world there gradually emerged in Crete the brilliant Minoan culture (so named from Minos, a half-legendary Cretan king), the influence of which was ultimately disseminated throughout most of the eastern Mediterranean. Of its truly extraordinary story it is possible to note only a few facts apposite to this brief survey. The Minoan civilization, which reached its greatest height in the first half of the second millennium, was sustained by naval power which controlled the surrounding waters; it was stimulated by eastern impulses, chiefly Egyptian. There is good evidence that this civilization was non-Greek: its religion manifests a close affinity with eastern religious conceptions; and the language, preserved in several thousands of documents but thus far undeciphered, is apparently not Greek.[2] From its height this Cretan culture passed through vicissitudes of which the most notable are the shifting of the center of civilization to the Greek mainland in the fifteenth century and the occupation of the island by Dorian Greeks at the close of the second millennium. To trace the course of this development we must turn to the mainland.

Here the tangle of data and theories becomes exceedingly intricate. The main problem consists in the racial implications of the mainland culture called Mycenaean because of the discovery by Heinrich

[2] The nature of the language is beginning to emerge; see M. G. F. Ventris, "Introducing the Minoan Language," in *American Journal of Archaeology*, vol. XLIV (1940), pp. 494-520. Ventris regards Minoan and Etruscan as "variants of a single 'Pelasgian' language" and concludes: "Once a single theoretical foundation has been agreed on, based solidly on factual evidence, the initial obstacles disappear, and it is only a matter of time before a full decipherment has been achieved. In the case of Minoan this is no idle wish. It can be done."

Schliemann of rich remains of that civilization in the Peloponnesian town of Mycenae. The nature of the racial development in the long period extending from early in the second millennium through the Mycenaean Age (1400-1200) may perhaps most accurately be described in the familiar image of a melting pot. Out of it a predominantly Greek order ultimately emerged through the fusion of the Neolithic non-Greeks with Indo-European newcomers from the north, a fusion fired by strong Minoan cultural influence which itself may have been accompanied by racial intermingling. Such is the picture evoked by the slight differences which obtain between the Minoan and the Mycenaean cultures and by the marked dissimilarities between Mycenaean and historical Greek in such respects as writing, burial practices and religion. Certainly the terms Mycenaean and Greek may not simply be equated; apparently the Mycenaean was a composite civilization. Historically the evolution seems to have taken the following course.

Sometime in the first half of the second millennium there began a long series of immigrations and incursions, preponderantly from the north, by vigorous tribes which were Indo-European at least in speech. Linguistically it is possible to distinguish among these peoples the non-Greeks who arrived earlier and settled to the north and the Greeks whose increasing numbers finally penetrated the Peloponnesus. Likewise we can recognize among the dialects of historical Greek three roughly homogeneous dialectal groups which may reflect the presence of disparate ethnic elements among these early Greek immigrants: the Attic-Ionic, Aeolic and Arcado-Cyprian or, as it may be called in reference to prehistoric times, Achaean. A highly developed civilization has the power to mould and transform other peoples, even though they are physically stronger, a phenomenon which reappears approximately 1,500 years later in the cultural victory of Greece over Rome. Even so these newcomers felt the touch of Minoan advancement and under this tutelage developed their own high culture in the sixteenth and fifteenth centuries. They became the dominant force when Crete dwindled and from their centers, chiefly in the Peloponnesus, spread their products widely around the Mediterranean basin.

A theory based upon several bits of evidence suggests that the Achaeans constituted the predominant group in the late Mycenaean world. This view, at least, accords well with the fact that in the Homeric epics, which are probably late Mycenaean in basic origin, the term "Achaeans" is generic for "Greeks." It seems significant also that the Arcado-Cyprian dialect group, regarded by linguists as the remnant of the speech of most of the Peloponnesus before the arrival of later Dorian Greek immigrants, in historical times was geographically the least extensive of the four groups; on the mainland it was restricted to mountainous, isolated Arcadia in the center of the Peloponnesus. From this it is reasonable to suppose that the Achaeans held the position of power which passed into the hands of the Dorians, bore the main shock of the turmoil caused by their arrival and were finally compressed and circumscribed in the interior of the territory which they previously occupied.

Be this as it may, it is affirmed both by ancient tradition and by modern archaeological and linguistic research that in the twelfth century additional Greek peoples crowded down from the northwest; among these were the Dorians who appropriated the Minoan and Mycenaean centers. The unrest attendant upon these tribal movements had two important consequences: cultural progress was apparently retarded during the so-called Middle Ages of Greece until the eighth century; and the Greeks began to expand eastward across the Aegean, thus initiating the process of migration and later, from the eighth into the sixth century, of colonization from Greece. This movement ultimately carried the Greeks throughout the islands of the Aegean and the western littoral of Asia Minor, along the coasts of Macedonia and Thrace, to the shores of the Black Sea, to Cyprus, northern Africa, the coast of Gaul, southern Italy and Sicily.

The dispersion of the various Greek folk will appear from a rough description of the geographical distribution of the three most extensive dialectal groups in historical times. Attic-Ionic has been shunted to Attica in the eastern section of the central mainland and to the island of Euboea nearby. It also extends across the Aegean, in an arc which embraces most of the Cyclades and the northern Sporades, to Samos and that part of the Asia Minor coast which is bent around Samos, and in the north to Chalcidice, the southern coast of Thrace and the shores of the Hellespont, Propontis and Black Sea. Aeolic appears in Lesbos, on the northern coastland of Asia Minor east of Lesbos and, with a considerable admixture of West Greek, in Thessaly and Boeotia of Greece proper. Finally, the most extensive group, West Greek (including Northwest Greek and Doric), covers most of central Greece, all the Peloponnesus except Arcadia, the arc formed by the islands Cythera, Crete, Carpathia and Rhodes (below the Attic-Ionic arc), part of the southwestern shore of Asia Minor, the southern Sporades and some of the southern Cyclades. Such is the complex result of the centuries of development.

The image of multiplicity and diversity evoked by the examination of the Greek peoples is sharpened by consideration of the significant features of their physical environment. Greek geography, despite its comparatively small scale, is characterized by variety resulting from the rugged, disjointed structure of the land. This lack of continuity produces relative isolation in the interior and great accessibility on the coastline. Largely because of this geographical setting, sectionalism within Greece and influences from without are frequently manifest in Greek history. On the one hand, although no peak save Olympus rises above 8,000 feet, the average altitude is high and the branching mountain systems, covering the far greater part of the mainland, form natural barriers. This impediment to internal communications is not palliated by navigable waterways, for most of the streams are dry beds except in the rainy winter season when they are torrential. The extreme example of isolation in Greece is, of course, the Peloponnesus whose relatively compact structure facilitated Spartan dominion; the geographically apt term "island" applied to it by the ancients is consonant with the insularity which characterizes its history. In contrast to this, the Greeks were brought near the sea by the irregularly serrated coastline which marks the whole Aegean basin, especially the eastern edge of Greece; activity on the sea was favored further by the mildness of the currents and by the regular alternation of the winds, both daily and seasonal.

In other respects as well, environmental conditions both compelled and facilitated the great activity of the Greeks. The mediocre natural

THE PEOPLE AND THEIR EXPERIENCE

resources of the country required persistent labor: only a small proportion of the land was arable and the heavy concentration of precipitation in the winter made both drainage and irrigation imperative. There was continual warfare against the encroachment of scrubland accelerated by the sharp contours of the land, the sweeping rains and deforestation. Agriculture was almost exclusively on the subsistence level. The grain supply was inadequate even though a major proportion of the arable land was devoted to the cultivation of wheat and, especially, barley. Only fruitgrowing, particularly vine and olive culture, was an enterprise which provided exports to compensate for the necessary imports of grain. This reliance upon import had, of course, an important effect upon foreign policy. On the other hand, the clear, generally dry atmosphere was conducive to the efforts of the Greeks which were necessitated by such deficiencies, to physical toil and to an inquisitive awareness of the conditions of their life. This interrelationship of poverty and riches appears clearly in the words which the historian Herodotus puts upon the lips of Demaratus the Spartan (vii. 102): "Poverty is ever natural to Greece, but nobility is the acquired fruit of wisdom and severe law; through nobility Greece repels poverty and despotism."

Great caution must be exercised, however, in the attempt to determine more closely the function of these racial and environmental factors. Certainly neither environmental determinism nor racial determinism nor even a combination of the two provides a wholly adequate explanation of the Greek experience. It is important to examine this question, even though briefly, especially in regard to the concept of race, about which many inaccurate and perilous conclusions are ever current. In the first place, rarely does racial homogeneity among a whole people reach such a high level that strict racial terms can be applied in the analysis of phenomena; there was no such homogeneity among the Greeks. Nor is it known how consistently the influence of race operates. It is known, however, that this influence is no law unto itself; clearly there is close interaction between race and environment. And, finally, great complication is introduced by the factor of human action, a conglomerate of individual qualitative differences only partially accountable in terms of blood and habitat. Even so, of course, the factors of race and environment are very important. In summary it will suffice to emphasize that undoubtedly they contributed largely to the abundant alacrity, enterprise and creativeness of the Greeks and to their heterogeneity.

Largely as a consequence of this heterogeneity and the particularism which it bred, the ancient Greeks were never able to achieve real Panhellenic unity. This matter will receive close analysis in the succeeding chapters. It is introduced here only as a prominent manifestation in Greek history of a phenomenon which emerges clearly in the study of the past, that is, the high incidence of failure.

Failure has, of course, the important negative value of a warning. There is a common tendency, however, to extend this function beyond its proper limit, to regard the past as absolute prophecy of the future. Thus historical research commonly produces cynicism, often expressed in the view that "every generation will commit its own errors." This conception is very vulnerable to attack. Many would affirm that such cynicism is the equivalent of defeatism, because it defines inadequately the human spirit as this is widely felt by men and has been historically manifested in men. Only upon the opposite premise, that despite many conflicts the impulse to apprehend and to ameliorate is basic to that spirit, can we meaningfully explore this complex matter as it bears upon the function and scope of historical inquiry. This attempt is especially pertinent since the most significant Greek contributions will perhaps thus most clearly emerge.

The necessity of historical inquiry may be illustrated by a closer examination of the view that "every generation will commit its own errors." An important amendment must be made. Because of the great dependence of the present upon the past, to a considerable degree "every generation *can not* commit its own errors." That is, through various media the individual from birth is gradually initiated into the whole system of institutions and ideas inherited from his predecessors. This continuous process operates both for advantage and for detriment. It preserves what is valuable in past achievement and also what is unworthy in past achievement. In the latter respect it tends to inculcate a resistance to change which, if stubbornly and uncritically maintained, produces violent reaction and conflict. Man thus inherits error.

Clearly, therefore, the first requisite for advancement is a full understanding of the present. But this understanding can be achieved only with reference to the past, not merely the immediate but the distant past, the influence of which is well illustrated by the large contribution of the Greeks to Western European culture. Indeed, the influence of antiquity requires closer analysis than that of the immediate past. Paradoxical though it may seem, antiquity lies in a real sense closer to the core of the present. Because of their primary concern with the inner nature rather than the appurtenances of human life the ancients formulated first principles which, preserved through the centuries, have fundamentally shaped human thought and action—and continue so to do. Largely for the very reason that this influence is so basic, it tends to become obscured and unexamined. Historical inquiry re-examines the past to provide understanding of the present.

On the other hand, a serious limitation of historical inquiry, narrowly conceived, has emerged from the very statement of the reasons which necessitate such re-examination. We have observed that the dependence of the present upon the past effects the preservation of "what is valuable in past achievement and also what is unworthy in past achievement." The process of re-examination thus has two primary aspects: historical analysis for the determination of what is fact and critical appraisal for the determination of "what is valuable" and "what is unworthy." Historical fact expresses, but does not constitute, value or its lack. Then what are to be the standards to which historical fact is to be referred, against which it is to be critically evaluated? If these are to have any real validity, they must be formulated by scrutinizing and testing the values which have been conceived by men or revealed to them. Two sources which must be consulted in any adequate formulation of standards are Hebraism with its religious conception and Hellenism with its conception of man; it was in the fusion of these two complementary conceptions that Matthew Arnold found his "best that is known and thought in the world."[3] Certainly there is much to be derived from the past in

---

[3] As in *Culture and Anarchy*; the quotation is from *Essays in Criticism, First Series*, "The Function of Criticism at the Present Time." R. W. Livingstone, *Greek Ideals and Modern*

its dual role as a major determinant of the present and, more largely considered, as a rich body of experience, but only through the conjunction of historical analysis and critical appraisal in the re-examination of the past is it finally possible to achieve the perspective and insight which are required for real human advancement.

To this end Greek experience, at its best, makes a final contribution in the crucial sphere of interplay between practice and theory. These people are unique in that they tended not to distinguish between the provinces of thought and of action and, as a corollary, they possessed to an unusual degree the impulse to actualize what they considered to be valuable. They therefore offer challenging testimony in support of the utility and practicability of theory. Two Platonic dialogues, the *Apology* and the *Crito*, written concerning the trial and imprisonment of Socrates, provide a familiar illustration of this point. In the first, Plato presents a version of what Socrates said in defence against the charge "of corrupting the youth and not believing in the city's gods, but in other religious practices." In response to his accusers Socrates explains the origin of the prejudice against him and of the misunderstanding of his philosophical purpose, ridicules his official accuser and the indictment, defends his whole career, especially his effort, in some sense divinely sanctioned, to stimulate in his contemporaries the realization of their inadequacies, and, finally, expresses his refusal to compromise. The *Crito* is so named for Socrates' unphilosophic friend, who comes to the prison at dawn to inform Socrates that the time for his execution is near and to urge upon him the expedient of escape, for which arrangement can be made. The core of Socrates' reply consists in upholding the binding validity of his compact with the laws of his city. His execution followed.

Socrates, threatened as he was by a debased democracy acting in a spirit of recrimination after national disaster, thus affirmed two principles which, through his example, were adopted by Plato as the basis of his political theory and which are, indeed, basic to democracy itself: in the *Apology*, that the individual must have freedom for the realization of his worth; in the *Crito*, that this free-

Life (Cambridge, 1935), presents a forceful analysis of the complementary nature and value of Hebraism and Hellenism.

dom must be controlled if it is not to degenerate into irresponsible individualism. In the *Apology*, after his condemnation to death, Socrates thus concludes some informal remarks to the jury: "So much I ask of those who voted against me: when my sons come to maturity, punish them too, gentlemen, causing them this same pain which I inflicted upon you, if they seem to you to be more concerned either for money or for anything else than for virtue and, if they think that they are something when they are nothing, reproach them, even as I do you, because they do not care for what they should and think they are something although they are nothing worth. And if you do this, I shall have received justice at your hands, yes, and my sons too.

"But enough: it is now time to go away, me to die and you to live; and which of us go to the better thing is concealed from everyone except god."

II. FROM KINGSHIP TO DEMOCRACY

BY J. PENROSE HARLAND

MONARCHY, aristocracy, oligarchy, timocracy, plutocracy, tyranny, autocracy, despotism, anarchy, democracy, politics are all Greek words and by themselves show the imprint which the ancient Hellenes have left upon this phase of our modern civilization. But it is more than a matter of terms. The Hellenes seem to have been the first to develop, if not to invent, most of the forms of government mentioned above. Before the rise of Hellenic or Greek civilization only monarchy, autocracy and despotism may be said to have appeared among the peoples of the world.

Pausanias says that "kingdoms were everywhere established in Hellas of old" and much earlier the historian Thucydides had stated that the Hellenes "had hitherto been ruled by hereditary kings, having fixed prerogatives." These statements may be applicable to most peoples after they have passed from the primitive status of isolated family life and have come to live in communities or in association with other families. The kingship was doubtless in vogue throughout Hellas in early times. Presumably in the Neolithic Age (before 3000) the different communities or districts in Hellas had their respective kings or chieftains or whatever they may have been called.

In the first period of the Bronze Age—the Early Helladic Period (*ca.* 3000-2000)—there is at least indirect evidence of the kingship in Hellas. The presence in a settlement of a house, larger and of richer content than the others, suggests that the owner may have acquired this apparent superiority in material possessions by reason of his superior position in the community. In this period the term *basileus* (king) may have been introduced into Hellas. Basileus does not seem to be a Greek word and, since it is presumably non-Hellenic, it may well be pre-Hellenic. If so, its introduction may possibly be associated with those Early Helladic peoples who migrated from Asia Minor

FROM KINGSHIP TO DEMOCRACY

across to the Aegean islands and the Helladic mainland in the early part of the third millennium.

About 2000 the first people of Hellenic stock entered the southern part of the Balkan peninsula and introduced the Middle Helladic civilization which, with a later leavening from Minoan Crete, was dominant on the mainland down to *ca.* 1400. The "Minyans"—as it is convenient to label these Middle Helladic people—were doubtless ruled by kings, to judge by the rich contents of the Shaft Graves at Mycenae (*ca.* 1700-1500). Such wealth and artistry must be associated with a royal dynasty in this early time. The title of the various local rulers in this period is unknown, but the term basileus may have been in use. If it had not been taken over along with other non-Hellenic words from the previous population, now subject or assimilated, it might have been acquired from association with the Minoans of Crete or with the Islanders.

The Middle Helladic civilization was more or less uniform throughout Hellas, even if not so richly represented elsewhere as at Mycenae "rich-in-gold." Of course uniformity of culture does not necessarily imply racial similarity, but kingship is not peculiar to any one race or tribe and may well have been common to the Minyans of Attica as well as to those of the Argolid. Furthermore, what will be said below concerning the Homeric or epic evidence of kingship in the Late Bronze Age may also be applicable to this preceding period. There seems to have been no ethnic break between Middle and Late Helladic.

The Late Helladic Period (*ca.* 1400-1150), the so-called Mycenaean Age, *par excellence*, saw the peoples of Hellas attain a height in culture that was not to be surpassed until the classical Greek civilization of the sixth and following centuries.

That kings ruled the various tribes or separate localities throughout Hellas in this last period of the Bronze Age is indicated by both archaeological and literary evidence. The remains of the great Cyclopean fortification walls, palaces, roads and especially the great and elaborate *tholos* or beehive tombs attest not only an advanced state of culture but also the institution of kingship. None but kings could have appropriated for their families and retainers such fortified *acropoleis* as at Mycenae, Tiryns, Thebes and Athens. Though these citadels might serve as places of refuge for the people who dwelt below and in the country around, still they seem to have been given over to the kings for their private and official use. The tholos tombs, by reason of their size, remarkable construction and wealth of contents, can only have been the burial places of royalty. The Treasury of Atreus may not have been the tomb of Agamemnon, but it was certainly the sepulchre of a king of the fourteenth century. We may therefore be justified in assigning the title of basileus to the ruler in this period.

In addition to the deduction drawn from archaeology, there is in the Homeric epics evidence for the rule of kings during the Late Bronze Age. The civilization depicted in these poems is for the most part that of the Late Helladic Period. As Nilsson has clearly shown, the political system set forth in the Homeric epos is essentially Mycenaean and reflects the conditions of this age rather than that of the later Geometric Age when the poems were probably put into writing. The conception of Zeus as king of the gods ruling on Mt. Olympus is most likely to have arisen when an earthly king ruled over his people, enthroned in a magnificent palace situated on a well-fortified citadel, and this was the case in the Late Helladic Period. And it is to this Mycenaean Age that we may logically refer the already-quoted statements of Thucydides and Pausanias about kings in early Hellas. Aristotle, drawing doubtless from the Homeric poems, describes the rule in the Heroic Age as a "hereditary legal kingship over willing subjects." And he adds, "these kings used to come to the throne with the consent of the subjects and hand it on to their successors by lineal descent. And they had supreme command in war and control over all sacrifices ... and ... they were judges in lawsuits."

As time went on, the king's power seems gradually to have become more limited and in some parts of the epos he appears more or less in the status of *primus inter pares*. In war the nobles served as vassals and the king was their ruler, but in times of peace there was nothing to prevent the nobles from rising to power and they became virtual kings over their own domains. The kingship admitted of degrees, as Zimmern phrases it in his *Greek Commonwealth*. Thus we can understand the existence of the fortified sites, palaces and royal tombs at Midea and Tiryns, situated between Mycenae and the sea. The king at Mycenae must have held sway over the minor kings during the great period of that famous site. To judge by the *Odyssey*, which may reflect somewhat later conditions than the *Iliad*, the power of the kings gradually diminished and some nobles became lesser kings.

Another institution of the Late Helladic state was the Council of Elders, of which there is evidence in the epos. Whether this body of advisers arose as a result of the wish of the king or—and this is more probable—because of pressure brought to bear by the leading families cannot of course be ascertained, but it became the practice for the king to consult with this advisory board. This Council of Elders appears to have become an accepted constitutional element in the Late Helladic state and it is important in the study of political science as the precursor of such bodies as the *gerousia* at Sparta and the Council of the Areopagus at Athens.

Another constitutional form comes into being in the Late Bronze Age, as we also learn from the *Iliad*, and that is the Assembly of the People. It consisted of men capable of providing and bearing arms, but it possessed no real political power. Rather it had the privilege of hearing the king present his plans and of voicing its approval or disapproval. The king could and did act despite the Assembly's disapproval at times, as we infer from the account of Agamemnon's refusal to heed the wishes of this body when it loudly supported Chryses in the latter's desire to ransom his daughter. That the commons could express their opposition to the king is illustrated perhaps by the oft-cited episode of Thersites. However lacking it may have been in power in this early age, this Late Helladic Assembly was the first actual step in the direction of democracy and it was destined to be the forerunner of the popular assemblies of later times, notably the *ekklesia* at Athens and its modern descendants.

In a large and highly developed state some assistance must have been given to the king and among his retainers who lived on the *acropolis* there were doubtless officials whose titles and duties may well have survived into classical times. As an example one might suggest the *kolakretai* (the collectors of the pieces at a sacrifice), whom we meet later as financial officials. But whether or not there was a major official beside the king in the Late Helladic polity is a debatable point. There is no direct evidence of such in the Homeric poems. The legend that Ion, who came to the aid of the Athenian king Erechtheus in the war against Eleusis, became the first polemarch (war-leader) merely indicates that this office was a very old one. Aristotle dates the institution of the polemarchy before that of the archonship and, since the first archon was appointed after the reign of the last king (Codrus), clearly he was of the opinion that the polemarch was an official during the period of the kingship. The polemarch was "added because some of the kings proved cowardly in warfare," says Aristotle. Because no mention is made of this official in the epos, one might assign the introduction of the polemarchy to the period after the Dorian invasion and end of the Bronze Age but before the institution of the lifelong archons. This period would correspond to the Post-Helladic and early Proto-Geometric periods (*ca.* 1150-1050), when we may assume with some reason that the kings were becoming weaker as the nobles increased in strength and prestige. Incidentally, the death of the last king Codrus is dated *ca.* 1068, a manufactured date, to be sure, but still one that may have historical value.

The monarchical form of government in Hellas on the whole survived the Dorian invasion (*ca.* 1150), but it underwent changes in some regions and disappeared entirely in others. In Argos the kingship lasted into the early fifth century, in Sparta till the end of the third. It survived even later in Macedonia and in those regions, such as Aetolia and Epirus, where the geographical situation retarded cultural development. But these historical kings do not appear to have had the wealth or power to construct such splendid palaces and elaborate tombs as did those of the Bronze Age.

The reasons for the disappearance and the weakening of the power of the kings cannot be treated adequately in this chapter, but it is clear that economic factors as well as political conditions entered into the evolution or, as in some places, the revolution that effected the transition from the Late Helladic kingship to aristocracy or oligarchy. The decrease in the material wealth and power of the king, which had already begun before the Dorian invasion—to judge by the *Iliad* and still more by the *Odyssey*—was accompanied by the rise of some of the noble families. Though the king may have received a royal domain and the greater share of booty, yet he also had to support the royal, official establishment and retainers and divide his land among his heirs. Then, too, at his death considerable wealth was removed from this earth by the accustomed royal funerary equipment and paraphernalia. On the other hand, some nobles were gaining wealth and power through trade (a euphemism for catttle-raiding and piracy, in many cases) and by receiving under their protection the people unable to provide themselves with arms and armor.

As often happened in Egypt, a period of chaos might give the nobles the opportunity to contend among themselves and also with the royal house for the supremacy. A noble might set himself up as king, but since he lacked the hereditary right to the royal scepter he in turn was liable to be displaced by a stronger noble. But the various kingdoms fared in various ways. At Sparta one powerful family, the Eurypontids, was able to demand co-regency with the royal house of the Agids and henceforth Sparta had two kings. At Athens, it would seem, the kingship disappeared only gradually.

This study may now well be limited to one representative state and Athens is the obvious choice. Almost every form of government was devised or experienced by the early Athenians and, besides, there has been preserved from antiquity more information about Athens than about any other Hellenic state. Aside from the material found in the historians (notably Herodotus and Thucydides) and in other writings, particular attention should be called to two works of Aristotle, *The Constitution of the Athenians* and *The Politics*. The last two treatises, written in the second half of the fourth century, were based largely upon a scientific study of sources now lost. However, one must not expect to find the great scientist in his political works purely objective and unprejudiced by his pro-oligarchical feelings.

Aristotle's statement that "the Athenians originally had a royal government" is, in the light of our other evidence, applicable at least to the last part of the Bronze Age. The Neolithic people, who have left their traces on the northwest slope of the Acropolis and elsewhere around Athens, may have had a king and, as suggested above, the Early Helladic inhabitants in Attica and at Athens may even have used the term basileus as the title for their rulers. The

Middle Helladic civilization (*ca.* 2000-1400) is well represented in Attica, even if not so richly as at Mycenae, and these Minyans may likewise have had their *basileis* at Athens and at other Attic sites.

Despite the fact that the Athenians are rarely mentioned in the Homeric poems, Athens was a flourishing state in the Late Helladic or Mycenaean Period (*ca.* 1400-1150). The scanty references to Athens in the *Iliad* (in the Catalogue of Ships) and in the *Odyssey* are probably later interpolations and mark the attempt of the Athenians to gain a place in the glorious past of Hellas.

However, the great Cyclopean wall atop the Acropolis and the remains of the palace and other buildings which this wall encloses, the Mycenaean tomb discovered in 1939 at the south end of the Agora and numerous other finds attest to the greatness of Athens in the Late Bronze Age. The tombs and other remains at Menidi, Thoricus, Eleusis and other sites show that Attica must be reckoned along with the Argolid and Boeotia as an important region of Mycenaean culture. Therefore, it seems permissible to hypothesize for Late Helladic Athens the same constitutional organization as that indicated by the Homeric epos for the Argolid and elsewhere.

Moreover, for Athens we have a legendary list of seventeen kings, from Cecrops to Codrus. Of course some of these kings were doubtless gods originally and some may be purely the figment of the later chronographers, but there may be an historical kernel at the base of some of the figures. At any rate, the very existence of such a tradition argues for the rule of kings in early Athens. It is interesting to note that the dates of the kings, which may be derived from the Parian Marble and from Eusebius, Castor and others, though manufactured, do cover the Late Bronze Age as well as the periods immediately preceding and following, namely from *ca.* 1556 to *ca.* 1068. When we consider that the supposedly "made" dates for the fall of Troy (1209 and 1184) and for the Dorian invasion (1104) come within a decade or two of the approximate dates for these events as indicated by the archaeological evidence, one may wonder if the early chronographers did not have more evidence before them than some scholars have been willing to admit.

A word or two must be said about Theseus, who seems at least semilegendary, even semimythical, by reason of his "labors" and his associations in mythology. But Thucydides treats him as an historical personage, a king who improved the administration of the state and brought about the union of the different communities of Attica. Aristotle also credits Theseus with the first change or reform in the Athenian constitution. The Parian Marble continues this tradition and credits King Theseus with establishing the democracy at Athens. Still earlier, on a wall of the Stoa Poikile at Athens, there was a painting of Theseus, Democracy and the Demos and Pausanias adds that Theseus is supposed to have bestowed sovereignty upon the people and that from this time the Athenians continued under a democratic government until the time of Peisistratus. Theseus is dated by the Parian Marble and the chronographers *ca.* 1259 and 1234 respectively, that is, in the Late Helladic Period.

There may have been a king named Theseus and he may well have reigned in the thirteenth century, but one may question the historicity of his constitutional measures. The presence of the Assembly, evidenced in the Homeric epos, and even its participation in the affairs of state may be implied in these traditions. Even a union of several communities or minor states may have been effected by a king of Attica in the Late Bronze Age, but, of course, the number twelve is too suspicious to be taken literally. However, it is too much to credit Theseus with founding the democracy at Athens. A king by the name of Theseus may have shown democratic leanings in his administration. Political measures, like heroic acts, tend to cluster around a legendary figure of the past. Even the institution of ostracism is credited to Theseus and this should warn us to be critical of the traditions associating political actions with Theseus. To credit Theseus with an institution was perhaps tantamount to ascribing a very early date to that institution—to saying that it began "way back in the Bronze Age." The surprising statement of Aristotle that the first change in the constitution took place in the time of Theseus does not alter the opinion just stated. How could Aristotle know that this reform in the time of Theseus "was a slight divergence from the royal constitution"?

If the union of the Attic towns was effected in the Bronze Age, there would certainly be a concomitant constitutional change and there is no reason why such a union could not have been achieved in the Late Bronze Age. On the other hand, this tradition of the union of Attic communities may reflect the rise of the city-state which is thought to have taken place after the end of the Bronze Age. An increase in the population of Athens around the beginning of the Proto-Geometric Age (1100-950) seems indicated by the American and German excavations in the Agora and Ceramicus respectively. Was this increase due to a union or to the influx of refugees who were driven from other lands by the Dorian invasion? The latter seems the more reasonable explanation.

The kingship came to an end in Athens with the death of Codrus, whom tradition makes the last king of Athens. The date of his death has been calculated to have been *ca.* 1068, roughly a generation after the traditional date for the Dorian invasion. It must be admitted that, however much we may distrust the "made" dates, this is the period when one should expect constitutional changes or, to be more specific, the change from kingship to aristocracy.

A college of three archons, appointed for life—apparently by the aristocratic Council, the successor of the old Council of Elders—succeeded the king. Various reasons were given in Athenian tradition for this change, but they are specious and conceal a constitutional reform about which the ancient historians knew as little as we today. Probably the same evolution or revolution took place at Athens as elsewhere in Hellas where the kingship disappeared or was modified. The fact that the lifelong archons were chosen from the Medontids may indicate that this noble family was involved in the abolition of the kingship. So aristocracy or oligarchy supplanted monarchy at Athens, probably within a half-century of the Dorian invasion or end of the Late Helladic Bronze Age, that is, between 1100 and 1050. Acastus was probably the first archon,[1] for later the archons swore that they would perform their oaths even as in the time of Acastus. So Medon, who heads the traditional list of lifelong archons, is probably only the eponym of the Medontids inserted as the son of Codrus in the Attic mythology.

The title basileus does not disappear entirely, for the second archon was known as the archon basileus (an official largely in charge of

---

[1] The term "archon" alone is used to distinguish the principal member of the college from the archon basileus and the polemarch.

religious matters) and the heads of the tribes were called *phylobasileis* (tribal kings) in Aristotle's time. The third archon was the polemarch. If Aristotle was correct in assuming the existence of this office prior to the institution of the lifelong archons, one might date the polemarchy back to the Bronze Age or to the period between the end of the period and the abolition of the kingship. The silence on the part of the Homeric poems regarding the polemarch cannot be considered valid grounds for rejecting an origin in the Bronze Age for this office. Attic saga remained almost completely beyond the pale of the great Aeolic-Ionic epics which drew chiefly from Thessaly and the Peloponnesus.

What these lifelong officials were called is unknown. Aristotle implies that Acastus was an archon, but in a passage of Plato and in the Parian Marble these pre-Solonian officials are described as "reigning" or "being kings" at Athens. It has been suggested that they were called *prytaneis* (princes, rulers, presidents). They were doubtless elected by the Council and from the house of the Medontids. The names of twelve lifelong archons, exclusive of Medon, are preserved, from Acastus to Alcmeon, covering the period from *ca.* 1068 to 752.

The popular Assembly probably existed, but with as little importance as it had had under the monarchy. Perhaps it possessed still less power for, otherwise, the economic condition of the people would not have been allowed to become so wretched as time passed. The Assembly may have represented the four tribes into which the Athenians had early been divided, according to Aristotle. The government was really controlled by the Council which selected the leading officials. This Council—it is not known when it came to be called after its meeting place, the Areopagus—gave an oligarchical character to the constitution.

About 752 another change was made in the Athenian constitution, namely the reduction of the term of archons to ten years. This change occurred in the second (or third) year of the reign of Alcmeon, but it is unknown whether Charops, the first of these archons, interrupted Alcmeon's reign or succeeded him at his death. If the former were the case, the change would appear to have been all the more revolutionary in character. Was this a move on the part of the nobles to get rid of the Medontid oligarchy or could the economic plight of the people, given expression in the Assembly, have induced the aristocracy to make the change from lifelong to ten-year term? These are questions which may now only be asked. The fact that the fourth decennial archon, Hippomenes (a Medontid), was said to have been deposed by the nobles (but at the end of his ten years) and was succeeded in turn by three archons selected from all the eupatrids (nobles), lends support to the idea that the reform of 752 was instigated by the nobles alone. The change in 712, which opened the archonship to all nobles, was a step from oligarchy to aristocracy in the true sense of the word.

About 682, after seven decennial archons had held office, a notable constitutional reform was effected whereby the term was reduced to one year. Thenceforward annual tenure became the rule at Athens. At the same time six new officials were added, the *thesmothetai* (lawgivers). These were "to perform the function of publicly recording the ordinances and to preserve them for the trial of litigants." The nine archons—the term archon was applied to the thesmothetes also—were elected by the Council of the Areopagus (to use its later name) which virtually controlled the Athenian state. According to Aristotle, "the Council of the Areopagus had the official function of guarding the laws, but actually it administered the greatest number and the most important of the affairs of state." At this time began the practice of recruiting the members of this Council from the ex-archons, who on the expiration of their year of office entered the Council and remained members for life.

Nothing is known about the Assembly in this period. The institution of annual tenure of office and the appointment of the six thesmothetes to be guardians of the laws may indicate a slight trend toward giving consideration to the people. Though the Assembly may not have acquired power, it is possible that the economic condition of the people may have caused rumblings which the nobles deemed it unwise to ignore. Most of the land was in the hands of the few; those tenants who were unable to pay one-sixth of their produce in rental eventually found themselves, their wives and children reduced to slavery. "Thus," says Aristotle, "the most grievous and bitter thing in the state of public affairs for the masses was their slavery; not but what they were discontented also about everything else."

Creon appears to have been the first annual archon (*ca.* 682) and this year may have seen a slight swing toward the movement which was to culminate in Solon's efforts to help the multitude. But the government was essentially oligarchical. It appears that appointment to office depended not only upon birth but also upon wealth, since apparently only those nobles could hold office who were financially able to maintain a certain standard and to equip themselves.

About 632, a young Athenian noble, Cylon, tried to seize control of the state. Besieged on the Acropolis, he escaped, but his followers were slain at the instigation of Megacles of the Alcmeonid family. Cylon had won a victory at the Olympic Games (in 640) and a statue of him had been erected on the Acropolis at Athens, where it was seen centuries later by Pausanias. The fact that this bronze statue was allowed to survive "in spite of his plotting a tyranny" may indicate that his attempt did not seem so outrageous in the eyes of the people. Perhaps Cylon anticipated Peisistratus in championing the cause of the people and his escapade may have been in part at least dictated by altruistic motives.

In enumerating the changes or reforms which were made in the Athenian constitution Aristotle gives as the second change, after the first one made by Theseus, "the reform in the time of Draco, in which a code of laws was first published." The reforms of Draco are dated by Aristotle in the archonship of Aristaechmus, *ca.* 621, when Draco was probably a thesmothete. To quote Kenyon, they "were the outcome of a long conflict between the rich and the poor, arising from the miserable condition of the poor laborers and agriculturists, who had sunk by the pressure of debt into the position of serfs attached to the soil." Despite lack of mention by Herodotus and Thucydides, Draco can hardly be denied historical existence. It is difficult to ignore Aristotle's detailed description of the Draconian constitution and the tradition about Draco's laws which became proverbial for their severity. Later oligarchical influence may have colored Aristotle's description of Draco's political measures, but the constitution ascribed to Draco may at least depict the pre-Solonian constitutional organization at Athens. As such, it forms a step in the development of the Athenian constitution.

All persons who could provide themselves with arms had become citizens and these formed the Assembly which now elected the various magistrates. It appears that before the time of Solon the citizens were divided into classes on the basis of income. Certain property qualifications were specified for the important magistracies such as the nine archons, the treasurers, the generals and the hipparchs (masters of the horse or staff-officers). A new body was formed, the Council of 401, selected by lot from those of the citizens over thirty years of age, probably 100 from each of the four tribes plus one extra man. Also citizens over thirty were eligible for election to the minor offices and for selection by lot for certain other offices. The outgoing officials had to stand an audit at the completion of their term and the archons were ineligible for re-election.

Despite the political gains made by the people, the constitution was still of an aristocratic character for, to quote Aristotle, "the Council of Areopagus was guardian of the laws, and kept a watch on the magistrates to make them govern in accordance with the laws." Hence Kenyon is led to surmise that "the change in the constitution was more apparent than real." Incidentally, it may have been at this time that the aristocratic Council (of ex-archons) received its designation "of the Areopagus" to distinguish it from the new Council of 401.

This pre-Solonian constitution ascribed to Draco marks a step in the direction of democracy. However, it dealt only with political measures and failed to remedy the economic situation of the people. Though seeming quite democratic in character, the reforms neither rescued the poor from debt and slavery nor enabled them to acquire arms which would have allowed them to avail themselves of the new political privileges.

"Such being the system in the constitution and the many being enslaved to the few, the people rose against the notables. The party struggle being violent and the parties remaining arrayed in opposition to one another for a long time, they jointly chose Solon as arbitrator and archon and entrusted the government to him." Thus Aristotle introduces the great statesman who is credited with being

-the actual founder of the Athenian democracy and with instituting the third change in the constitution of Athens. One should read the extant poems of Solon to appreciate the conditions of the times and the problems which Solon was called upon to solve in his year of archonship (594/3). It is a tribute to his character and political astuteness that he was chosen by both nobles and commons, rich and poor, to be arbiter in their strife at a time of impending revolution. It is also a compliment to his statecraft, though a questionable one sometimes, when a modern senator is dubbed a "Solon" in the newspaper of today.

Solon's reforms show the many-sidedness of the man, touching as they do on the economic, social, political and judicial phases of life and involving also a change in the monetary standard and a reform of the calendar. Moreover, they reveal the statesman's keen insight into human nature as well as politics. Solon's "New Deal" was nothing if not thoroughgoing; it involved both radical innovations and revisions of existing institutions.

His most radical moves were the cancellation of debts—*seisachtheia* (or the shaking-off-the-burdens)—and the prohibition against enslavement for debt in the future. Solon supplanted Draco's laws except those relating to homicide and published the new code, setting it up for all to see on prisms in the Royal Stoa in the Agora. As before, the people were classified on the basis of annual income of produce in terms of dry and liquid measures: the 500-measure-men, the 300-measure-men, the 200-measure-men, and the lowest class, the thetes (laborers). Only those of the three upper classes were eligible to hold office. The nine archons were chosen from the two upper classes, only 500-measure-men might become treasurers, and other officials were selected from the appropriate classes.

In one passage of *The Constitution of Athens* Solon is credited with instituting the practice of sortition, that is, selection by lot, in choosing the state officials. But in another passage Aristotle says that the lot was first used for the selection of the archons in the year 487 and this seems the more accurate statement in view of the fact that a generation after Solon, in the period of the tyranny, these officials were elected.

The four tribes, each with its tribal king, were retained and each tribe was subdivided into three *trittyes* (thirds), which were further divided into four naukraries (ship-boards). These forty-eight naukraries, each under a ship-commissioner, had charge of raising funds and making expenditures for the Athenian navy. They were administrative districts, each of which was responsible, at least in later times, for the equipping of one war vessel.

Solon is also said to have formed a Council of 400, for which each of the four tribes selected, apparently by lot, 100 members. In this connection it is interesting to note a seeming corroboration from archaeology. In 1937, on the west side of the Agora near the site of the later *bouleuterion* (Council House), Homer Thompson discovered the remains of a building which he identifies as the "primitive Bouleuterion" and dates in the time of Solon or in the years immediately after his reforms. This Council of 400 did not, however, attain the importance of the old aristocratic Council of the Areopagus, which Solon preserved and "appointed to the duty of guarding the laws, just as it had existed even before as overseer of the constitution, and it . . . kept watch over the greatest number and most important of the affairs of state."

It is noteworthy that Solon was determined that the democracy should not only be safeguarded, but also be literally maintained. Not only was the Council of the Areopagus empowered to try persons who sought to put down the democracy, but Solon made it a law that anyone who did not participate on one or the other side, when civil strife prevailed, should be disfranchised and cease to be considered a member of the state.

In the eyes of Aristotle the three most democratic features of Solon's constitution were the prohibition against mortgaging a person for a loan, the privilege of appearing in court on behalf of a wronged or injured person and the right of appeal to the jury-court. Although the thetes were ineligible for office, they could participate in the Assembly and serve in the law courts. Thus the way was paved for popular sovereignty, for the Assembly directed the policy of the state and the courts reviewed the conduct of every magistrate at the end of his term of office. In the *Politics* Aristotle states that Solon "restored the ancestral democracy with a skilful blending of the constitution: the Council of the Areopagus being an oligarchical element, the elective magistracies aristocratic and the law courts democratic."

Solon pursued the middle course and while he gave consideration to both rich and poor he incurred the enmity or criticism of both. Though he recognized the fact that the rich were largely to blame for the wretched economic conditions of the people, he saw that it was unwise to institute an entirely democratic form of government. He did not think it safe to allow those who were neither rich nor in any way distinguished to hold the higher offices, but, on the other hand, he thought it dangerous not to admit them to deliberative and judicial functions.

Such a prodigious amount of legislation and organization may have required more than the year assigned to Solon by tradition, but there is no evidence of any extension of tenure. It is said that on conclusion of his reforms Solon was immediately beset with persons of both parties urging him to modify this or that measure. But he knew human nature and went abroad (in particular to Egypt) for ten years so that his constitution would be given a chance to exist and become accepted. Whatever disappointment was felt by his fellow-Athenians, rich and poor, Solon came to be regarded in later days as the founder of the Athenian democracy and also as a man of great character and ability, "the first and original champion of the people."

But the nascent democracy at Athens was not destined to develop uninterruptedly to its bloom. Five years after Solon's archonship, party strife broke out and no archon was appointed. A few years later the same thing happened and, later, in 581 the archon Damasias refused to relinquish his office at the end of his term. He retained the office another year and even served two months of a third term before he was ejected. A coalition government, composed of ten archons—five elected from the nobles, three from the farmers, two from the artisans—seems to have finished the year. But internal dissension continued as three factions gradually evolved: the Men of the Plain, the aristocratic landholders living on large estates and at Athens; the Men of the Hills, the poorer farmers on the little fields in the rocky districts; and the Men of the Coast, a conservative party which included in its number those engaged in overseas commerce.

Peisistratus, a member of the nobility but "an extreme advocate of the people," became the leader of the popular party, the Men of the Hills, and as champion of the people seized control over the government at Athens (*ca.* 560). By this act he effected the fourth change in the Athenian constitution. Twice Peisistratus was expelled, but by ruse and force—and with the help and connivance of the people—he succeeded in re-establishing his tyranny and remained in power until his death (*ca.* 528). Because of the opprobrious connotation attached to the words, it is better to transliterate *tyrannis* and *tyrannos*, for in the case of Peisistratus the translations "tyranny" and "tyrant" are not truly applicable. In fact, it would seem that, in the opinion of the people and of at least some of the nobles, the regime of Peisistratus might best be characterized as a benevolent dictatorship.

Peisistratus inaugurated the first great, brilliant period of Athens —if we may except the last period of the Bronze Age—and his regime was not surpassed either materially or culturally until the Age of Pericles and possibly only by that period. Artists and poets were attracted to Athens; the drama, festivals and games were introduced; the city was embellished with temples and statues. The people were kept busy by the great building program—that age-old practice of dictators so prevalent in many countries today—and they were not concerned by any theoretical loss of political liberty. The brilliant court life, the artistic productions, all must have appealed to many of the upper class. Hence we can understand Aristotle's statement that the majority of the notables and of the people were willing for him to govern.

Although Peisistratus obtained his position unconstitutionally, yet he made at least a show of constitutional government. All the Solonian laws and institutions he seems to have retained in form, if not in function, but he contrived to have the chief offices held by members of his family. It was the people in Assembly who voted him a bodyguard of fifty men and if, as is thought, he organized several bands of fifty, he arranged that more than fifty guards were never seen together. Aristotle says that Peisistratus carried on "the public business in a manner more constitutional than tyrannical" and that his "administration of the state was moderate"; that he himself was popular and kindly, so that men often spoke of the tyranny of Peisistratus as the Golden Age of Cronus.

On the whole, even allowing for a bias on the part of Aristotle, it seems that the majority of the Athenians were satisfied with the tyranny of Peisistratus and with the early part of that of his son and successor, Hippias. To the thinking man this might seem to be a dictatorship, benevolent or oppressive according to his party affiliations or political experience, but to the many Athens probably seemed as free a state as the Solonian Athens and as democratic. Doubtless the ordinary citizen then, as today, cared little about constitutional forms so long as his stomach and purse were not empty.

The tyranny left an impress on the later Athenian constitution, for the undemocratic character of the later influential Board of Ten Generals may have been due to the rise of the generals at the expense of the archons during the tyranny. Furthermore, the *poletai* (finance officials) may have made their first appearance in this period and Beloch would also ascribe to Peisistratus the division of the country into ten tribes. At the death of Peisistratus (528), his sons Hippias and Hipparchus carried on the tyranny in the same form and manner. In 514 an attempt was made on the lives of the two by Harmodius and Aristogeiton. Hipparchus was assassinated, but Hippias escaped. The attack was an act of personal vengeance, but was later exalted to a patriotic deed performed by the "Liberators of Athens." However, it did at least indirectly affect Athenian constitutional history and so should be mentioned.

Thenceforward Hippias became suspicious and the severity of his rule make the terms tyranny and tyrant, in the modern unfavorable sense, applicable to the rule and ruler respectively in the period 514-510. Strong sentiment against tyranny developed in Athens and the Delphic Oracle was influenced—not to say bribed—to induce the Spartars to help rid Athens of the tyrant. Ever ready to install an oligarchy in another state, the Spartans under Cleomenes came to the aid of the Athenians and besieged Hippias on the Acropolis. After five days Hippias came to terms and was allowed to leave Athens with his family and go into exile.

Two years of factional strife followed (510-508). One faction was led by Isagoras, whom Aristotle calls a friend of the tyrants, but who might more correctly be designated as the leader of the oligarchical party. Cleisthenes, an Alcmeonid, championed the cause of the people and eventually triumphed over his adversary, whose enlisting of Spartan aid succeeded only in arousing the people and accomplishing the defeat of the oligarchical party. So Cleisthenes who, like Solon, Peisistratus, Pericles and others, came to be designated "champion of the people," took the leadership in re-establishing the democracy at Athens. His reforms of 508/7 mark the fifth change which Aristotle lists in the development of the Athenian constitution from the beginning down to *ca.* 402. "Fifth was the constitution of Cleisthenes, following the deposition of the tyrants, which was more democratic than the constitution of Solon."

First of all, Cleisthenes saw the need of eradicating the local party feeling which had caused so much factional strife within the state. So he abolished the old four tribes, which were based on family and religion, and redistributed the citizenry into ten tribes which were political units of a geographical character. For he subdivided the tribes into trittyes (thirds), one trittys being taken from the Coast, one from the Plain and one from the Hill district. No trittys was contiguous with another within the same tribe. "Each tribe consequently included within itself representatives of each of the rival districts, and the party feeling was spread over three local divisions, and the old feuds between the different districts of Attica became impossible." The country was divided into demes (wards or townships) and these were assigned to the tribes by lot. The deme became the unit of political organization and demarchs were appointed to be presidents of each deme.

Along with the institution of the ten tribes a change was made in the Council. Instead of 400 Cleisthenes "made the Council to consist of 500 members, fifty from each tribe." Further, he increased the number of citizens by enrolling in the new tribes many resident aliens who had been foreigners or slaves. That no discrimination might be shown with regard to the newly enfranchised, Cleisthenes ordained that the people should henceforth be designated, not by their father's name, but by their deme. Otherwise, in the case of an ex-alien, the naming of his father would reveal that he was not of an old Athenian family. Thus the deme became a social group as well as a political unit.

The nine archons appear to have been elected by the ekklesia and election rather than sortition is what one should expect at this time. It would have been dangerous to trust to selection by lot, when so many of pro-oligarchical leanings were around, not to mention those who still favored the tyranny. The *boule* (Council) doubtless prepared measures for the Assembly and acted as its executive committee. The Council of the Areopagus existed, but popular sovereignty was now assured by Cleisthenes' organization.

In addition to other new laws Cleisthenes is credited with the institution of ostracism. But it is remarkable that twenty years elapsed before this law was put into effect and then it was to banish Hipparchus, a relative of Peisistratus, "the desire to banish whom had been Cleisthenes' principal motive in making the law." This has led Beloch to object to crediting Cleisthenes with the institution of ostracism. However, there may have been circumstances which caused Cleisthenes to withhold this political weapon against Hipparchus. Aristotle explains all this on the ground of democratic leniency: "the Athenians permitted all friends of the tyrants who had not taken part with them in their offences during the disorders to dwell in the city—in this the customary mildness of the people was displayed."

As Aristotle says, "these reforms made the constitution much more democratic than that of Solon." After Cleisthenes the Athenian democracy underwent little change until it reached its height of development under Pericles. About 501, "they began to elect the generals by tribes, one from each tribe, while the whole army was under the command of the polemarch." And so, at the battle of Marathon (490), the polemarch Callimachus had an equal vote with the generals and occupied the post of honor (the right wing). In 487, the year after the first recorded case of ostracism, a noteworthy change in the constitution was made: "in the archonship of Telesinus, they selected the nine archons by lot, tribe by tribe, from a preliminary list of 500 chosen by the demesmen. This was the date of the first selection on these lines after the tyranny, the previous archons having all been elected by vote." Since the archon could not be reappointed and the hazard of the lot left too much to chance, the archonship rapidly declined in importance. The Board of Ten Generals continued to be elected and, since re-election was permitted, the generals soon became the most important magistrates under the new constitution.

The forty-eight ship-boards, which even before Solon had been apportioned among the four tribes, were now probably increased to fifty and continued as administrative units to raise funds with which to equip the fleet. In 483 the profit to the state from the silver mines in southern Attica, in amount 100 talents, was on Themistocles' proposal given to the hundred wealthiest citizens. These, suggests Beloch, were the two richest men of each ship-board. At any rate, the money was used to equip 100 triremes which were very conveniently ready for use against Xerxes' fleet at the battle of Salamis three years later. In this year (480) all persons ostracized were allowed to return and a boundary was fixed thenceforth for those under sentence of ostracism. The year 480/79 is a natural dividing point in Hellenic history and may well mark the close of this historical survey. "At this date," as Aristotle says, "the state had advanced to this point, growing by slow stages with the growth of the democracy."

This sketch of the early constitutional history of the Hellenes supports Zimmern's statement that "The Greeks invented politics." For in ancient Hellas are the origins of many present political institutions. But there is more than an historical interest in the study of Hellenic experience in politics. With profit one may take to heart—better, to mind—their successes and be warned by their failures.

It is essential to avoid the pitfall of the loose use of terms and in the light of the Athenian experience to recognize that constitutional forms may differ in degree. Democracy and monarchy are not necessarily antithetical terms; monarchial Sweden is in the opinion of many more truly democratic than democratic America. A benevolent dictatorship may produce a more contented citizenry than some forms of democracy. The regime of the tyrant Peisistratus produced an apparently prosperous state which to the majority was probably indistinguishable from a democracy. Tyranny may emerge from democracy or from oligarchy, yet its life is usually brief. When democracy has become a vital institution, it seems destined to be more long-lived and stable than oligarchy, as Aristotle has said. To those who prefer the tempered democracy of Solon to the less restrained democracy of the fifth century Aristotle's statement that middle class government is the best practicable seems confirmed by history.

An anecdote, doubtless apocryphal, which is preserved in Plutarch's *Solon*, presents the Hellene in a cynical and pessimistic humor. Anacharsis, finding Solon at work on his laws, laughs at the statesman for imagining that the dishonesty and covetousness of his countrymen could be restrained by written laws, which were like spiders' webs and would catch, it is true, the weak and poor, but could easily be broken by the mighty and rich. And again there is that discouragingly apposite comment of Pausanias, anent the undeserved fate of Demosthenes, "I heartily agree with the remark that no man who has unsparingly thrown himself into politics trusting in the loyalty of the democracy has ever met with a happy end."

Of course, the great problem then as now was human nature. For democracy, or any form of good government, calls for unselfishness and will not prove successful if too much power is given either to the wealthy upper class or to the poor and the uneducated. Solon might well be taken as a model. He chose the middle course at the cost of incurring the displeasure of both nobles and commons and thereby created at least the framework of a great democracy. And so in politics as in other fields appears that idea which permeated all Hellenic life and civilization, namely, the "Golden Mean" or, as the Hellenes have expressed it, "nothing in excess."

III. DEMOCRACY AT ATHENS

BY GEORGE M. HARPER, JR.

To the Greeks democracy meant a city-state governed by the people gathered in assembly. It mattered not whether such a city-state was weak and insignificant or, like Athens in her heyday, mistress of a great empire; each was a democracy. In a limited democracy class distinctions, usually based on property, were observed; in an extreme democracy these distinctions tended to disappear except where common prudence forbade. Athens at various stages in her history favored now the limited, now the extreme, form of democracy. Since democratic imperialism is considered in a later chapter, the Athenian Empire and the vicissitudes of Athenian foreign policy are important here only as they reflect or influence the internal constitution of Athens herself. But it should not be forgotten that Athens encouraged and fostered democracy in subject communities. Beyond the limits of her empire, moreover, her influence and example were at work. Athens comprehensively illustrated democratic principles and forms and served as a pattern for other states.

During the years separating Marathon (490) from Crannon (322) the Athenian political way of life affected the Greek world most widely and yet most intimately. These years afford adequate illustration of the interaction of conservative and revolutionary forces, of the interplay of economic conditions and public policies and of the essential stability of Athenian democratic institutions.

The composition, competence and disposition of the Athenian Assembly or *ekklesia* are especially noteworthy, since it was in this body and in the popular law courts that the sovereignty of the people found its clearest expression. Roughly one person in ten in Attica was qualified to attend the ekklesia. Slaves and resident aliens and, of course, all women and minors were ineligible. Thus of a total population of some 400,000 perhaps 40,000 constituted the nucleus from which the ekklesia drew. Thucydides states that during the Peloponnesian War attendance at the Assembly never rose to

5,000. Residents of the city and its immediate environs naturally found it easier to attend than those dwelling in remote districts of Attica and so dominated the ekklesia. Only by a system of representation, not by a primary assembly, could this inequality have been avoided.

The dominance of the ekklesia over other organs of government became increasingly evident. In Cleisthenes' day ten regular meetings were held each year, in Aristotle's the number was forty. The Council of 500 or *boule*, established by Cleisthenes, was never in any sense comparable to the upper house of a bicameral parliament. Its function had always been to frame proposals for consideration by the ekklesia, where they might be disregarded or modified beyond all recognition. Its second task was to supervise the execution of the decrees of the ekklesia. The role of the boule was ancillary. One sure safeguard against usurpation of excessive power by the Council was that its members were chosen by lot to serve for a single year. The Council, moreover, was divided into ten tribal executive committees, each functioning for one-tenth of the year. The presidency of these executive committees (*prytaneis*) rotated daily. Continuity of policy and effective leadership in the Council were thereby prevented. The members of the boule had no special political aptitude. Statesmen and popular leaders were to be sought elsewhere, either among the incumbents of the few elective offices or in the Assembly. Members of the Council represented neither special classes nor special interests. Doubtless their duty to execute the will of the Assembly during their year of office gave them an added sense of responsibility above that of the ekklesiasts. The Council, moreover, disposed of much routine business. The true dependence of the boule was long disguised by its habit of agreement with the ekklesia. Thus on the eve of the Sicilian expedition it imposed no check upon the passions of the ekklesia. In the fourth century the Council declined in importance, a fact illustrated by the transfer of many of its former financial responsibilities to officials elected by the people. The boule remained, however, in its tribal organization an attractive and symbolic replica of the state. As will appear later, the Council of the Areopagus, ancient and revered though it was, in no way restricted popular supremacy and eventually became only a court limited to the hearing of cases of manslaughter.

Equally effective in securing the sovereignty of the ekklesia were the checks put upon the power of magistrates. Generally speaking, election to office depended upon lot. From 487 onwards even archons, previously the chief officers of state, and their associates, the *thesmothetai*, were so chosen. Tenure of most offices was limited to a year. Many magistracies were shared by ten incumbents, one from each tribe. The mere number of major and minor officers, of assistants, clerks and special commissioners, inevitably lowered the prestige of office. Magistrates had neither the confidence that a flattering popular vote inspires nor its corresponding sense of obligation. The magistrates and Council did not constitute a responsible ministry. No campaign promises bound them. The theory underlying choice by lot was that any citizen of proper age, not specifically disqualified, was equally fit as councillor or magistrate to execute the people's will. In practice men so selected might help to shape policy and to direct the state's course; in theory it was theirs not to command, but to obey. Those who were chosen by lot to hold office had to submit to a preliminary proving, in which their family life and religious and civic conduct were scrutinized, to a monthly review of their acts by the ekklesia and to a final audit of accounts at the year's end.

The whole aim and tendency of the formal constitution seems to have been to insure equality. Such equality might well involve mediocrity, although the annual infusion of fresh blood into the administration must have given strength and health to the body politic. At all times persuasive orators were free to exert great and continuing influence in the Assembly. But more than this, if the state was to employ the special talents of its ablest men, it had to find dignified and authoritative governmental posts for them. Chance must not determine every choice. At least one office, whether held singly or in commission, must be filled by popular election. Re-election must be legal. In the fifth century, as was natural for a community living continuously under the threat of or in an actual state of war, this exceptional office was the *strategia* or generalship shared by ten colleagues. Thus Pericles was repeatedly re-elected general. Since financial, imperial and international questions were closely related to military policy, the general's sphere of interest was wide and in practice his powers were extensive. But he was not a responsible party leader. Subordinate political positions were not held by his lieutenants and henchmen. Like the other generals he called special sessions of the ekklesia to vote upon his proposals and to pass enabling acts. The ekklesiasts, not being the elected representatives of political parties, were completely free to support or to oppose him. The general's ascendancy was personal.

Following the Peloponnesian War the generalship declined in prestige. On the other hand, the economic stringency of the times required a more systematic control of finance. When drafts upon imperial tribute were no longer available to meet domestic demands, pay was extended from members of the boule to ekklesiasts, while distributions to the people, already conspicuous in the fifth century, were increased in the fourth. Under such conditions a careful and continuing study of new sources of revenue and of new methods of raising funds had to be made, while government expenses wherever possible had to be curtailed. Here was a field for experts, a field in which such men as Eubulus and Lycurgus rendered notable service to Athens. By virtue of the various financial offices to which they were popularly elected and re-elected they secured to themselves an authority comparable to that of the great generals of the preceding century. Yet even more than the generals they must have felt the pressure of public opinion, always most sensitive where money is concerned.

Beside the general and the expert financial administrator appears a third type of leader, the so-called demagogue, better described perhaps as the independent orator. Holding no office under the recognized constitution of the state, the demagogue found his opportunity in the extraordinary scope given to individual initiative in the ekklesia, which made it possible for a skillful pleader to redirect or to pervert the recommendations of the magistrates and Council or even in effect to propose administrative measures of his own. Indeed there are periods in Athenian history, notably the time of the Peloponnesian War, when eloquent demagogues, without office or formal party ties and free from the restraints imposed upon responsible magistrates, dominated the ekklesia and so the state. Such men were dangerous. Pericles as general might persuade the ekklesia, largely composed of urban tradesmen and artisans, to submit each year to the ruin of the Attic harvest by Spartan invaders, but all the while he knew that this ekklesia, grown impatient and swollen by refugees from the countryside, might repudiate his leadership by an impeachment—which in fact it did. A demagogue such as Hyperbolus, on the contrary, might as a private citizen with impunity urge the Assembly to vote reckless military adventures overseas, knowing that the penalty for possible failure would fall upon the heads of the generals appointed to command.

It is an interesting paradox that the history of a state dedicated to the principle of equality should be so largely the record of the achievements of a succession of distinguished individuals who formulated and executed policy and swayed the Assembly by their eloquence. This paradox is the more striking, when we recollect that a dread of tyranny had called into being the institution known as ostracism, whereby a citizen whose political designs were suspect might be banished for ten years by a popular vote. Ostracism was to prove a convenient means of removing minority leaders, but it argues well for the moderation of the people that this expedient did not quickly degenerate into an abuse and that when it did, in the last quarter of the fifth century, it was practically discarded. Nor should we fail to observe that Athenian statesmen often had the courage to propose and the Assembly the wisdom to adopt unpalatable measures looking beyond immediate self-interest to future security or solvency.

The Assembly had final authority in the departments of diplomacy, war and finance. It also controlled import and distribution of grain. The pages of Thucydides establish the fact that the ekklesia, at least in the fifth century, made full use of its power, being neither passive nor uncritical. Thucydides has many harsh things to say about the unseasoned judgments and factional spirit of the ekklesia, but his comments serve to point out the more clearly that sovereign power resided in that body. We should observe in this connection that measures, such as posting the *agenda* four days in advance, were taken to guard against the consequences, possibly unfortunate, of a surprise vote. Furthermore, if public opinion seemed dissatisfied by a vote, an opportunity for reconsideration was afforded by a special session. Thus in 427 the ekklesia modified its initial vote to execute all adult citizens of Mytilene. It was in the ekklesia that the generals and financial administrators already mentioned, together with many of their subordinates, were elected by a show of hands. Here also officials charged with religious duties and many special commissioners were elected. The ekklesia, moreover, met as a court to grant to individuals special exemption from ordinary legal restrictions or to pass judgment on individuals suspected of damaging the state.

Theoretically the Assembly had no direct or independent power to make law. In practice, however, pronouncements of far-reaching or permanent administrative policy might be hard to distinguish from legislative acts. Nevertheless, respect for the established law, much of which went back to Draco, Solon or Cleisthenes, served as an effective check upon revolutionary legislative proposals—a check having as its sanction the dreaded *graphe paranomon* (indictment of illegality), threatening a serious penalty, even death, to the original sponsor of such legislation.

But change and growth are the law of life. Some provision had to be made for the amendment of written law. While the ekklesia itself could not directly vote changes in the law, it could at least appoint commissions to consider such changes. At first these commissions were small and appointed only under circumstances of special urgency. In the fourth century, however, proposals leading to revision of the law could be made each year at one of the regular sessions of the Assembly, while the ultimate decision was given to a panel, oft n numbering 1,000 members, chosen by lot from the dikasts of the popular courts. Thus without infringement of popular sovereignty impulsive restlessness in the Assembly was checked.

It is in the popular courts themselves that democratic philosophy was most perfectly reflected. This is seen both in their organization and in their processes. In earlier days judicial power was divided between the Council of the Areopagus and the various magistrates. The Areopagus, by reason of the fact that it was composed of ex-archons sitting for life, was doomed to a role of diminishing importance as the democratic current set strong. Nor is it surprising that, as the power of the people grew, the competence of the magistrates, notably the archons, as judges was restricted to the imposition of small fines for offences against their own magisterial authority. These magistrates, however, prepared cases for trial and presided in the courts, so retaining an influential place in the administration of justice.

The judgment itself, from which there was no appeal, was rendered by the so-called dikasts, who were at once jurors and judges, determining both the fact and the law in each case and sentencing the defendant found guilty. From a total of 6,000 dikasts, drawn by lot each year from citizens not less than thirty years of age, the several courts were constituted. The dikasts' integrity was encouraged by an oath and by increasingly elaborate precautions against bribery. Responsible to no one, the dikast was shielded from intimidation by the use of a secret ballot and by the very size of the court, the number of his colleagues never falling below 200 in a given case and sometimes running as high as 2,000 or 2,500 and possibly 6,000. Each court was a law unto itself, free from the restrictions of precedent. Proceedings even in capital cases, such as that of Socrates, were limited to a single day. No discussion among the dikasts preceded their vote. A simple majority determined the verdict. Execution of sentence was prompt.

In these courts large sections of the people got a heady draught of power. Even routine provings of the annual magistrates must have flattered the vanity of the dikasts. Furthermore, the modest remuneration of the dikasts proved attractive, if not indispensable, to many indigent citizens. These facts, coupled with the hope present in the mind of any citizen bringing an action before the court that he might share in the fine imposed upon the defendant or in the confiscation of his property, combined to give to the Athenians that love of litigation which Aristophanes never wearies of lampooning.

The unprofessional character and summary methods of the Athenian courts should not be too lightly condemned. Athenian legal practice was founded on a serious belief that the first and instinctive reaction of a large court to evidence which was sufficiently restricted in amount to be comprehended as a whole was not likely to be wide of the mark. But it was dangerous that a simple majority sufficed for conviction; and the litigants' habit of appealing to the sympathy of the dikasts suggests that emotion might overrule reason. Our own jury system, however, has absurdities and dangers no less real. How, for example, in well publicized cases can the pretence be maintained that the jurors, often selected in the very locale of the alleged crime, come to their duty with no foreknowledge or predisposition? Again, how can the jury in many long and complex hearings be expected to bear in mind more than a small part of the evidence presented for their consideration?

In all states there is more or less conscious antagonism between rich and poor. Not later than the last quarter of the fifth century democracy was defined as the rule of the poor, oligarchy as the rule of the rich. The vigor with which the proponents of these two forms of government strove for mastery in many cities strongly suggests that each group hoped to exploit the other. In Athens this struggle was singularly free from physical violence. The early agricultural economy of Athens produced few conspicuous private fortunes. With the transfer of capital from land to trade and industry, which, despite the conservative prejudice of landed citizens, inevitably accompanied the maritime expansion of Athens, fortunes were made and unmade more rapidly than in earlier days. The rift between rich and poor widened.

So long as Athens was mistress of an extensive maritime empire, however, this increasing economic divergence did not seriously disrupt internal political harmony, for imperial tribute was available to meet the public charges. Grants of pay to more and more persons in government service and subsidies for the entertainment of the populace at religious festivals might be voted with comparative levity. The allies could defray these costs as well as the expense of the great building program undertaken by Pericles. Special charges, the so-called liturgies, were, it is true, levied upon the wealthiest citizens, but in the expansive days of empire they seem to have been cheerfully borne. Rich men may well have felt genuine satisfaction in equipping war galleys at their own expense or in furnishing choruses for dramatic competitions in the theatre. On the other hand, Athens sent out thousands of colonists to various parts of her empire. Here was an economic and political safety valve, for the colonists were largely the poor and the dissatisfied.

With defeat in the Peloponnesian War and loss of empire, the opposition between rich and poor was bound to become more bitter. Although Athens was able to establish a second confederacy in the fourth century, it was barely self-sufficing. Meanwhile the poor of Athens and Attica had come to feel that the state was ultimately responsible for their support. In 378/7 a property tax, formerly employed only in times of special need, was regularly instituted. This impost somewhat resembles the graded income taxes of today. Apparently it took into account both the actual or estimated income and the assessed value of the property held by each citizen, but taxed only the largest holdings at their face value. Deductions were granted to intermediate holdings, while the smallest were completely exempt. This tax was equitable in itself. The state, however, devolved the responsibility of assessment and collection upon the taxpayers themselves. The people were divided into twenty *symmoriai* or groups of approximately equal aggregate wealth and with equal tax quotas. Assessments within each *symmoria* were made by its members. This was a sufficiently irresponsible method of handling taxes; but in 374 the evil was aggravated by a provision which was at least burdensome and must often have proved costly to the rich. Of the wealthiest citizens 300 were required to pay in advance the full amount of the tax. They were then entitled to recover this sum as best they might from their respective symmoriai. Evasion and subterfuge, however, thwarted all efforts of the state to collect its due and arrears steadily mounted. In this same period, moreover, recourse to a legal action known as *antidosis* seems to have become more common, a process whereby a person upon whom a liturgy had been imposed might be relieved, if he could establish the fact that another richer citizen was available to bear it. On the whole the people do not seem to have resisted the temptation to place disproportionate burdens on the rich.

The very smallness of Greek city-states provided an essential condition for a closely knit corporate life. Citizenship itself, in the presence of resident aliens and slaves, gave to those fortunate enough to claim it a certain *esprit de corps*. The application of the lot and the grant of pay to many categories of public service assured and facilitated the association of men of diverse economic status. At any one moment a very large proportion, perhaps one-third to one-half, of Athenian citizens was engaged in public service, either civic or military. The citizen's private business was often interrupted by the claims of public duty. In addition to serving the community as a whole he participated in the local affairs of his *deme*, whether it was a village in Attica or some portion of Athens. A citizen did not choose, as we often do today, between a public and a private career. Pericles boasted that in Athens a man who took no interest in public affairs was regarded as useless.

Furthermore, the diversified training and experience of Athenian citizens helped to make them sound judges of a policy or at least imparted vigor and point to their discussions in the Assembly. This is seen for example in many lively debates about the details of military and naval expeditions. He must have been an exceptional citizen who could not count at least one campaign to his credit, for the obligation to serve in either the army or the navy rested on all. Although assignments to the various departments of military or naval service were based on property ratings, common experience of trials and dangers must have welded together these citizen-soldiers and sailors. Ancient critics, however, appreciated that the development of sea power hastened the advent of extreme democracy, since those who manned the fleet, drawn from the lowest economic level, demanded their price. Absence on duty, however, minimized this influence except perhaps in winter.

One should not be misled by skeptical philosophers and philosophic poets into underestimating the place which religion held in public and private life. Indeed the many festivals, annual or at least periodic, which punctuated the Athenian calendar, afforded unparalleled opportunity for free association and admixture of all classes of society under most happy auspices. In festival season a broad spirit of tolerance prevailed. What the ekklesiast or councilman had not dared to say of his opponent was said for him by the comic poet in the theatre of Dionysus. The foibles of particular social classes were openly recognized and ridiculed. Emotions, political and social, found safe release. In a deeper sense common religious belief and worship united the people.

The Athenian people established a proud record. At Marathon, on the threshold of their greatness, and again at Salamis the Athenians showed Greeks and Persians what democracy disciplined and devoted might accomplish. Discipline and devotion are most clearly shown in the evacuation of Athens on the advice of Themistocles. After the Persian withdrawal from Greece the Athenians alone had the vision and the energy to press home the victory and to guarantee its permanence on the eastern shore of the Aegean. We have already mentioned Pericles' patient strategy on the land in the early stages of the Peloponnesian War, which bears witness to the discipline of the people. Most impressive is the vigor with which Athens threw off the oligarchic regime imposed by victorious Sparta, re-established democracy and set about regaining a dignified place in the Hellenic world. Finally, it is notable that Athens, more courageously than other Greek city-states, resisted the encroachments of Macedon; and displayed a larger recognition of the common ties which should bind all Greeks together. This record of fidelity and constancy should not be forgotten when we are confronted by the charge, formulated most effectively for the ancients by Polybius and repeated in substance by many modern historians of Greece, that the Athenians were by temperament peculiarly volatile and unstable.

This short survey of Athenian democracy may well conclude with a review of judgments passed upon this form of government by leading statesmen and philosophers of the fifth and fourth centuries. A wide divergence of opinion is evident. Statesmen were influenced by their associations and experience or by the circumstances in which they were speaking either to praise or to censure democracy somewhat extravagantly. Philosophers, on the other hand, were more nearly united in disapproval of democratic forms and objectives.

The most eloquent defence of democracy is put into the mouth of Pericles by Thucydides. Pericles regards equality, liberty and fraternity as the distinguishing traits of democratic Athens. He reminds the Athenians that citizens are all equal before the law and asserts that advancement in the public service depends solely on merit. The citizen is free to do as he likes without fear of his neighbor's opinion; but reverence for the law prevents liberty from degenerating into licence. Most important of all, Pericles shows how the state may exercise its superior authority without prejudice to individual liberty. To Athenagoras, the popular leader at Syracuse, Thucydides attributes the claim that in a democracy there is room for the rich to control finance, for the wise to guide counsels and for the masses to render decisions. Such flattering comments, if scarcely justified by the facts, at least reflect the ideal present in the mind of democratic sympathizers—an ideal whose influence must not be discounted.

A wholly contrary point of view is accredited to Cleon and Alcibiades. Cleon asserts that a democracy is incompetent to control an empire, since it relies on good will to secure obedience. Furthermore, it encourages too great fondness for talk and breeds indecision. Alcibiades, in his turn, explains to the Spartans, with whom he is attempting to ingratiate himself, that he with other sensible men has long recognized the follies of democracy.

The most cynical account of democracy that has come down to us is contained in a political pamphlet, *The Constitution of the Athenians*, written, perhaps in 423, by an unknown author commonly styled "The Old Oligarch." The author congratulates the Athenian democracy on having found the surest means to preserve itself. By insisting upon the equality of all citizens, democracy secures the mastery of a poor, ignorant and unprincipled majority over a more well-to-do, educated and virtuous minority. The untutored masses, having no desire for or capacity to appreciate good government, inevitably cling to democracy.

"The Old Oligarch" anticipates many of the strictures of philosophers. Although completely loyal in his personal relation to Athens, Socrates regrets that the city is controlled by an ignorant assembly and that the magistrates being chosen by lot have no special qualification for leadership. To Plato also extreme democracy means the rule of ignorant amateurs, a state in which no regard is paid to intellectual capacity or to special aptitude and training. Plato, unlike Aristotle, would grant the masses no part in the original drafting or subsequent revision of the constitution. In democracy and in the democratic citizen Plato discovers a disastrous want of discipline, for desire, not reason, is master. Individualism runs riot, subverting order and stability. The principle of equality upon which democracy rests is wholly false, for men are not by nature equal. Aristotle treats existing democracies as aberrations from a superior type of democracy, which he on the whole prefers to other forms of government. In this preferred democracy the citizens, most of them farmers and shepherds, being too busy to convene frequently, place responsibility for the conduct of government squarely upon the magistrates, who in their turn recognize the sovereignty of law. Inferior democracy arises, however, when commercial interests supersede agricultural and when the city proper grows at the expense of the surrounding countryside. The urban proletariat flock to the assembly and, holding established law in contempt, rule by decree. Extreme democracy, moreover, like extreme oligarchy fails to accord adequate recognition to the middle classes.

Hellenic democracy and oligarchy represented no clear-cut antithesis. They differed in degree, not in kind. Each was the government of a privileged minority. In Athens privilege was extended but never abolished. Certain distinctions based on property continued to distinguish citizen from citizen in most democracies. At the same time resident aliens, jealously excluded from the franchise, and slaves were sharply contrasted to the citizenry. But these inequalities did not disturb ancient writers. Xenophon, if he be the author of the interesting essay, *Ways and Means* or *Concerning Revenues*, recommends the introduction of more resident aliens into Athens, regarding them as a source of added economic strength. Again, in proposing that the state should increase its activity in the silver mines at Laurium, he discusses slave labor without a trace of humanitarian sympathy. Plato also regards resident aliens as almost indispensable to a community, since by their efforts ample leisure to contemplate the purposes of life and of the state are secured to the citizens. Aristotle, in his turn, discovers nothing unnatural in slavery. The fact remains, however, that residence in Athens proved attractive to aliens. Citizens in increasing numbers condescended to work side by side with aliens in industry and trade once held beneath a citizen's dignity. Meanwhile the enslavement of Greeks came to be regarded as unbecoming. Thus barriers still recognized by theorists were broken down by the uses and habits of everyday living.

Athens is the best example of Greek democracy. The distinctive merit of the Athenian regime lay in the fact that each citizen directly and vitally and, it would seem, contentedly shared in communal services without impairment of individual freedom of action and thought. Providing for the import of needed supplies, notably grain, the Athenian state sought by payment for many public services to put each citizen in a position to satisfy his minimum requirements. Beyond that, however, the state did little to foster the material welfare of the people. Thus in the economic field, that is in the management of his household and of his business, the citizen was neither hindered nor helped by government. Because the Athenian seems to have been well satisfied with modest living, because the climate was genial, because such occupations as farming and seafaring were seasonal and because the citizen's land or at least his dwelling ordinarily lay at no great distance from the seat of government, the demands of public and private life were happily reconciled.

IV. ATHENS AND THE DELIAN LEAGUE

BY B. D. MERITT

ATHENS in the best days of her Golden Age offers a heartening example of the strength and resiliency of the democratic system. The rise of the Delian League gave proof that democracy could rule an empire. But the story of the Delian League is also the story of imperialistic Athens, whose fall exemplifies the fate of any government which yields to too great ambition.

The Persian invasion of mainland Greece was turned back by the victories of Salamis and Plataea. The sea power of Persia was broken by the victory of Mycale. From the Greek point of view one main purpose of the Great War had been achieved, but the fight had to be continued for the liberation of states still under Persian control in Thrace, the Hellespont and Asia Minor. When Sparta failed to realize the opportunity and the duty of this leadership, the direction of military operations fell principally to Athens and she became quickly the first state in a new Hellenic league. Although first, she was still among equals. The declared purpose of the union was the prosecution of the war. A common treasury and a common meeting place were established on the sacred island of Delos, from which the coalition came to be known as the Delian League. The sanctuary of Delian Apollo was the home of one of the oldest Panionian festivals and its choice as center for the organization reflects the Ionian character of the League's original membership.

Contributions for the maintenance of the confederacy were levied to the amount of 460 talents a year and it was decided which cities should furnish ships for the navy and which in lieu of ships should supply money. Individual amounts, recognized by everyone as fair and equitable, were fixed according to the assessment of Aristides. There have been much discussion and much difference of opinion about the amount and method of payment of this first levy. Fortunately, the epigraphical record of later years is now well enough established, so that one may say with confidence that the total sum of 460 talents covered both ships and money. In the early years the contributions in money represented a relatively small proportion of the total, but in spite of this the total itself had to be expressed in the common terms of money value. In the light of the documentary record the statement of Thucydides that the "first tribute assessed" amounted to 460 talents must be interpreted in this way.

Within a quarter of a century this voluntary league had become an empire with the democratic city of Athens at its head. Policy was no longer determined through consultation among the members, but was dictated by the Assembly in the city of Athens. The process by which Athens obtained this supreme and dictatorial leadership has been admirably described by Plutarch in his *Cimon*. Many of the smaller cities were unwilling to furnish ships and men for distant campaigns and they willingly made a cash payment to relieve them of such contributions. Athens was glad to supply the ships and the men which small cities were unwilling to furnish. In so doing she gained a powerful navy at the expense of her allies and the time soon came when the contributions of money were no longer voluntary. Athens could compel payment from any state which wished to withdraw from its association with her. She could also round out her empire by compelling cities that had not yet become members of the League to cooperate with her and to pay her tribute.

The subjugation of Carystus on the island of Euboea offers an example of enforced expansion. The first test of strength within the League of which Thucydides informs us was the revolt of Naxos. The revolt was suppressed and the tribute of Naxos was fixed thereafter at an annual figure of six and two-thirds talents. This sum (or more) was paid under duress with consistent regularity during the following years, reaching a peak of fifteen talents during the Peloponnesian War. Other states which revolted suffered similar fates and with each conquest the chance of successful revolt among those still nominally free was more and more diminished.

Athens was able to build her empire, therefore, because of her own willingness to bear arms and because of a general desire of her former allies and neighbors to follow the ways of peace and to disarm their forces. The unhappy fate of small states which were not willing to maintain efficient armed forces and which thought that their individual will to peace would guarantee them peace is not without its parallel in modern times. Athens gained her empire because she became strong and was able to suppress or intimidate any ally which opposed her hegemony.

All this came about largely without plan on the part of the Athenians themselves. They did not set out to win an empire, but by the middle of the century an empire, so to speak, had been thrust upon them. A huge concentration of Persian ships off the coasts of Phoenicia in 454 led to the transfer of the treasury from the island of Delos to the city of Athens, where, it was presumed, it would be safer. The change was made at the suggestion of the Samians. This fact implies still a certain amount of consultation among the allies, but soon after, it appears, even the pretext of the old organization was abandoned. The *hellenotamiai*, who were stewards of the League's treasury, had always been chosen from the citizens of Athens, but after the transfer Athenian control of the money became absolute. Matters came to a head several years later, when terms for a cessation of hostilities and the demarcation of spheres of influence between Athens and Persia were agreed upon by a treaty known as the Peace of Callias. The conflict with Persia was now at an end. The incentive and sustaining cause of the Delian League no longer existed.

No historian reveals the reaction to this Peace among the members of the League, but the Athenian tribute-quota lists enable one to make some deductions. These quota lists have been in large part preserved on stone upon the Acropolis at Athens. When the treasury of the League was moved from Delos, the Athenians consecrated each year one mina from every talent of tribute (one sixtieth part) to the goddess Athena. The first annual record belongs to the first year after the transfer in 454/3. The records were continuous, except for a brief period from 414 to 410, down to the defeat of Athens at the end of the Peloponnesian War. Year by year one may follow in the quota lists the control exercised by Athens over the cities which paid tribute to her. Every name was listed each year and opposite was posted the amount of its quota consecrated to Athena. Whenever the Athenians felt the need to justify the existence of their empire, they could always claim that their fleet gave necessary protection from foreign domination to those who paid tribute to them.

It is a curious fact that no known quota list is preserved for the year 449/8. When this discovery was first made, it was assumed that possibly no tribute was collected in that year. The absence of payment seemed definitely to be connected with the Peace of Callias and its implications. And yet tribute was paid in subsequent years. The record of 448/7 can be restored almost in its entirety, so that the amount of tribute collected is approximately known. Compared with the years before and after, it was a meager sum amounting only to 280 talents as against 350 talents in 454/3 and 375 talents in 444/3. In the present state of knowledge it would perhaps be best not to claim that the absence of a quota list in 449/8 means that no tribute was collected. There are too many uncertain elements entering into the problem of the missing list. A more probable view is that Athens collected some tribute and that she may have transferred all of it, not merely a quota, to Athena. What does seem certain is that a crisis was at hand in the development of League affairs and that many cities felt themselves released by the Peace from the obligation to pay. The low payment of the following year is evidence that this was so. On the other hand, the payments for 448/7 prove that Athens intended to collect her tribute even after the Peace and that she was moderately successful in doing so. The League for War against Persia had ceased to exist and the Athenian Empire had come into being. The die was cast with the continued exaction of payments after 449.

The grip of Athens upon her subject states was tightened in still another way. A monetary decree was passed by the Athenian Council and Assembly, which regulated standards of coinage, weights and measures. The text of this decree is still partially preserved. Until quite recently it has been given a date of about 423, but a new fragment found in the island of Cos, written in early Attic letters on Pentelic marble, shows that the decree belongs approximately to the same era as the Peace of Callias. The Athenians not only had determined that tribute should still be paid, but they also had decided that the economic life of their empire was to be scaled to an Athenian pattern. It was directed that a copy of the monetary decree should be placed in the market of every city of the empire. The Athenians hoped that this would be done voluntarily by the now subservient cities. It happens that fragments have been found at Smyrna (brought from some city near by), Siphnos, Cyme and Aphytis, all apparently of local workmanship. The people of Cos were less compliant. The Athenian decree provided that, if any city did not erect the decree as desired, the Athenians themselves should erect one for them. This they did at Cos; and it is for this reason that the copy from Cos is in Attic script and on Attic marble.

At about this same time the Athenians passed a new law regulating the collection of tribute, parts of which have been known for many years, but new fragments of which have now been discovered on the Acropolis. The orator who sponsored the motion in the Council and Assembly was Clinias, in all probability the father of Alcibiades. Since he lost his life in the battle of Coronea in 447, it seems reasonable to connect the decree with the other measures of imperial reorganization which followed the Peace of 449. Furthermore, both in this decree and in the monetary decree reference is made to a fourfold division of the empire. It is well known from the tribute-quota lists that between 446 and 438 Caria was recognized as a fifth and separate subdivision. There is all the more reason, therefore, to date these reforms in the period of fourfold division which existed from 450 through 447.

The democracy of Athens was now full-grown. Its strength as a form of government had increased steadily with the growing power of the city. Aristotle describes its characteristics as follows: "the election of officers by all out of all; and that all should rule over each and each in his turn over all; that the appointment to all offices or to all but those which require experience and skill should be made by lot." The generalship, obviously, was one of the offices which required skill and experience; and for years Pericles held this office as representative of his tribe Acamantis. After the death of Ephialtes he became the leader of the popular party. The great respect in which he was held and his unrivalled powers of persuasive argument enabled him to shape the destinies of the state. Plutarch cites as an example of his breadth of vision and high purpose the plan to send invitations throughout the Greek world for a Panhellenic congress, so that ways and means might be discussed for restoring shrines and temples destroyed by the Persians a generation earlier. The delegates were to discuss other matters of common interest, including freedom of the seas and general peace. But it seems evident that the Athenians realized almost at once that there was little prospect of a successful congress. The refusal of Sparta alone made any real unanimity impossible.

But Pericles was determined that at least the shrine of Athena on the Acropolis of Athens should be restored. In 448/7 the building of the Parthenon as we now know it was begun. There were still those in Athens who believed that imperial funds should be used for the purpose for which they were originally intended and Pericles was charged with improper diversion of this money for the beautification of the city. The expense accounts for the Parthenon as preserved for the years 447 to 432 do not show that any money was drawn from the imperial treasury. Sums contributed by the hellenotamiai amounted only to the quota which belonged to the goddess Athena. The heavy expenditures were borne by the Treasurers of Athena from their own resources. A justification for the indictment made against Pericles can be found only if title to the imperial funds or to substantial parts of them had been vested in these treasurers. That such transfers had in fact been made is evidenced by the terms of another Athenian decree. In 434 a motion was brought before the Council and Assembly by Callias on the subject of financial reform: he proposed the creation of a joint board of Treasurers of the Other Gods. This board was created and it functioned thereafter down to the end of the century, side by side with the board of Treasurers of Athena. Callias mentioned incidentally that 3,000 talents had been brought to the Acropolis by an earlier vote and given to Athena. He called attention to the fact that the way was now clear for certain repayments to the Other Gods from funds designated for that purpose. The first item specified as a designated source was the money stewarded by the imperial treasurers.

Evidently the Athenians in 434 were using these revenues at their pleasure as a source of domestic credit. They were able to do this at the moment because a previous obligation had been fulfilled. One must suppose that the 3,000 talents given to Athena had come also from the reserves of the imperial treasury. The evidence is that from time to time considerable sums of money were transferred to the Treasurers of Athena. The accumulation of the 3,000 talents must have begun at least as early as 443. It was suggested above that perhaps the reason why there is no quota list for 449/8 is that under the new imperial policy the money of that year was all regarded as belonging to Athena. The quota lists of subsequent years served the convenient purpose of a record of empire; but the transfer of the quota represented only a small part of the funds available to the Athenian treasurers. After the expenses of the fleet had been met, the balance was probably handed over in lump sums or by decree authorizing the transfer of annual surpluses.

There is now new evidence from an old source, the famous Strassburg papyrus, which throws considerable light on this policy of transferring funds. A scholiast on one of the speeches of Demosthenes reports that in 450/49 Pericles introduced in the Assembly a motion to allow the Athenians to use the balance of 5,000 talents, which had been collected in the imperial treasury according to the assessment of Aristides, to help to defray the expenses of his building program. The papyrus does not state how the money was made available, but there is a strong probability that it was taken from the treasury of the hellenotamiai and given to the Treasurers of Athena. It is clear that such transfers were made; even the date of the first installment is now known. It is a significant fact that the purely Athenian use of imperial funds began precisely at the time when other evidence shows that the Delian League had become in fact an Athenian Empire.

The issue of misappropriation of funds brought to a head the rivalry between the conservative and popular parties in 443. The policy of Pericles was ratified by the vote of ostracism which exiled his rival Thucydides, son of Milesias. A closer organization of empire in 443 is proved by the tribute-quota lists. There was a new assessment of tribute in that year. The names of the cities were divided into five geographical districts. The time of assessment was unusual, for it was not a Panathenaic year. The secretary of the hellenotamiai was given an assistant who continued his services through the year 442. It is of interest to note that the chief hellenotamias in the year of reorganization was Sophocles of Colonus. The great dramatist "who saw life steadily and saw it whole" was a man of affairs as well as a poet. He helped to reorganize imperial management in 443; he produced his *Antigone* in 442 or 441; and he served as a general against Samos in 441. One source of his personal wealth was the successful manufacture of arms.

This military and economic control was accompanied by political control which gave to Athens an opportunity for direct supervision and intervention in the affairs of individual cities. From the lexicographers we learn of overseers and of Athenian magistrates who were quartered in the various cities of the empire. These magistrates, or local *archontes*, are mentioned occasionally in the extant inscriptions. Both overseers and archontes appear in the early lines of the decree of Clinias, which has been dated about 449. They were there charged with supervising the collection of tribute. Another decree indicates that it was the duty of some tributary states to support Athenian magistrates, whom they were compelled to entertain. The decree of Clinias and a subsequent decree moved by Cleonymus in 426 give further details which show that infraction of rules applicable to the tribute were tried in the Athenian courts. These are only a few of the types of cases referred to Athens, but they show how thoroughly the life of the individual cities was made dependent on the will of the Athenian people. Colonies, like those at Brea and Amphipolis and on the Thracian Chersonese, were sent out as bulwarks of the empire at strategic points; and colonies and tributaries alike were required to participate in the celebration of the Great Panathenaea in Athens with the offering of a cow and a panoply of arms.

Athens had thus acquired a complete military, economic, political and juridical control of her empire. The last great threat of revolt before the outbreak of the Peloponnesian War was the defection of Samos, but this insurrection was suppressed by the vigorous action of the Athenian fleet and an effective blockade under the leadership of Pericles. The Athenian state entered upon the Peloponnesian War with a unified empire; Athens itself was a democracy under the leadership of its foremost citizen, but had autocratic control over its subject states. Only Chios and Lesbos still furnished ships but no money.

The conflict which broke out in 431 between Athens and Sparta had its roots deep in the disparity of economic interest between the maritime empire of Athens and the states of mainland Greece. The empire had every reason to face the issue with confidence. It had ample revenues, a considerable reserve upon the Acropolis, a powerful fleet which controlled the sea. It would have to contend with the highly disciplined army of Sparta, but the Athenians were prepared to suffer invasion of their country, to hold their lines of communication with the Piraeus and to wear down the resistance of the enemy. In an address to the Athenian people Pericles outlined the reasons for his confident optimism about the future. It was the judgment of Thucydides that this optimism would have been justified, had Pericles lived to carry out the policy with which he initiated the war.

The advantages to Athens of her power at sea were again emphasized by Pericles in his oration for the fallen soldiers at the end of the first year of the war; and this oration, as reported by Thucydides, portrayed the many advantages of the democratic way of life which the Athenians enjoyed and which made their city the one most worth fighting for in all Greece. Athens was the center of culture, of liberalism, of freedom in thought and action, a worthy exponent of the dignity of the individual. The state was strong so long as its citizens were not false to these ideals. Pericles stressed especially one asset of democratic government—the opportunity for debate on public issues. Jowett translates his speech as follows: "The great impediment to action is, in our opinion, not discussion, but the want of that knowledge which is gained by discussion preparatory to action." The student must admire the comparative efficiency of Athenian debate, when he remembers that only rarely was any discussion prolonged in the Assembly for more than one day. When the time for legislative action came, Athenian democracy was capable of making a decision without spending weeks or even months upon the same topic. Thus it did not fail as completely as do modern democracies to achieve the promptness and efficiency which despotic governments count among their greatest advantages.

The first ten years of the Peloponnesian War were not decisive. The Peace of Nicias was no real peace. Fighting continued in northern Greece and was soon resumed closer home. The death of Pericles was a great tragedy; the loss of his wise counsel and persuasive logic was worse than military disaster. Lesser demagogues obtained control and there grew up in Athens in the last quarter of the fifth century a spirit of imperialism which yearned for conquest for its own sake. Thus the empire was transformed by the extremists into an empire without mercy, one which asked no justification save that of force and one for which far horizons had an irresistible appeal in spite of many unsettled problems near at home.

The debate in the Athenian Assembly over the fate of the citizens of Mytilene shows the contrast between a ruthless and a humanitarian attitude in dealing with subject states. This was in 427. The Athenian Assembly had condemned to death all citizens of Mytilene and then, repentant at the enormity of their crime and the injustice of it, they sent forth messengers to stay the execution of their order. In 416, when the Athenian fleet invested the small island of Melos, the records tell of no such debate. Certainly there was no repentance. Melos was a small state which wished to remain at peace. It did not suit the convenience of the Athenians for her to do so. She was given a choice of submitting or of being destroyed and the Athenians offered no justification except that they had the power to carry out their plans. Melos had the courage to resist. The Athenian conquest was not long delayed and the destruction was complete. Athenian desire for power had become insatiable and her imperialism had taken on the complexion of world domination. Covetous eyes were then turned toward Carthage and there was hope in the minds of some that even this far away nation might be conquered. In 415 the Athenians embarked upon the foolhardy adventure of an invasion of Sicily.

This expedition was the beginning of the end of the Athenian Empire. Athens had undertaken to conquer a strong people, democratic in their way of lives, resourceful and steadfastly determined to resist aggression. The attempt was made across an expanse of ocean comparable in extent to the barrier which the Atlantic places between nations today. The huge armament sent to Sicily in 415 and later reinforced was disastrously defeated within two years; and

Athens found herself beset by revolt among her allies, by a new and powerful enemy overseas and by the growing threat of intervention from Persia. Even so, the unequal struggle continued for many years. The Athenians sought desperately for allies. During the dark days before Syracuse the generals in the field dispatched a ship to Carthage to try to make friends with their one time intended victim. Later the Carthaginians invaded Sicily and preoccupation of the western Greeks with their Carthaginian foe did much to prevent them from throwing their full force into the final attacks upon the Athenian Empire. An Athenian decree found recently on the Acropolis indicates that diplomatic negotiations were being carried on in 406 between Hannibal and Himilco, whose headquarters were in Sicily, and the Athenian people. Nothing is known concerning the outcome of these parleys. It is doubtful whether they achieved any result of importance, but they prove the eagerness of the Athenians in the last years of the war to win any possible friends to help them in a cause already almost lost. The Athenians finally exhausted all possible reserves of money and their empire was doomed when their fleet was destroyed on the beach of Aegospotami.

MAP OF GREECE
TO ILLUSTRATE
the Peloponnesian War

From the Cambridge Ancient History

V. SOCIALISM AT SPARTA

BY P. R. COLEMAN-NORTON

WAS Sparta a monarchy or an aristocracy or an oligarchy or a democracy? This question often has been asked and can be answered thus: Though certain features of such governmental forms existed in the constitution under which Spartans lived for generations, yet these aspects were merely the outer trappings concealing the inner workings of a socialistic order, for the Spartan government, unique among Hellenic constitutions, was a despotism in which the state was exalted above the individual.

Tradition informs us that about the end of the twelfth century the Dorians, who were perhaps distinguished by the quality of "character" from other branches of the Greeks, descended into the Peloponnese and conquered its southern and eastern sections. Those invaders who subjugated the inhabitants of Laconia settled in little communities, which eventually were united into the city-state called Sparta. Of the natives some were reduced to serfdom and were named helots (caught or conquered); but others, who found refuge in the hills near the Eurotas River, by which Sparta lay, were deprived of political rights (though in a semi-independent status allowed to manage their local affairs) and were designated perioecs (dwellers-around).[1] The new lords of Laconia distributed the land among themselves: when the requirements of the chieftains had been met, the other Dorians partitioned into equal shares what tracts remained. As elsewhere in Greece, so here it is believed that these lots belonged to families. But in the course of generations with the disappearance of patriarchy and in the struggle for wealth both rich and poor appeared in Sparta. As elsewhere also, increase of the population here precipitated a demand for redistribution of estates

[1] However, the "Dorian Invasion" of the Peloponnesus, if there was such an incursion, antedates our earliest notice of perioecs and helots by so many generations that some reject the pre-Dorian descent of these subjects and consider them politically and economically less fortunate members of the conquering race.

by the disinherited and by the ejected who did not emigrate. Need for farm land, then, impelled the Spartans to look for *Lebensraum*, that the dispossessed might be satisfied. Therefore, in the latter half of the eighth century the Spartans turned westward and after two decades subdued Messenia. The victors divided this land into lots and put the victims into the caste of helots. These new serfs (we are informed by Tyrtaeus in the next century) were herded "like asses laden with heavy loads, forced to furnish from the fields the half of all the harvest." After the conquest of Messenia life became more abundant for the Spartans, who were now contented in respect to land—at least for the moment—and who deported most of those still disgruntled to Italy, where a colony was founded at Tarentum.[2]

During the first half of the seventh century Sparta in some ways was the cultural center of Greece. Hither came Terpander from Lesbos, from Gortyn Thaletas, Tyrtaeus from Athens, Alcman from Sardis, from Colophon Polymnestus. These were the men who as musicians and poets pointed the Spartans to a lighter side of life. Moreover, the existence of early Laconian schools in clay, metal, stone and wood is clear from the evidence of archaeology. It was not till the close of this century that a decision to transform the state into a military despotism turned Spartan interest from arts to arms. Then poetry was banned as enervating, but versifiers were introduced occasionally and were instructed to write only "odes to obedience and chants to concord"—that is, to concoct propaganda for use by the administration in its management of the citizens, whose singing (when they sang) was typically and patriotically choral. Industry and trade were assigned to the perioecs, who either manufactured or imported those articles which the citizens were permitted to acquire.[3]

How was this change in Spartan life attained? Through almost a century of oppression the Messenians endured the Spartan yoke and at last considered the time ripe for rebellion, when they believed that

---

[2] Of negative significance for the method in which the Lacedaemonians sought to relieve their burden of a mounting population (common to all Hellenic states in the eighth century and for generations afterward) in a period of diminishing returns from arable land is the fact that in the era of colonization (*ca.* 750-*ca.* 550) Tarentum was the only transmarine foundation of the Greeks for which was claimed a Spartan origin.

[3] But Lacedaemonian simplicity was not what historians once imagined, because it is now suspected that here, as in other countries, the wealthy could afford to collect outlawed *objets d'art*.

luxury had weakened their overlords. Though assisted by other Peloponnesians, the Messenians suffered one defeat after another and were compelled to resume their thralldom. After this subdual of the rebels in the latter half of the seventh century, when antagonism between master and slave had become so acute that it could be remedied only by insurrection, the Spartans finally comprehended the import of their position. Faced with the choice between retaining their industrial and cultural interests and governing a population about ten times that of their own, they renounced everything which might have impeded their survival as well as their dominance. So after a few decades their old way of life vanished. Nothing mattered now except to retain supremacy over both perioecs and helots and to construct a state powerful enough to repress its subjects. As the population under Spartan rule at the turn of the seventh century appears to have been as follows: 25,000 citizens (landed proprietors and soldiers), 100,000 perioecs (industrialists and traders), 250,000 helots (serfs and slaves), it seems then that of the inhabitants in the Spartan dominions two-thirds were denied the Rights of Man. But the Spartans had now perceived that they were living on a volcano, if not within its crater. For protection they shielded themselves behind the *Eunomia*, the famous code wherein posterity discerned the handiwork of Lycurgus the nomothete—for to him has ever been ascribed the reform of the Spartan polity. On the ground of its unanimity this testimony has been suspected by certain historians, who therefore think that the Lycurgan system was not original with Lycurgus. But none has proposed an acceptable substitute, if indeed to any one man must be assigned the authorship of this legislation. It is difficult to untangle the work of Lycurgus from that of subsequent lawmakers, but this is of minor importance, for those who set themselves to perfect his constitution were trained in his spirit and trod in his steps. Furthermore, about Lycurgus nothing authentic is now ascertainable and what we are told by ancient authors about him is largely legendary. In antiquity none knew when he had lived among men; but the ancients declared that he was of royal degree. Whether Lycurgus was a god or a gangster or a hero or a king—he has had partisans for each role—we know not;[4] nor can we tell with assurance what earlier ideas he adopted or how the helots and the perioecs were controlled before his labors.

By and large the Eunomia subordinated life to an administration "as rigid as any religious rule." So basal was this reorganization that the very nature of Spartan civilization was altered by the organic law, which was designed to deal with a tetrad of factors: citizens, perioecs, helots, foreigners. Though the Dorians had been separated into three tribes (Dymanes, Hylleis, Pamphyloi), the Lycurgan reform apportioned them among five tribes (Amyclae, Conooura, Limnae, Mesoa, Pitana), which were territorial units.[5] It is not known why this regrouping was made, but apparently more citizens could be included in the five new tribes than in the three old tribes. This rearrangement seems to have been at the base of the reform, which embraced three significant fields: martial, political, social.

The first field touched martial affairs. Five companies recruited by district instead of three companies mustered by lineage henceforth formed the army. This citizen-corps was drilled by a discipline unparalleled in history, a system beginning in childhood and ending with senility.[6] A citizen at twenty could be called for military service, until thirty he slept in barracks, till sixty he dined at mess. Provided that he was not engaging in politics or inspecting his estate, it seems that all his time was occupied with exercise, drill, marches, patrols, manoeuvres, when it was not wanted in war, which was greeted as freedom from routine, for on campaigns—averse from the practice of other nations—discipline was relaxed. The Spartan, then, was a part of a military machine prepared for action anywhere and anytime.[7]

The second field concerned political matters. The polity, long before Lycurgus reformed it, had four parts: kings, elders, commons, overseers. Of these the last was exceptional among Greek govern-

---

[4] The likeliest rationalization about Lycurgus regards the legislator thus: first accepted as a gangster, then acclaimed as a hero, finally acknowledged as a god; if he was a king, his kingdom was not of this world.

[5] Amyclae was a suburb and the others were districts forming the city of Sparta.

[6] The curious reader may find description of Spartan training as well as information about domestic life at Sparta in the ancient documents listed in the Bibliography.

[7] Aristotle, however, tells us that the father of three sons was exempt from military service and that he who had four sons was immune from all public burdens.

ments, existing only at Sparta. Under the Lycurgan scheme the principal changes appear to have been the revocation of some prerogatives of the Assembly and the enlargement of the Council's powers.

The Spartans were ever notorious for their conservatism. Hence in their political system persisted survivals of the old order, among which the most remarkable was kingship. While it is true that next to no evidence about the development of the Spartan state before the seventh century has been found, yet it may be supposed that it followed the same lines as in other city-states. However this may be, the Spartan was one of the few Hellenic governments wherein monarchy remained for generations, though its authority was diminished not only by other institutions but also by its unique character. For here there had been two sovereigns ever since the memory of man. It is conjectured that this dual dynasty (Agid and Eurypontid) grew from a union of two communities and it is notable that, probably because each king served as a restraint upon his colleague, the royal dignity was not degraded into mere magistracy, as in some states, though by the sixth century the regal power had been circumscribed. After the reform the rulers kept beside several prequisites some of those religious, military and judicial functions which had been exercised by all Greek monarchs. Among these activities may be mentioned: superintendence of religious observances, command of the army, jurisdiction over minors in certain instances.

As the conservatism of Sparta was manifested in retaining its kings, so also was it evident in the organization of its Council. Membership in the *gerousia* (as the synod was termed) was limited to the two kings and to twenty-eight lords chosen for life from those beyond the age of sixty. Although all Spartans were called *homoioi* (peers or equals), under the Lycurgan provisions only those of aristocratic lineage whose citizenship antedated the Messenian rebellion could be selected and, when vacancies occurred, only those candidates whose civic virtue was attested could be elected. The latter quality Xenophon explained as "laboring strenuously at submitting to the laws." However, one can hardly imagine that the citizens submitted to all the ordinances, even in a land of spies like Sparta. Probably penalties were exacted only from those in disfavor with "the organization." Certainly any citizen who survived for sixty years without yielding to the temptation to disobey the laws or (more likely) without being detected in lawbreaking was worthy of a seat in the Council; but some have suggested that one who was *persona gratissima* to "the Old Guard" won a place in the senate anyway, except when he was exposed by the opposition. The councillors advised the magistrates on political matters, prepared the *agenda* for the Assembly and formed the tribunal for important criminal actions involving citizens. Thus the gerousia gave an aristocratic aspect to the state.

All citizens above the age of thirty constituted the *apella* or Assembly, which supposedly expressed the sovereign will of the people and was thus considered the democratic organ of the government. But this body was democratic only in theory, for in practice its powers were limited. It is true that the Assembly met to elect ephors and other magistrates and gerousiasts, to adjust contested successions in the dynasties, to vote for war or for peace, to enact or to reject measures proposed by councillors and magistrates. But only on bills laid before it could the apella vote and no discussion about these was permitted. Moreover, the Assembly could be prorogued by the ephors and its acts could be nullified by the elders, if they thought that the commons had made "a crooked decree" in perverting the sense of propositions by addition or omission of words. That the apella submitted to such interference may seem strange; but protest by the citizens was rare, since the state controlled them from the age of seven and deliberately suppressed any tendency to independent thought.

That the ephorate existed before the Eunomia was professed by the ancients, who discovered eponymous ephors (overseers) as early as the eighth century (757). But the college of ephors, as it appears in classical times, began at the end of the seventh century, when the tribes were enlarged from three to five, one ephor being chosen from each tribe. Prior to this time the ephors had been authorized by the sovereigns (who were occupied with their other duties) to judge citizens involved in civil actions, but about the middle of the sixth century and after a conflict of indistinct origin between the classes the kings were superseded in the presidency of both the gerousia and the apella by the ephors, whose power came to be supreme in the state. Though annual election to the ephorate was open to all citizens, yet re-election seems to have depended on the Council's attitude. To their management of civil suits these magistrates added jurisdiction over criminal actions in which perioecs were litigants, over helots they held complete authority, they exercised some control over the kings in the city as well as in the field and occasionally even drove them into exile by threats of prosecution, negotiations with other states they conducted, they commanded expulsion of foreigners from time to time, against recalcitrant serfs they engineered organized hunts, they ordered exposure of malformed and defective babes soon after birth,[8] they supervised education of minors of each sex, from citizens they exacted strict discipline. Their annual mandate that "the citizens shave their upper lips and submit themselves to the laws" has amused moderns; but it had its serious aspect, for the condition of the upper lip was a test of compliance with the laws (on the principle that disrespect for one law provokes disregard for all laws) and he who had a mustache was held a lawbreaker and consequently the magistrates could prosecute him. In the ephorate some see, therefore, the oligarchic element of the state.

The third field treated social conditions. To full citizenship were admitted those Greeks (partly pre-Dorian, partly Dorian, partly non-Dorian), who by distinguishing themselves in the conquest of the rebels had deserved well of the state. These persons were now given shares of land, since citizenship was held only by tenant-farmers of the state. Knowledge of Lacedaemonian tenure of land is not as full as one could wish, but there is general agreement that an effort to protect the interests of the state was made by guaranteeing to its citizen-soldiers a revenue sufficient to meet their needs and that such income came from farms belonging to the state. Apparently the land was divided into two parts and for each part there were different rules. The civic land was in the center and around it lay the perioecic land. The portion of state land granted to the citizen could be bequeathed only to his eldest son, for it was considered an entailed leasehold. From this farm (*kleros*) the Spartan provided his

---

[8] This custom achieved more notoriety than another practice in the Spartan program of eugenics: the improval of progeny by the encouragement of women to bear the offspring of biologically superior citizens—whether or not these were their husbands.

share for the military mess (*syssitia*) and failure to do so lost him his citizenship. Perioecic land could be purchased, sold, partitioned and devised. Though perioecs owned most of it, yet much of it belonged to citizens. It was thence that younger sons of citizens could take some of their patrimony, so far as real property was concerned. What became of his land when a childless Spartan died is not known, but it is suspected that in such rare cases the state resumed it pending its disposal to another citizen. Also it is not clear whether farms were leased to sons who in their fathers' lifetime were sufficiently adult to serve in the army or to vote in the Assembly. Surely the system must have been elastic enough to count these as citizens by some settlement. And the ephors, we may suppose, could either cause the eldest son after his father's death to maintain his younger brothers not yet of age or arrange the support of minors from state land still undistributed. Nor do we know what measures about the lots were taken by the state, when the number of citizens decreased owing to wastage in war, forfeiture of citizenship, decline in birth-rate. But we do know that from generation to generation the disproportion between the exploiters and the exploited became more decided. To Plataea (479) Sparta could send 5,000 citizens, but only 2,000 Spartiates to Leuctra (371). And as the soldiery diminished numerically, the Spartans became more suspicious of and harsher toward the perioecs, who were being influenced by democratic ideas received from other Greeks. So the citizens began to fear the perioecs almost as much as the helots. And at last discontent separated the Lacedaemonians themselves. The equality among them was intended to be maintained by the inalienability of the state land, but some grew wealthier than others through ownership of property both real and personal. Since citizens who had only their original lots could not sustain themselves and their families and in addition contribute their portions to the mess (on a revenue unchangeable under the law), when their fields became less fertile, to retain their citizenship they borrowed on their future income, hoping against hope, and, when finally they were permitted to alienate their land, they transferred it to their creditors. Such Spartans were called *hypomeiones* (inferiors) and, because they had not managed their allotments efficiently, they were degraded from citizenship and were relegated

SOCIALISM AT SPARTA

into the landless class without, however, release from military obligations. Moreover, according to Aristotle, almost three centuries after the constitution was adopted, women had secured title to about two-fifths of the land by inheritance and through dowry, of the citizens some had large holdings of civic land and others were almost landless, ownership of the soil had fallen into the hands of a few persons.[9] Thus the socialistic features of the Lycurgan system were gradually erased by a capitalistic scheme, which apparently retained the worst characteristics of the old order. The socialism created for the citizens became only superficial and the constitution, elaborated to secure the equality of superiors (citizens) by the denial of this right to inferiors (perioecs and helots), resulted in the inequality of the citizens.

But what about the other classes in the population: the perioecs and the helots? Under supervision of the state agricultural activities were in the hands of the helots and upon the perioecs were placed manufacturing and merchandising.

The helots were owned by the state, allotted among the citizens and condemned to perpetual serfdom unless the state should ordain otherwise, for no Spartan could dismiss or manumit or sell his helots. The lots were large and the rent, paid in kind to the masters, had been regulated for all time at a period when returns from the land were small. Any improvement in agricultural methods, therefore, benefited the workers, because to helots was left all produce beyond the annual revenue, which the state had fixed the same for all serfs, which no citizen could alter, which was unvaried according to the harvest. Ordinarily the economic situation of helotry was not below that of peasantry in other parts of Greece apart from Attica. Moreover, though helots were enrolled in the army as retainers (seven to a Spartan), they were allowed to keep what booty they could gather, probably as an incentive to courage. Occasionally and chiefly for

[9] This acquisition of large estates (*latifundia*) first appeared about the middle of the fourth century, for, though unmentioned by Xenophon, it was noted by Aristotle (his younger contemporary), who recorded the passage of legislation allowing Spartans to convey their farms by gift or by will. According to Plutarch, who dated the corruption of the Lacedaemonians from the fall of Athens (404), this change was caused by the influx of capital into victorious Sparta. So the introduction of latifundia into Sparta anticipated the system in Italy by more than a century.

heroic service helots were freed by the state. But the more essential they were, the more was it necessary to hold them in subjection. Not without reason has it been observed that the discipline of the state necessitated the existence of the helots and their existence necessitated such a discipline. Their agricultural services and their intrepidity as campaigners were profitable, but their presence in the population (conspicuously outnumbering all other classes) was also dangerous, for the helots were ready to rebel at any opportune moment. So national militarism was partly a measure of protection. An important check on the helots was the *krypteia* (secret police). Spies toured the fields to execute any serf whom they suspected and these agents were held innocent of manslaughter, since the ephors annually proclaimed war against the helots. But all to no avail: rebellion was succeeded by repression again and again.

In the social scale between the citizens and the helots were the perioecs. About four times more in number than the Spartans early in the sixth century, they were grouped into a few fair-sized cities and about 100 villages, where, though subject to Sparta, they had at least home-rule. They were required to furnish soldiers, who were occasionally rewarded with citizenship for conspicuous gallantry. Perioecs enjoyed certain advantages which were at the same time disadvantages. On the one hand, their persons were not subjected to the discipline exacted from the citizens and their estates were held in fee simple and could be sold and devised. Some were farmers, but these were generally poor peasants, for the best land belonged to the state and was cultivated by helots for citizens; others supported themselves by herding; most engaged in commercial and industrial enterprises, which were unlawful for citizens and to helots forbidden. As a class, then, perioecs alone displayed initiative and interest in all phases of economic livelihood. On the other hand, the Spartans never attempted to foster trade, because they believed that the country ought to be self-sufficient. To attain this condition, though barter was elsewhere being replaced by coinage as a medium of exchange, Lycurgus restricted Spartan currency to iron bars. Also the state closed its frontiers occasionally, as when the ephors promulgated their order (the notorious *xenelasia*) that aliens, whether transient or resident, must leave Laconia. Inhospitality was an integral part of the self-sufficiency professed by Spartans, who cherished an isolation which was not splendid but stupid, because by excluding foreign ideas it forced upon them rigorous standardization. In a nation so suspicious of aliens and so disdainful of coinage it is no wonder that trade and politeness languished. And so perioecs were unable to make full use of their monopoly in trading with foreigners.

From this review of the state may be drawn three conclusions. First, the city was in reality a military camp. Second, the polity can not rightly be called either a monarchy or an aristocracy or an oligarchy or a democracy. Third, the system, which existed without grave alteration until the fourth century, was socialistic, so far as the citizens were concerned, and was well suited to this militaristic society wherein all the masters were also slaves.

Lycurgus had striven to organize a state fit for heroes, nor did he fail, for none save heroes could have endured his system. As Xenophon asserted, "Seeing that those who wanted to train in virtue were not sufficiently numerous to enable the state to become strong, Lycurgus compelled all in Sparta to work at practising all the virtues." And this compulsion came from the Delphic oracle, through whose divine mandate Lycurgus persuaded the citizens to accept his reforms: thus to disobey was to defy not only the government but also the god. Even in antiquity Spartan virtue attracted attention, to which Xenophon testified in an oft-quoted epigram: "All admire Sparta, but all are averse from adopting their system." Whence arose this admiration? Possibly because Spartans so often defeated other Greeks in battle. For centuries Spartan virtue was victorious, if we except the tragic engagement at Thermopylae, where Leonidas and his 300 men sacrificed their lives in obedience to the laws. Probably because in other Hellenic nations *stasis* (class strife) produced intermittent revolutions of government, but the Spartan ship of state almost alone weathered such storms. For generations Spartan rule survived intact, because it was established on a system which both ennobled and enslaved. If Sparta inspired the admiration of outsiders, one may conjecture the emotions of Spartans proud of their efficiency and conceited over their perfection.

In what did these exemplars of virtue boast themselves proficient? In warring with their neighbors, in keeping their helots in slavery, in restricting their perioecs to industry and commerce, in making their citizens obey the ordinances. But if there were Spartans whose minds had not been stultified by what little education was permitted them, they might have perceived that their fatherland would secure some fame as the paradise of prohibition and as the Elysium of efficiency and they might have mourned that they had no leisure to tell their city's story, for they were too occupied to spare time for its transmission. But the omission was rectified by foreigners, who, in weighing this society which forced its members to excel in virtue, found it wanting not, indeed, in efficiency, which caused much ill for itself as well as for its contemporaries, but in imagination, which by judicious importation of "sweetness and light" could have enhanced the richness of its life. And it was precisely its "grand disregard for human nature" which was the most notable feature of this *Herrenvolk*, a characteristic explaining not only its marvellous efficiency and its deadly inflexibility but also its consequent decline and its eventual catastrophe.

The Spartan system worked well—too well; for in its remarkable success at home were the seeds of its ruin abroad. After the Spartans, for generations supreme in southern Greece, had won the World War of 431-404, they failed to construct an enduring empire, chiefly because of defects in the character of the statesmen who tried to maintain it. That there were other reasons is true;[10] but it was the want of character in the harmosts (governors) which went far to impair the leadership claimed by Sparta after Athens had lost the

[10] Among these may be counted: active opposition against Sparta emanating from the peace settlement of 404; encouragement of Sparta's enemies by Persia; formation of the Second Athenian Confederacy to defend Greek cities from Spartan oppression; decrease in Spartan prestige evidenced in the increasing ability of other Hellenic states to withstand Sparta successfully; Spartan refusal to acknowledge Theban hegemony in the Boeotian League; decline in number of Spartiatai and decadence of their stock; discontent among and danger from hypomeiones, perioecs, helots; Spartan lack of experience in imperial finance, in maritime affairs, in commercial and industrial matters, in administration of oecumenical justice; no broad and sympathetic object of Spartan policy, which extended and fostered oligarchy among states averse from it; no Spartan program to restore prosperity to a war-ruined world; poverty of intelligence among Spartan politicians and inferiority of education in all Spartans when compared with other Greeks, particularly with Athenians; no Spartan vision of an imperial or a federal organization of Panhellenic scope.

war. The generals who governed cities like kings could not conform themselves with the laws either at home or abroad. Regimentation had made men, indeed, iron men, but men without morals and men without manners; for inoculation with the vaccine of virtue when at home did not noticeably safeguard Spartans from infection with the virus of vice when at large. There are those who think that the Spartan venture in a new imperialism succumbed, ironically enough, because of their use of iron currency in Laconia. In Greek states bribery was sufficiently widespread to evoke no surprise; but the ease with which Spartans were corrupted excited universal amazement. It has been stated that Lycurgus, in view of this national failing and "considering the corruption which the chemistry of coinage moves in men," legislated against temptation by banning all currency except iron bars. Whether removal of temptation or aversion from trade (or both) was his real reason, this prohibition was evaded when Sparta exacted tribute from the states once dominated by Athens and again when citizens first deposited gold and silver coins in temple-treasuries beyond the border and then imported these ostensibly for the service of the state—at any rate that was the answer when any one in authority asked about it. This situation induced an ancient humorist to insinuate that Spartans were obedient merely for lack of opportunity to be lawbreakers. And an Athenian ambassador, speaking to Spartans, declared: "Not only do you live at home regulated by prescripts and by customs incompatible with those of outsiders, but also when abroad you are neither heedful of your ordinances nor mindful of those institutions recognized by the rest of the Hellenes." Self-control, so glorified by other Greeks, was patently not a Spartan virtue in money matters, for their avaricious harmosts, who endeavored to maintain the Spartan hegemony over other peoples fighting for freedom from imperialists, took more interest in their personal gain than in the well-being of their subjects. So despotic, so insolent, so tactless was their conduct and so deficient were they in genius for ruling others, who had lived in more liberty than their masters either could endure for themselves or would grant to others—in short, so detested was the Spartan regime that this imperial experiment outside the Peloponnese collapsed after a generation of determined resistance, when, thanks to the Thebans, the Spartans were vanquished in the battle of Leuctra (371). And the event was more impressive, when it was learned that King Cleombrotus had been killed in the conflict, because after Leonidas at Thermopylae (480) no Spartan sovereign had fallen on the field.

A little over a century later Phylarchus drew a sad picture of Sparta, which now contained only 700 citizens. The old order of lots was obsolete, for the few had acquired most of the land; the military mess was abandoned; the rich oppressed the poor; the propensities which Lycurgus had attempted to extirpate by legislation reasserted themselves; discipline failed and equality vanished. It was now apparent that the Spartan, sloughing his skin, so to speak, had "at long last both ascended and descended to the measure of a man."

Social revolution was recurring in other states and escape for Sparta did not this time seem possible. Indeed, circumstances were quite propitious for revolution. Economic and social conditions could be improved, many believed, only by adoption of a program including cancellation of debts, equality of allotments, confiscation of property for the general welfare, emancipation of helots to rally support for the project. Particularly strong for reform were those who believed that Sparta's troubles arose from disregard for the laws, under which the citizens had once lived simply and harmoniously.

In the crisis a leader appeared in the person of Agis IV, a conscientious ruler as well as a cautious reformer, who was eager to restore the system of Lycurgus. Some called him a philanthropist, because he avowed sympathy with the poor, or a socialist, because he favored public ownership of land; others hailed him as a conservative patriot, who wanted to eradicate stasis, or as Plato's philosopher-king, supposing that he had "come to the kingdom for such a time as this." Though the nobles rejected Agis' measures, by which debts were to be cancelled and land was to be apportioned among 4,500 citizens (of whom some would be drawn from perioecs and from aliens sympathetic with his plans), nevertheless Agis secured the election of magistrates pledged to his reforms and with them contrived the outlawry of his colleague Leonidas, the leader of the opposition. But during the former's absence in war the latter regained his sovereignty. When Agis returned, his only option was fight or flight and so, averse from civil strife, in his turn he sought asylum, whence by a trick he was decoyed and murdered. Thus perished a lover of his country and again the few controlled the fortunes of the many.

Though Agis was dead, his program was destined to be accomplished by Cleomenes III, both the heir of Leonidas and the husband of Agis' widow. By his tutor first and then by his wife Cleomenes was trained in the ideas to which Agis had subscribed. But not until fifteen years after Agis' death did Cleomenes believe that the opportunity for action had arrived. In 227 (the tenth year of his reign) when he had returned from a campaign, accompanied by his mercenaries but having left the citizen-soldiers in camp, Cleomenes inaugurated his *coup d'état* by executing four ephors along with ten of their supporters and by exiling eighty of the opposing faction. The administrative functions of the ephors he assumed, though he may have transferred their judicial powers to new magistrates (*patronomoi*), and, though he did not dissolve the gerousia when he abolished the ephorate, he curtailed the political authority of the elders. Cleomenes next remitted the debts, redistributed the land, recruited the citizenry with several thousands of perioecs and of metoecs (foreigners whether sojourners or settlers), reorganized the army along Macedonian lines, reinstalled the military mess, revived the strict training of the young, reintroduced obsolete or obsolescent regulations—in fine, restored Lycurgan Sparta so far as he was familiar with it and so far as it was feasible. But his ambition to be a second Alexander beguiled him into warfare for five years in the Peloponnesus, until finally certain free city-states, determined to preserve what little liberty yet remained among Greeks overshadowed by their northern neighbor, conferred upon the Macedonian monarch, Antigonus III, the direction of the war against Cleomenes. From the field of Sellasia in 222, where the Spartans made the last bid for their hegemony, Cleomenes fled to Egypt to end his self-imposed exile by suicide. As the price of defeat Sparta relinquished the kingship and accepted a governor, deprived Cleomenes' new citizens of their estates and joined the Hellenic League.

Social revolution appeared yet again in Laconia. In 207 a tyrant of royal rank named Nabis, who was more ambitious than Agis and more courageous than Cleomenes, usurped the sovereignty and inaugurated a drastic program. Not only did he ruin the aristocrats, but he also seized the property of the citizens and gave it to his henchmen, distributed land among the poor, apportioned the womenfolk of proscribed nobles among his followers and manumitted as well as enriched many helots. When the details of this "New Deal" were broadcast through Hellas, to Sparta flocked the lowest elements of the world (according to ancient authors)—assassins, bandits, conspirators, filibusters, fugitives, pirates, profligates, slaves, thieves, villains—all of whom Nabis enlisted as mercenaries to uphold his despotism. Moreover, he prepared to execute Cleomenes' plans for building an empire: constructing walls at Sparta, enlarging the army with adventurers, creating a fleet manned from coastal towns. It is unnecessary to linger over the career of Nabis: how his early achievements in the Peloponnese, made possible because of the preoccupation of Philip V, the Macedonian king, and because of the weakness of the Peloponnesians, eventually aroused hostility to him; how to defend his position he allied himself with the Romans, who championed the Hellenes against Philip; how, after the defeat of Philip, when the Romans had organized the Greeks against himself and besieged Sparta with allied troops, he surrendered and accepted the Roman terms; how the Aetolians persuaded him to break his treaty with the Romans, whom they regarded as repressers of his and their rights; how the Achaeans thereupon attacked him and, repulsing his forays, hemmed him in Sparta, while they devastated Laconia; how on the pretext of rescuing him the Aetolians assassinated him (192). But it should be noted that throughout his tyranny his "reforms" continued secure. Such is the ancient picture of Nabis' regime. However, he may not have been so bad as he was portrayed, for it is thought that he had "a bad press" seeking to discredit him.

Turmoil at the death of Nabis provided a chance for the Achaeans to interfere in Spartan affairs and this intervention resulted in Sparta's entry into the Achaean League. But Spartan pride disdained this inferior role and in 189, urged by intrigues of exiles wanting to regain their rights, the Spartans seceded from the union. In the next year an

Achaean army, conducted by many whom Nabis had outlawed, advanced into Laconia, where they murdered the exponents of Spartan separatism. Too weak to fight, the Spartans beheld their fortifications dismantled, their laws abolished and replaced by Achaean ordinances, their marauding gangs and their enfranchised helots banished, their outlaws enriched by recovery of property from those serfs and hirelings whose refusal to leave the country resulted in their capture and auction as slaves, their state retied to Achaea by treaty. Thus the Achaeans hoped to offset the threat which the Spartan system from Lycurgus to Nabis had offered to the social security of other Greek nations. But by their treatment the Achaeans only nourished the menace, for in 180 they interposed in Lacedaemonian affairs to suppress Chaeron, whom they considered another Nabis. At last the Achaean attitude toward Sparta excited such displeasure among the Romans, whose participation in Hellenic politics had grown momentously, that in 178 with Rome's acquiescence the Spartan constitution was restored and the city was refortified. Sparta now seemed content and for some years remained quiet. But in 149, before the Achaeans could launch an attack strong enough to reduce Sparta which had again become resurgent, the Romans determined to control a people who could no longer live and let live. In the final settlement (146) Sparta became merely a part of another province and only a relic of another experiment in political theory and practice.

VI. TYRANNY

BY MALCOLM MACLAREN, JR.

To the Greeks of classical times, who valued highly their independence and their constitutional rule, tyranny was an unnatural institution. Yet tyrants occasionally appear in Greek political life. It is the intention of this chapter, not to present the history of these Greek tyrants, but rather to describe the more important aspects of Greek tyranny and to show how the Greeks regarded this form of government.

Tyrannos, the Greek word for tyrant, has had a singular history. In origin it was probably not Greek. It made a comparatively late appearance in the Greek language and in all likelihood was borrowed from an Asiatic language, such as Lydian or Phrygian. The sophist Hippias reports that the Greeks began using the word "in the time of Archilochus," that is, fairly early in the seventh century. The earliest reference to tyranny in extant Greek literature is contained in a fragment of Archilochus, which runs, "I do not care for wealthy Gyges, . . . I do not desire a great tyranny."

From this time on tyrannos is used as a general term for "ruler," carrying no evil implications and reflecting in no way upon the ruler's constitutional position. Tyrannos is applied to gods as an honorary title by the poets Aeschylus, Aristophanes and Herondas; and inscriptions as late as the Christian era use the word to describe the Asiatic god Men. Human beings as well as gods receive the appellation. Sophocles in his *Oedipus the King* describes Laïus, a legitimate monarch, sometimes as *basileus* (king) and sometimes as tyrannos, using the terms synonymously. Herodotus also applies both tyrannos and basileus to the same man indiscriminately.

The word tyrannos, however, was also used in a more restricted sense to designate a special kind of ruler, namely one who has usurped the governing power. Here nothing is implied as to the kind of government provided by the tyrant, who is not necessarily a harsh oppressor. Modern historians tend to regard this as the Greek definition of the tyrant *par excellence*—a supposition which needs to be modified. Aristotle, it is true, implies that this was a widely accepted definition of tyranny, when he says, "If anyone makes himself ruler by force or deceit, this is considered to be tyranny." Aristotle's own definition of tyranny is very different.

The definition of a tyrant as a usurper, pure and simple, was extended and modified. Thucydides, who contrasts tyrannies with "hereditary kingships having fixed prerogatives," seems to regard a tyrant as a usurper who rules without regard for law. Other writers see tyranny as a monarchy ruling without the consent of the governed. The Socrates of Xenophon regards kingship as "government of willing subjects according to the laws of the state" and tyranny as "government of unwilling subjects not in accordance with the laws of the state, but in accordance with the will of the ruler." Plato states that it was usual to regard willingness or unwillingness of the subjects and lawfulness or unlawfulness of the rule as criteria for distinguishing kingship from tyranny. These popular conceptions of tyranny seem to Plato inadequate. In the *Politicus* Plato's definition of the tyrant emerges from his attempt to discover an ideal government. The true statesman in Plato's view is the man who actually knows the science of government. If a ruler is truly wise in this sense, it is indifferent whether or not he rules in accordance with written laws and whether his subjects are willing or unwilling. Such a wise ruler will never do wrong. Governments other than that of the wise ruler are not legitimate and not really existent; they are imitations of ideal government; those states that imitate it best are governed best. Here Plato characteristically makes value a criterion of reality. It is a hard saying, Plato admits, to maintain that good government may contravene the laws. Yet, he argues, it is better for a wise man to rule than for laws to rule, since laws are hard to change and can seldom make allowances for special cases. A wise ruler should be allowed sometimes to disregard the laws, for the good of his subjects. A government of this kind is best; a strictly law-abiding government is only a second best. Genuine political wisdom can never be gained by a large number of men. Consequently in an ideal state there will be a monarch or at most a few rulers. The ruler who really knows the art of government is called by Plato a king. Plato gives the title of king also to a monarch, lacking true knowledge, who imitates the scientific ruler;[1] but such a king's lack of knowledge makes it imperative that he shall never act contrary to law. After thus defining the king Plato gives his definition of the tyrant in the following terms: when a monarch, motivated by *desire* and *ignorance*, acts contrary to laws and customs, he is a tyrant. When describing an ideal government Plato dismisses legality of rule as an irrelevant consideration, but he admits that such a government is unattainable by man here and now. With reference to attainable kingship and tyranny Plato has to revert once more to the principle of legality in drawing his distinction between these two governments. The tyrant, as opposed to the king, is a monarch whose rule disregards the law, but in Plato's sight the tyrant's breaking of law is less significant than the fact of his being swayed by his appetites and his ignorance. One may fairly say that Plato considers the moralistic aspect of his definition of tyranny to be primary, the legalistic aspect secondary.

Aristotle, as well as Plato, makes ethical considerations paramount in his definition of tyranny. This is natural, for Aristotle maintains that government should exist in order to make a good life possible for the citizen. In his *Politics* Aristotle lists six forms of government: monarchy, aristocracy, *politeia*, democracy, oligarchy and tyranny. He states that in monarchy and tyranny there is a single ruler, in aristocracy and oligarchy there are a few rulers, in politeia and democracy there are many rulers. Monarchy, aristocracy and politeia seek the good of the entire commonwealth and are considered by Aristotle to be good forms of government. Tyranny, oligarchy and democracy seek the good of the rulers only and are regarded by him as perversions of the three good forms. Aristotle thus defines a tyrant as a monarch who rules for his own advantage. This implies that a tyrant is not necessarily a usurper; in fact Pheidon of Argos, a legitimate monarch, is classed by Aristotle as a tyrant because he ruled despotically. Despotically implies a relation like that of a master to a slave, a relation which Aristotle regards as primarily in the master's interest. After laying down this definition Aristotle modifies it considerably. In a later passage he apparently thinks a tyrant to be

[1] B. Jowett and H. N. Fowler in their translations miss the point of this passage; it is correctly interpreted by L. Campbell in *The Sophistes and Politicus of Plato*, note on the *Politicus* (Oxford, 1867), p. 158, l. 26.

a monarch who rules lawlessly over unwilling subjects in a despotic manner. Still later he mentions a sort of super-tyrant, defined as a monarch who exercises irresponsible rule over subjects who are his equals or his betters, with a view to his own and not to his subjects' advantage.[2] From this definition Aristotle deduces that a tyrant rules over unwilling subjects, since no free man willingly endures such rule. Aristotle's treatment of tyranny is confused. All the same, it is evident that he believes the essence of tyranny to lie in the conduct of its rule and not in the manner of its acquisition. Furthermore, his various definitions of tyranny have one common feature: they regard self-interest as an integral aspect of tyranny.

Apparently, as time went on, the conception of the tyrant as a usurper was virtually supplanted by the view that the earmark of tyranny is in the character of its government. To Polybius kingship means a monarchy voluntarily accepted by the people and directed by reason rather than by violence and terrorism; tyranny is the evil counterpart of kingship. Thus we see that Polybius must regard tyranny as a monarchy lacking the consent of the governed and maintaining itself by violence. Cicero, too, in his *Republic* thinks of the tyrant from an ethical standpoint. He writes: "When a king begins to be unjust, that form of government [kingship] ceases then and there and that king becomes a tyrant." Finally, we must quote a significant statement made by Nepos. He says of Miltiades: "In the Chersonesus . . . he had been called a tyrant, but he was a just one." Evidently Nepos expects the notion of a "just tyrant" to seem paradoxical to his readers. And so he adds, by way of clarification, that a ruler may be classed as a tyrant if he holds permanent rule in a state which has previously enjoyed liberty. We may conclude from this passage that when Nepos was writing it was usual to regard injustice as an essential feature of tyranny and that a strictly constitutional definition of the tyrant was no longer generally current.

It should be pointed out that "tyrant," "tyranny," "tyrannize," etc. were often used as abusive epithets in cases where these terms were not literally applicable. Strictly speaking, a tyranny was a monarchy. Nevertheless, we find nonmonarchic governments described loosely

---

[2] By "betters" Aristotle seems to mean those more noble; he defines nobility as "ancient wealth and virtue."

as tyrannies by hostile writers. For example, a democratic regime in Corinth, which owed its establishment to a massacre of political opponents, was likened by Xenophon to a tyranny. Aristotle characterized as a tyranny the rule of the Thirty who misgoverned Athens in 404; this government, of course, was actually a narrow oligarchy. Hermodorus described as tyrants those who were responsible for the death of Socrates. In a similar spirit Thucydides made both Pericles and Cleon, with a downrightness not far removed from cynicism, call the Athenian Empire a tyranny.

We have seen that tyrannos has both a general and a special meaning. It may denote a ruler, in the broadest sense, and it may designate a special kind of ruler, in a more restricted sense. These two uses of the word exist side by side. Sophocles uses tyrannos as a colorless term for "ruler" in his *Oedipus the King*. In the same play he uses tyrannos in the opprobrious sense when he says, "Sinful pride begets the tyrant." So too Herodotus uses the word *tyrannis* to mean monarchy in the general sense, as when he describes the rule of Astyages now as a kingship and again as a tyrant; but he constantly uses tyrannis in the special sense also, as when one of his speakers voices the sentiment that there is nothing on earth more unjust or more bloodthirsty than tyranny. One should not be startled by this dual employment of the words in question. To the founding fathers of our republic kings and lords were an abhorrence. And yet it is highly improbable that they would have shrunk from hailing their Maker in scriptural language, as "King of kings and Lord of lords."

It is now time to consider the causes that produced tyranny and the methods employed by tyrants in gaining their power. Whether or not usurpation be regarded as the essence of tyranny, the fact is that a vast majority of the men ordinarily classed as tyrants were usurpers. This study is not particularly concerned with legitimate rulers whose conduct in power sufficed to class them as tyrants according to some definition of the term. It is confined rather to conditions which made it possible for an individual to seize absolute control of a government.

It must be admitted that there is very little specific information about the early tyrants' rise to power. There is no doubt, however, that in the seventh century landowning aristocracies were in a privileged position politically, economically and socially. Small farmers, finding it increasingly difficult to make a living, were becoming poverty-stricken and debt-ridden and were even being reduced to serfdom and slavery. Relief seemed impossible to obtain under existing conditions, since government and the administration of justice were in the hands of the aristocrats, who formed the creditor class. With the growth of commerce and industry a new class of workers came into being and not a few individuals made fortunes. The interests of the workers were disregarded by the aristocrats. As for the *nouveaux riches*, some succeeded in winning political equality with the aristocrats and some actually married into noble families and thus attained social standing; but many men of outstanding ability and energy failed to gain any sort of political and social recognition. Probably in some states the nobles differed racially from the commoners and this distinction promoted ill feeling. The exclusiveness and the oppressiveness of the aristocracies were bringing about a situation ripe for revolt.

In many states a revolution led by a popular champion, who not infrequently was a dissatisfied noble, overthrew the rule of the aristocrats. The masses, largely uneducated and lacking in political experience, could hardly begin to cope with the problems of self-government immediately after the fall of the aristocracies. Quite naturally the revolutionary leader assumed control of the state, thereby making himself a tyrant. These tyrannies resulted largely from the struggles of the underprivileged elements to win some measure of political, social and economic betterment.[3] Many tyrants so improved the condition of the lower classes that the citizens became both desirous and capable of self-government—a result hardly intended by the tyrants. These tyrannies may fairly be reckoned as marking a necessary stage in the political evolution of their states.

[3] Professor Prentice, in his book *The Ancient Greeks* (Princeton, 1940), doubts whether the seventh century tyrannies were caused principally by class struggles. These conflicts, he holds, did not become serious until the commercial and industrial classes grew numerous and powerful. That the seventh century saw no great development of commerce and industry he believes to be demonstrated by the persistence of emigration from Greek states throughout this period. He suggests that the seventh century tyrants may have been military dictators who owed their positions to national crises caused by threatening foreign enemies.

The later history of many Greek states was disfigured by bitter partisan struggles between rival oligarchic and democratic factions. All too often these animosities produced rioting, bloodshed and civil war. Ostensibly the issue at stake was the form of government, but, as Aristotle realizes, the struggle was fundamentally one of the rich against the poor. Here we see something rather different from the earlier class struggles, in which certain oppressed groups striving to win relief were opposed by a long dominant nobility attempting to maintain its supreme position. The strife about to be considered is not a constructive stage in the development of the city-state, but is rather symptomatic of dissolution and decay.

Wealthier citizens feared that a radical democracy might confiscate their property and divide it among the mob. The lower class had reason to fear the establishment of an oligarchy which might curtail their civic rights and prove oppressive. An ambitious man seeking to make himself tyrant could, like Euphron of Sicyon, win over the masses by promising to grant all their desires. Again, a nervous oligarchy sometimes employed mercenaries for its protection; whereupon the mercenaries' commander might, like Timophanes of Corinth, surprise his employers and make himself tyrant with the help of his troops. A threatening foreign enemy often proved a factor in the establishment of a tyranny. Faced with danger from without, a state might feel it necessary to dispense with the luxury of untrammeled political squabbling. Then an individual might exploit the danger and win supreme power, perhaps by force or perhaps with more or less general consent. Dionysius the Elder at Syracuse was believed to have nursed along a Carthaginian menace deliberately, the better to establish and to perpetuate his tyranny.

Another cause of tyranny, external rather than internal, was foreign intervention, which often foisted a puppet government upon a weaker state. Thus Peisistratus set up Lygdamis as tyrant in Naxos.

The actual process of setting up a tyranny often followed a fairly uniform pattern. Somehow the potential tyrant acquired an armed bodyguard, possibly, as in the case of Dionysius the Elder and of Peisistratus, by direct grant from unsuspecting governmental authorities. Frequently a surprise attack by these troops captured a city's acropolis. Thereupon, possession of the entire city was a usual but not an inevitable result, as Cylon of Athens learned to his cost. Naturally the revolution had a better chance of success if its leader were a military man like Peisistratus or Orthagoras—to name but two of many. Another important factor in a tyrant's success was wealth, owned by the tyrant himself or by the state or by citizens whom he could despoil. Money made it possible to hire a bodyguard; and the average tyrant required large sums for carrying on his government, as we shall see. The geographical distribution of early tyrannies testifies to the importance of wealth. Greek tyranny appears to have originated among the Asiatic cities. The chief regions in which it next appears are certain Aegean islands, Athens, Corinth and some neighboring states, northwest Greece, Sicily and Magna Graecia. All these regions lie along important trade routes. In regions like Laconia and Boeotia, which were poor, backward, out of the way and predominantly agricultural, we find no tyrannies in the earlier days. In backward Thessaly tyranny was late in appearing and significantly it had its beginning at Pherae, the one Thessalian city with easy access to the sea. Unless supported by an outside power a tyranny could hardly exist in a poor state. The importance to a tyrant of financial and commercial power is well emphasized by Ure in *The Origin of Tyranny*, but this writer goes too far when he discounts, with great arbitrariness, political and military power as factors in the establishment of the earlier tyrannies.

An account of the way in which tyrants governed is also pertinent to this discussion. It is probably doing them no injustice to say that they were not a group of starry-eyed reformers, eager to right the wrongs of the world. They were, rather, ambitious self-seeking men whose principal object was to win and to maintain power and to pass it on to a son or a near relative. A tyrant might choose to adopt one of two general policies. Either he could apply repression and terrorism in order to keep himself in power or he could use conciliatory methods in the hope of winning popular approval. Aristotle states that oppression is the time-honored policy which most tyrants have employed. He gives a description of standard oppressive measures, most of which, it may be noted, can be illustrated in history. A tyrant, Aristotle remarks, destroys his outstanding citizens, for he hates the proud and the independent. Xenophon declares that a tyrant fears the brave lest they make a bold bid for freedom, the intelligent lest they plot and the just lest the people desire to be ruled by them. Dio Cassius in a rather rhetorical passage says that under a tyranny no citizen wishes to have any outstanding capacities or possessions. One is reminded, in this connection, of the anecdote of the tyrants Periander and Thrasybulus told by Herodotus. Periander of Corinth, desiring advice as to how he should conduct his rule, sent a messenger to consult Thrasybulus of Miletus. Thrasybulus took the messenger into a field of grain and slashed down the tallest and finest stalks, saying never a word. The messenger returned home perplexed and told his story. Periander, however, understood what was meant and acting on the advice he proceeded to kill or to banish his leading citizens. The anecdote may be unhistorical. Aristotle tells it with the roles of Periander and Thrasybulus reversed and the tale appears in Roman tradition with reference to Tarquinius Superbus.

Aristotle next says that tyrants limit the citizens' freedom of association, that they discourage education and that they frown upon men's clubs, in the belief that discussion groups and common meals engender self-respect and self-confidence among the people. We are told that Polycrates of Samos destroyed the palaestrae where his subjects had been accustomed to assemble for exercise and companionship. We hear that Dionysius the Elder prevented his son from receiving an education and from playing with other boys. Aristodemus of Cumae is said to have killed his aristocratic enemies and to have planned a massacre of their sons. Dissuaded from this, he sent the boys into the country to do farm work, denying them the education and training proper to freeborn children. Also he put an end to assemblages in the gymnasia.

Aristotle mentions that tyrants employ spies, sometimes female, to give information about chance sayings or doings of individuals. Dionysius and Hieron of Syracuse were apparently notorious for their secret police; in fact Pindar gives Hieron friendly advice not to listen to the whispers of such spies.

A tyrant, Aristotle continues, desires his citizens not to be prosperous, for financial independence may give them free time in which to plot against him; this Aristotle asserts to be one motive which prompts tyrants to levy taxes. Doubtless the financial policies of many tyrants were objectionable. The Greeks usually resented direct taxation and tolerated it with a good grace only in emergencies. To raise funds the tyrants resorted to confiscation, to taxation and even to temple-robbery, a measure adopted by Euphron. The situation must have been particularly galling when money wrung from the people was spent on the mercenary force which held them in subjection and on the tyrants' personal pleasures. Tyrants were given to lavishing money on expensive women, on elaborate and prolonged feasts, on debauches and on gaudy costumes.

Aristotle remarks that a tyrant stirs up wars in order to keep the people occupied and convinced of his indispensability. We may point to Dionysius the Elder as an outstanding warmongering tyrant, although we must credit him with freeing a large part of Sicily from Carthaginian domination.

Aristotle summarizes the oppressive policies of tyranny by stating that they aim to keep the people meek, to make the people distrustful of one another and to render the people politically powerless.

As an alternative, Aristotle shows how a tyrant may keep his power by following a policy of mildness. The method, generally speaking, consists in doing the reverse of what the oppressive tyrant does. Perhaps it will be enlightening to consider the reign of a typical beneficent tyranny, that of the Peisistratids in Athens.[4] More is known about them than about any other Greek tyrants.

Peisistratus ultimately succeeded in conciliating both the upper and the lower classes. In rising to power he showed some ruthlessness, particularly toward the nobles. By the time that he was permanently established, some of his opponents had been killed, others were in exile. Probably he took over the property of some or all of these victims and certain modern historians suppose that he distributed confiscated lands among the poorer peasants. A blow was struck at the judicial powers of the nobility when Peisistratus organized deme-courts. Nevertheless, Peisistratus at length won the support of most of the aristocracy by means of friendly social intercourse, as Aristotle tells us. Certain noble exiles were finally allowed to return.

---

[4] After the assassination of Hipparchus this tyranny was oppressive for a short time.

Some acts of Peisistratus were designed to help the peasants, as when he advanced them money. Also much was done for the skilled and unskilled laborers. Work was provided for them by a program of public buildings and municipal improvements. Taxes were declared by Thucydides to have been moderate—for a tyranny. Considerable income was derived from Peisistratus' Thracian possessions. The conquest of Sigeum and the establishment of a protectorate in the Thracian Chersonese furthered the economic welfare of Athens, for thus the city gained control of the western end of the Hellespont, a vital point on the trade route from the Black Sea. The Peisistratids tried to maintain friendly relations with adjacent states, hoping, no doubt, that their neighbors would refuse to serve as bases for any possible attempts to overthrow the tyranny.

By making a magnificent spectacle of the Panathenaic festival Peisistratus appealed to the citizens' religious feelings and gratified their taste for pomp and display. Credit probably should go to Peisistratus for the introduction of tragic contests at the City Dionysia. His son, Hipparchus, who invited Anacreon and Simonides to Athens, subsidizing Simonides generously, was a distinguished patron of literature.

Peisistratus made a point of maintaining constitutional forms. Elections were held as usual, but somehow the tyrant's candidates always won. Peisistratus once allowed himself to be charged with homicide and he actually appeared for trial. It is almost superfluous to add that the prosecutor let the case go by default. Aristotle thinks that the prosecutor lost his nerve. How he ever had the nerve to start proceedings is a mystery. Perhaps he and the tyrant were in collusion from the beginning of the affair.

Many of these activities of the Peisistratids can be matched in other tyrannies, both benevolent and oppressive. The Corinthian Cypselids won a colonial empire in northwest Greece. Polycrates of Samos, the Cypselids and Dionysius the Elder were particularly noted for their splendid monuments and buildings. Cleisthenes of Sicyon in promoting the worship of the rather plebeian god Dionysus recalls the religious innovations of Peisistratus. Polycrates entertained the poet Anacreon at his court. Theron of Acragas and Hieron presumably made it well worth Pindar's while to celebrate their athletic triumphs in his odes; Hieron had Pindar as a guest. Clearchus of Heraclea founded a famous library. Dionysius the Elder was, among other things, a playwright whose career included a victory in an Athenian tragic contest. Cleisthenes of Sicyon, who won chariot races at the Olympian and Pythian games, was an athlete to compare with Hieron and Theron. Whatever else may be said about the tyrants as a class, there is no denying that there were brilliant, colorful and versatile individuals among them.

An account should be given of the circumstances under which tyrannies came to an end. Not a few of them survived the deaths of their founders, but it was an unusual tyranny that lasted, as did the Orthagorids, the Cypselids and the dynasty of Clearchus in Heraclea, beyond the second generation. Tyranny was an unnatural institution to the Greeks, who generally valued their independence. An unconstitutional rule affronted their best political thinking; an oppressive rule tended to defeat its own ends; even a mild tyranny was hardly to be endured with equanimity. When political and economic conditions were improved by a tyrant, an important reason for his existence ended. The actual overthrow of a tyranny might be facilitated when a successor to the power proved less able than his predecessor. Assassination sometimes ended a tyranny. Quarrels in a tyrant's family and foreign intervention might lead to the fall of tyrants. A tyranny might be followed by a democracy, as in Athens, or by an oligarchy, as in Corinth.

We cannot fail to notice that to an extraordinary degree the policies of ancient tyrants have counterparts in those of modern dictators. Practices common to both groups include: ruthless elimination of outstanding citizens, employment of secret police, curtailment of educational privileges, limitation of freedom of association, extortionate financial exactions, construction of great public buildings, patronage of art, interference with established religious activities, maintenance of empty constitutional forms (especially by means of farcical elections) and promotion of wars.

Having seen how Greek tyrants operated, we can better discuss the ancient definitions of tyranny. The definition of a tyrant as a usurper had its advantages, for it was simple and easy to apply.

And yet it is not surprising that there was a tendency to supersede this definition, since it ignored aspects which must have seemed most significant to the tyrant's subjects. Picture a man, living under a tyranny, who had seen friends exiled and killed, property confiscated, women outraged and civil liberties flouted. Such a man, if asked to indicate the most noteworthy feature of his government, would most likely have dwelt on the tyrant's behavior in power, not on the means by which the tyrant rose to power. The philosopher, no less than the man in the street, was disinclined to be satisfied with a strictly constitutional definition of tyranny, as we have already seen. And yet, if this definition is abandoned and if a tyrant is defined as one whose rule is either unacceptable to his subjects or in his own interests, the problem of determining degrees of unacceptability or of self-interest may arise. Aristotle, who apparently considers self-interest to be an essential aspect of tyranny, classifies Peisistratus as a tyrant, although he seems to describe the rule of Peisistratus as benevolent on the whole. It is not improbable that Peisistratus, in Aristotle's opinion, was something of a hypocrite and that Peisistratus or his like was in the mind of Aristotle, when he suggested in the *Politics* that a tyrant may keep in power by cleverly acting like a king and thus making his tyranny appear regal (*i.e.*, disinterested). No doubt hypocrisy can be seen in Peisistratus' career. His maintenance of constitutional forms and his submitting to a trial for murder may be regarded as pure humbug. Aristotle asserts that Peisistratus was acting in his own interests when he helped the peasants, for he took a percentage of their products. One feels that Peisistratus was shrewd enough to make self-interest coincide frequently with popular interest, that he was in general well-disposed toward his people, but that in any serious clash between his own interests and those of the state he would not have been the one to suffer. In this way, Peisistratus might be regarded as a "self-interested" ruler and therefore as a tyrant according to Aristotle's definition of the term. Although the Greeks seem not to have evolved any altogether satisfactory definition of tyranny, they were in substantial agreement as to who was a tyrant and who was not.

The general Greek attitude toward tyranny as expressed in our literary sources is one of bitter hostility. Xenophon in his *Hieron* seeks to demonstrate that the tyrant despite his wealth and power is less happy than the private citizen. Both Plato in his *Republic* and *Politicus* and Aristotle in his *Politics* consider tyranny to be the worst form of government.[5] This list of witnesses need not be extended. Nevertheless, one tyrant, Peisistratus, succeeded in winning a good reputation with posterity. People looked back upon his reign, Aristotle states, as though it were a second Golden Age. Only an occasional voice, like that of Isocrates, speaks in condemnation of Peisistratus. Regarding Cypselus we have two rather contrary traditions: Herodotus considers him mild; Aristotle and Nicolaus of Damascus regard him as oppressive. This suggests that our literary evidence may be unduly prejudiced against some of the tyrants.

Actions which are recorded, however, give eloquent testimony to the Greek hatred of tyranny. An Athenian decree quoted by Andocides provides that all citizens shall swear to kill anyone attempting to establish a tyranny; that a tyrannicide shall not be counted as a murderer and that he shall receive the slain man's property; that anyone slain while attempting to kill a tyrant shall together with his descendants be given certain honors. Harmodius and Aristogeiton, popularly but mistakenly regarded as liberators, were celebrated in sculpture and in song. The living heads of their families were granted in perpetuity seats of honor at public assemblages and meals in the Prytanaeum. Xenophon and Aristotle speak as though it were a widespread practice to honor tyrannicides. Tyrants' names after their fall were commonly erased from monuments. Ostracism at Athens and similar forms of temporary banishment elsewhere were originally devised as safeguards against tyranny.

Finally, in assessing tyranny's contribution to Greek political life various considerations should be kept in mind. Some tyrannies did great, if unintentional, service to the cause of popular government. They broke the power of the aristocracies and provided stable regimes during which the people could develop an ability to rule

---

[5] In Plato's last work (the *Laws*) it is said that a good government would be most readily established in practice, if a young, high-minded tyrant were brought under the influence of an able legislator.

themselves. To do tyranny full justice it must be admitted that some states enjoyed more power and prosperity under tyrants than at any other periods of their history. On the other hand, many a tyrant must have done incalculable harm to his state by his shameless misuse of its resources both material and human.

VII. FEDERAL UNIONS

BY CHARLES ALEXANDER ROBINSON, JR.

THAT remarkable manifestation of the human spirit known as Hellenism was a product, by and large, of the city-state, hence we have been inclined to focus our attention upon that form of government. Yet it is true that the city-state failed conspicuously to solve certain fundamental problems of life and that it was reserved for federalism to create the best type of government in the Greek world.

Various factors, active and otherwise, influenced Greek thinking on the subject of union. A powerful state, such as Athens (which in addition had the good fortune to be situated in a relatively large district), could not possibly be as eager for federation, even when only the memory of her former greatness was left, as a small city-state. Since the Greeks were always ready to dominate their neighbors, it was natural for weaker states to band together in common defence. Thus many Greek leagues were formed to meet specific needs and tended to disappear with the passing of these crises.

There were, in general, two main reasons why more of these leagues did not strive for permanent union and, with it, for a broader citizenship than the city-state could offer. The first, at once the weakness and the strength of ancient Greece, was the particularism of the city-state—that love of autonomy which insisted on complete control of foreign affairs and which was often the equivalent of race suicide. Second, it frequently happened that in spite of the solemn oaths with which treaties of free alliance had been undertaken the leading state of a league attempted to subordinate the other members to itself. Party strife, class struggle and the imperialistic scheming of powerful states often impelled the Greeks, however, to experiment with union. But the chances of permanence were not good unless the league was founded on the solid rock of a common *ethnos* (tribal group) or at least upon a community of interests. Such a league was still more likely to succeed if it also contained within its borders no state of sufficient strength to control the collective will. And, finally, if a league hoped to be both successful and democratic it must have a common citizenship and a primary Assembly whose effectiveness was not vitiated by, say, the infrequency of its meetings or the difficulties of attendance.

Of the three important types of leagues created by ancient Greece the Peloponnesian League illustrates an alliance of free cities with its own organs of government; the League of Corinth was a confederation of sovereign states formed by a king; and the Aetolian League, developing from a cantonal commune, became a federation with its organs of government based on a common citizenship. The Thessalian League, long a puppet of the Macedonian king, and similar leagues in Asia Minor during the Hellenistic Age had little real significance.

From early days there had existed in Greece religious leagues whose origins went back to festivals or to fairs. The only one of these associations to acquire political importance was the Amphictyonic League, which had grown up at the sanctuary of Demeter Pylaea at Anthela and came to be known after its seizure of Delphi (*ca.* 590) as the Delphic Amphictyony. The basis of this union was the tribal group and not the city-state. Each of the twelve communities in the League furnished four "speakers" to the Council and a recorder; the speakers proposed measures and the recorders voted upon them. In a rudimentary way the League organized international justice and provided compulsory sanctions against offending members; for example, it was forbidden to destroy a member city or to cut it off from running water. The antiquity of Delphi, no less than the fame of its oracle, gave the League considerable authority in the Greek world, but because of the temptation to extend this authority into the political sphere the Delphic Amphictyony never rose to its fullest opportunity of moulding the Greeks into a nation. Its chief importance in later Greek history lay in the prestige it gave its suzerain, particularly newcomers such as Philip II or the Aetolians, who might hope to use it as a stepping stone to more ambitious schemes.

Neither the Delphic Amphictyony nor the more famous Peloponnesian League was a federation in the sense that the organs of government were based on a common citizenship. It will be worthwhile, nevertheless, to examine the structure of the Peloponnesian League which, as the stabilizing force in the Peloponnesus for many generations, brought security to its members and gave a stimulus to the federal idea. The Peloponnesian League was officially styled "The Lacedaemonians and Their Allies," but for the sake of convenience we may think of it simply as a symmachy, a coalition or alliance of autonomous states with an Assembly or other permanent organs of government. The Greeks commonly resorted to a league of this sort to obtain unity of action, particularly in the field of foreign relations.

The Peloponnesian League, as such, probably began about 505.[1] A half-century earlier Sparta had been forced to abandon her policy of naked conquest and to turn to a system of separate alliances with various states. Her allies soon included the entire Peloponnesus (except Argos and Achaea), Megara and Aegina. About 506, however, Sparta called on her allies for help against Athens, whereupon Corinth and other states demanded that a congress be held to consider a more satisfactory method of alliance. We must imagine the former group of allies sending representatives to the congress and agreeing upon certain general principles—a constitution, as we might call it—which the individual states later embodied in treaties and swore to support.

The new League was to be permanent and provided chiefly for collaboration in foreign policy; in other words, its purpose was purely general and was not directed against any specific state. The chief feature of the League was the Assembly of representatives of the constituent states. Its approval was necessary before the League could take any action, such as the declaration of a defensive or an offensive war or the admission of new members (by means of treaty), and it could pass decrees, some of which occasionally went beyond ordinary matters to what were, in effect, constitutional amendments. We have here the federal idea, for it must be stressed that the decisions of the Assembly were binding on all members and that Sparta could not call on others for help without the approval of the Assembly. Sparta enjoyed the double advantage of having her

[1] J. A. O. Larsen, *Classical Philology*, vol. XXVIII (1933), pp. 257-276; vol. XXIX (1934), pp. 1-19.

officials the sole executives of the League and of being able to thwart a member by the simple process of refusing to call a meeting of the Assembly. Against this advantage, however, may be placed the fact that a member state apparently could escape from its obligations by appealing to religious scruples. Sparta insisted upon a local aristocracy or oligarchy as the form of government of the constituent states wherever she could, but otherwise they were quite independent in their domestic affairs; they were not subject to tribute, although occasionally they had to make financial contributions.

The Peloponnesian League was undemocratic since it lacked the one absolute requisite of ancient democracy, a primary Assembly. Its achievements were very great, nonetheless, for it brought together many scattered cities and persuaded them that autonomy in their own affairs could be maintained and security won if they surrendered to a central authority a measure of control over their foreign relations. For nearly 200 years (550-370) Sparta dominated the Peloponnesus and on two occasions almost succeeded in turning her union into an Hellenic League—during her heroic role at the time of the final Persian invasion and again after the Peloponnesian War when the excesses and failures of Athenian democracy seemed clear to all. But isolation and apparent security had made Sparta insensitive to her ideals, and instead of rising to the opportunities of her victory over Athens she eventually made a mockery of the cry that she had come to destroy the tyrant.

The Greeks were not ready in the fifth century to reconcile, in a large federation, municipal autonomy and international co-operation. Even where a union existed, as in the case of the Peloponnesian League, there was often little common government and no general citizenship. There is abundant evidence, however, that man was becoming less narrow in his outlook. A common literature and art, national meeting places, such as Delphi and Olympia, and the dominance of things Athenian are examples. But above all, perhaps, we may point to the fact that events in the fifth century were tending toward some scheme of unity. For better or worse, Pericles had built his empire, as Sparta had hers, and to the north, in Boeotia, there existed still another union.

Boeotia, with its ethnic basis, its annual religious festival and its need for security, provided fertile soil for federation, but in the rivalry of the individual states it also possessed the rock on which Greek federalism often foundered. The persistent political issue in Boeotia was federalism against autonomy and, because the leading state, Thebes, was oligarchic and looked to Sparta for support, the advocates of autonomy were democratic and pro-Athenian.

About the middle of the fifth century the Boeotians, urged by Sparta, reformed their old League to resist Athenian aggression. Their union was an oligarchic confederacy; the mere fact that the chief organ of government was a representative Council, rather than a primary Assembly, stamped it at once, in Greek eyes, as aristocratic. The whole district of Boeotia was divided into eleven electoral regions, four of which were assigned to Thebes. It was proper for Thebes with its greater population and wealth to have the largest representation and the heaviest burdens, but it meant, too, that the smaller states (lacking, for example, the protection afforded by the United States Senate) were responsible for decisions in which they had little voice. Each of the eleven electoral regions furnished one Boeotarch for the central executive board, sixty members for the Council and a proportionate share of the judges on the federal court. Thus Thebes had four of the eleven Boeotarchs and 240 of the 660 Councillors—not enough to give her a majority, though she could generally control the votes of smaller communities—and in return she contributed proportionately to the federal army and to the occasional levies on property which took the place of a regular tax. It seems likely that active citizenship at Thebes was restricted to those financially able to equip themselves as hoplites. The Council of the League met at Thebes; ordinary business was conducted by one of its four rotating committees, though any important decision had to be ratified by the entire body. The duties of the Boeotarchs were concerned chiefly with military and foreign affairs; it is not known to what extent the federal court was a tribunal of appeal or of the first instance. The Boeotian League, it may be fairly claimed, was popular and successful, bringing, as it did, unity to an entire district without destroying local self-government, but it remained sectional and offered no solution for the political problem of Greece.

Its whole tendency, moreover, was toward greater Theban hegemony, so that in the fourth century Boeotia became, in effect, a Theban city-state.

Perhaps the Greeks of the Chalcidice, situated on the very border of the barbarian world, were in a position to think, even more acutely than some others, on the futility of the fratricidal warfare of the day; perhaps, too, their proximity to Macedon opened their eyes to the efficiency of monarchy. Be that as it may, in their effort to resist Athenian imperialism in the period before the outbreak of the Peloponnesian War, they came together in a strong and remarkable confederacy, which might almost be called a sympolity (in a sympolity every man kept his own local citizenship and acquired an additional citizenship in the league). The constituent cities were internally free and at the same time equal, or proportionately so, in the new federal authority that assumed a large control of common affairs. In the Chalcidian League every citizen of a town was guaranteed freedom of commerce and intermarriage in every other town; thus there was civil equality but not common citizenship. The cities were essentially free in their own affairs, but surrendered to the federal Assembly control of their foreign and military policy. The coinage was federal and the head of the League was an elected general. The League was limited geographically to a small district and the attendance at the meetings of the Assembly suffered from poor communications and the poverty of many of its members. Thus it developed that the Assembly of Olynthus, the capital, more and more came to be identical with the Assembly of the League. A wise and moderate leadership of a league by a single city could be an offset to Macedonian monarchy, but inevitably Olynthus became domineering and threatened other states, until Sparta disbanded the League in the course of the fourth century (379).

It would be easy to create a false impression of Greece in the fourth century. An economic depression, the growing attractiveness of a mercenary career, the interference of the Persian king in Greek affairs and the well-nigh constant warfare must be balanced against undoubted achievements in art and literature. The tyrannical rule of Sparta, following the collapse of the Athenian Empire, was itself succeeded by the short-lived hegemony of Thebes under Epaminondas. It is little wonder that the fourth century witnessed many a peace congress, the recrudescence of old leagues and the birth of new ones. The Second Athenian League, for example, was an attempt to bring together a great state and several smaller ones in a dual form of government. Authority was divided equally between the central Synod, in which each ally (excluding Athens) had one vote, and the Athenian Council and Assembly; a measure adopted by one body had to be ratified by the other. The Synod met at Athens and the executive was Athenian; and yet, by the guarantee of autonomy and the prohibition against Athenians owning land or establishing colonies in allied territory, an attempt was made to avoid some of the mistakes of the earlier Empire. The League had been formed to resist Spartan aggression and with the disappearance of that danger and with the increasing belligerency of Athens herself it passed out of existence.

It seemed to be beyond the political capacity of the Greeks to create a national state, although there were many people who meditated upon this and kindred problems. Demosthenes stood for the self-government and self-sufficiency of the city-state and harked back to a supposed Golden Age; an ever-growing body of opinion agreed with Isocrates that the city-states should unite against Persia; Plato and Aristotle instead of exploring the possibility of a new system, such as federalism, preached the need of reforming the city-state itself. As the struggle of the few against the many passed into an open contest between rich and poor, the propertied classes favored the arbitrary rule of an alien state (Macedon and, later, Rome). There were moments in the third century, however, when the masses themselves thought of monarchy as a protection against the misgovernment of the few.

Amid the confused conditions and conflicting theories of the fourth century Philip II brought unity to Greece under the Macedonian monarchy. The battle of Chaeronea (338) did not mean, however, the end of the city-state (the city-state lived on, as a reality and as an ideal, so long as hope of freedom existed in Greece), but it did mean the beginning of a new era. Given time, the Greeks might have solved the problem of cooperation themselves, but they had reckoned without Macedon. Henceforth the pattern of Greece was different. Great states, and even small ones, might stand aloof or give grudging and disloyal support to leagues, but from now on the league (or the king back of it), and not the city-state, was the moving force in Greece. Philip II had had the good fortune, as a youthful hostage, to study Boeotian federalism at firsthand. A remarkable man, and a statesman, he now planned to use his momentous victory to bring peace, unity and internal harmony to the Greek world.

It is customary to speak of the new union as the League of Corinth, for there it was organized and generally met, but officially it was called "The Hellenes." The Greeks under Persian rule were excluded, but the states of Greece proper (except Sparta) were united in what was essentially a Panhellenic union. The most important feature of the League was the representative Assembly, to which the various states sent delegates. The unit was not necessarily the city-state, for smaller states were grouped together or were actually merged with an entire district, an unpopular arrangement in spite of the fact that it gave the small states proportionate rights against the larger ones. Representation was in proportion to population or, perhaps, to the size of the military contingent which a state could raise. Each representative had one vote. A board of five chairmen, chosen from the Assembly, prepared the business for the meetings and acted as an executive committee.

Here one sees representative government in the strict sense of the term, for the delegates had full powers; but the absence of a primary Assembly, the large area of the League and its inability to form and express an Hellenic public opinion, no less than the particularism of the city-state and its reluctance to surrender sovereign powers, were among the reasons why the League did not call forth universal enthusiasm and loyalty. Macedonia itself was not a member, although its king and his descendants were to be the military commander and head (*hegemon*) of the League for life and the king or his representative (a general) was to enforce the decisions of the Assembly. The monarchical element was a new one in Greek experience and was resented by some as a thinly disguised alien rule, but, once we grant that the League had been formed by force, it must be said that the hegemon, no less than the members of the League, was bound by the decisions of the Assembly. Thus we may speak of the League of Corinth as a constitutional monarchy with a representative Assembly.

Philip, nevertheless, dominated the diplomatic affairs of the League; in this offensive and defensive alliance no member could war against another member or against Philip; and offenders against the League were to be tried by the federal court. Each state was required, on demand, to provide its share of funds for the government and to furnish its own quota of troops or be fined for every day its contingent was absent from the field. On the other hand, neither tribute nor garrisons (except those already established at Chalcis, Thebes and Corinth) were imposed upon the Greeks and each state was to maintain its existing form of government and be internally free. A contradiction, however, was embodied in the constitution (in the treaties, that is, which formed the League), for it was stipulated that the League might interfere in a state on the threat of social revolution, the threat, so familiar to Greeks, to free the slaves, confiscate property, divide the land and cancel debts. The League of Corinth, for all its weaknesses, had a popular appeal and was reconstituted at various times in Greek history.[2]

Alexander's world conquest and his habit, later in life, of treating the Greeks as subjects instead of as allies raised acutely the question of federalism in Greece. Could the League of Corinth, a creature of Macedon, be the answer? Could any league, indeed, prevent itself from becoming a pawn of one of the new large territorial states? Certainly the city-state was helpless before the powerful and efficient Hellenistic monarchies. As the Greeks poured eastward in search of golden opportunities, the homeland was robbed of much of its manpower. Many city-states, having surrendered the right to direct their own foreign policy, became in effect municipalities, so that men lost interest in political life, though never their fear of social revolution. In every city there were those who for selfish reasons

[2] It is possible that we have ascribed to the original constitution some of the details of Demetrius Poliorcetes' revival in 303. See J. A. O. Larsen, *Classical Philology*, vol. XX (1925), pp. 313-329; vol. XXI (1926), pp. 52-71.

favored Macedon or some other monarchy, but most people were determined to oppose a king's despotism. The answer, no doubt, was federalism, but a federalism which avoided the mistakes of the past. The new league must be neither limited geographically nor dominated by a single city; it must give local autonomy and yet centralize authority; it must be democratic and evoke loyalty from its members, giving them a satisfactory substitute for the responsibilities of the city-state; and it must promise security. Many Greeks of the Hellenistic Age felt the need of federation. Contact with the barbarian world had not only given them the capacity for world culture and co-operation, but had also emphasized their essential sameness.

The answer to the problem of the day—indeed, the best answer which the Greek world ever found for the problem of government—was discovered by the peoples of Aetolia and Achaea, rural backward folk, who proved that a common citizenship could be extended over a wide territory. For purposes of federation they were doubly fortunate in forming an ethnos and in possessing no city of past or present glory, but, as will appear, the success of the Aetolian and Achaean Leagues was temporary and partial.

It was not till the end of the fourth century that the Aetolians reformed their League and based it upon the city, often no more than a group of villages about a fort, but a better arrangement, nonetheless, than the ancient tribal system. Between 301 and 298 the Aetolians, always a warlike people, captured Delphi. Although it was never incorporated in their League, they used it as a sort of second capital and gained much prestige from its possession. Further prestige came from their defeat of the Gauls in 279-278 and very soon the League grew to include all of central Greece and some of the Peloponnesus and Thessaly.

The Aetolian League was a sympolity: every man within it was a citizen of the League and of his own town. Citizenship was extended to all, as the League grew, but probably those living at a distance were given isopolity (an exchange of citizenship often amounting merely to commercial privileges) and had to move to a town enjoying sympolity to exercise active citizenship; thus the original members had no special rights. The primary Assembly was open to all the citizens and had the power of admitting new members, of forming general policy, of making peace and war. For the sake of convenience it ordinarily met before and after campaigns, since the membership of the army and the Assembly was the same. The spring meeting was moved from town to town in order to prevent the inhabitants of any town from regularly dominating the sessions and in order to solve, as far as possible, the problem of poor communications. The meeting in the autumn was held at the federal center, the temple of Apollo at Thermum. The League gained executive efficiency by the election of a single head, a general, but to block the rise of a tyrant re-election was possible only after an interval of several years. There were a few other officials for war, festivals and finance. The coinage was federal. The cities of the League were sovereign in their internal affairs and elected, in proportion to their military strength, the members of the federal Council. This body had little power; it attended to those things which could not await the Assembly and in general co-operated with the officials; it also served as a federal court for offenders against League statutes.

It was probably the growth of the League that spelled the doom of democracy in this healthy confederacy, for eventually the Council numbered 1,000 members. It was found necessary to organize a committee (*apokletoi*) of the Council, which should be in continuous session with the general; the Assembly, however, still kept the right to declare peace and war. The Council had too little power and was too unwieldy to be an effective instrument of representative government, whereas the primary Assembly, an apparent guarantee of democracy, did not meet often enough to provide that intensity of life which was the very pulse of the city-state; furthermore, the Assembly developed the faults of a mass meeting. The final result was that the Aetolian League was governed arbitrarily by the apokletoi and the general.[3]

About the middle of the third century the Achaean League reformed its structure and threw open its doors to others. Its extraordinary growth was due to Aratus, a young man of Dorian Sicyon, who added his city to the League and set upon his life work of

[3] W. W. Tarn, *The Cambridge Ancient History* (Cambridge, 1928), vol. VII, pp. 208-211.

ridding the Peloponnesus of tyrants and of all Macedonian influence. For almost thirty years (beginning in 245) Aratus was elected general in alternate years and, had he been a more honest constitutionalist, might have carved for himself and his League a greater niche in history. Even so, the Achaean League is remarkable among federations. It ultimately included most of the Peloponnesus. Sparta, though stubbornly maintaining her isolation, entered into an alliance with it (243), a particularly dangerous connection, for the seething ferment of Laconia was then headed, under the leadership of King Agis IV, toward communism.

This union of cities, like the Aetolian League, was a sympolity. Every man in the Achaean League was an Achaean and a citizen of his own town, though to enjoy private rights in another town he probably needed a special grant. As it grew, the League gave its citizenship to new territories, which were broken up into their component parts on joining. Secession was forbidden. There is some evidence that the cities had to model their magistracies upon those of the League, though otherwise they were internally free and enjoyed their own constitutions and law courts. They could mint coins on the League standard, but weights and measures were within the province of the League.

All citizens over thirty years of age were members of the primary Assembly (*synkletos*), which could meet on call at any city. The voting was probably by cities on the principle of one vote to a city, in order that the original eleven Achaean cities might not be swamped by the new large members. Though war could not be declared without its approval, the Assembly could pass only on measures submitted to it and did not have the right of initiative. The cities of the League, probably in proportion to their military strength, elected the members of the Council, perhaps 6,000 in number. The Council, unlike its Aetolian counterpart, had real power; it guided foreign policy, admitted new members, oversaw the army and treasury, served as the federal court of justice and in general conducted the affairs of the League. Large as the Council was—it amounted almost to an Assembly—and unwieldy as it must have been, nevertheless the Achaeans saw to it that this powerful body really represented the constituent cities. It is possible, however, that

FEDERAL UNIONS 105

the members of the Council were subject to a property qualification, for there is no doubt that moderately wealthy landowners dominated the League.

The head of the League was a general and re-election in successive years was forbidden. It was a disadvantage in that day of specialized warfare that the "general" did not have to be a man of military experience and that the citizens of the League did not receive regular military training. Other officers included an admiral, treasurer, secretary, and an inner committee (the ten *demiourgoi*), which formed with the general an executive board of considerable power. When the officials met with the Council, the joint body was called the *synodos*. The two regular meetings of the synodos were held in the autumn and spring at the federal center, the temple of Zeus Amarius at Aegium. Voting was probably by cities.[4]

By annually elected federal officials and a representative Council, with a primary Assembly based on a common citizenship but avoiding infringements on the local rights of the constituent cities, the Achaean League found a practical balance between autonomy and federation. This experiment in democratic federalism was marvellously suited to the Greek character and in its heyday it received enthusiastic support. It did, however, favor the rich. Attendance at meetings was impossible for some members on account of distance or lack of leisure. The limitation of membership in the primary Assembly, which had the power to declare war, to persons over thirty was unfair to many of those who had to do the fighting. The Achaean League, moreover, was not always true to its ideals nor did it hesitate to coerce other states into joining.

[4] The difficulty in regarding the synodos as a primary Assembly, as some would do, is chiefly that Polybius occasionally uses the word "Council" as a synonym; but, in that case, why does he use synodos at all, when there could be no doubt of the meaning of "Council"? Since the Achaeans had one Assembly (such as it was) in the synkletos and since we should normally expect to find a Council too, it is equally unsatisfactory to think of synodos as a generic term, meaning congress and used to describe a bicameral body composed of a primary Assembly and a Council of deputies. Our problem is probably solved, if we imagine the synodos as a body consisting primarily of a Council; this will also explain Polybius' ambiguous language. See A. Aymard, *Les assemblées de la confédération achaienne* (Bordeaux, 1938); M. Cary, *Journal of Hellenic Studies*, vol. LIX (1939), pp. 154-155; W. W. Tarn, *The Cambridge Ancient History* (Cambridge, 1928), vol. VII, pp. 735-739.

The Achaean League's dangerous connection with Sparta has already been mentioned. Under Cleomenes III a bloody revolution was carried through in Sparta, debts were cancelled and the land was redivided. By military victory, as well as by the hope which he appeared to hold out to oppressed masses everywhere, Cleomenes soon threatened the very existence of the Achaean League itself. In this crisis Aratus, who had spent his life opposing Macedon, appealed to Antigonus Doson for aid, but the Macedonian's price was the fortress of Corinth and, with it, the real independence of the League (224). Antigonus Doson now added the Achaean League to his Hellenic League of Leagues. The chief feature of the liberal new union, which took the League of Corinth as a model and which included, in addition to Macedonia and Achaea, the Leagues of Epirus, Acarnania, Thessaly, Boeotia and Phocis, was that important decisions of the federal congress had to be ratified by the constituent states.

The following years saw the deaths of Antigonus Doson and Aratus, the accession of Philip V to the Macedonian throne and the emergence of Rome as a world power. Because of their hatred of Macedon the Aetolians sided with Rome in her struggle against Philip; but, when the Roman victory at Cynoscephalae (197) did not produce the much-desired destruction of Macedon, the Aetolians were embittered. In the next year at the Isthmian Games the Roman consul, Flamininus, declared the Greeks free—an ironical expression typical of the Hellenistic Age—and this pronouncement meant the end of the Hellenic League of Leagues and the enrollment of its members (including the Achaean League) as allies of Rome. The Achaean League under the direction of Philopoemen now enjoyed an illusory era of importance and with the acquisition of Sparta controlled the entire Peloponnesus.

The mutual fears and ambitions of Rome, Macedon, Asia and Egypt quickly combined to end Greek freedom forever. In 189 Rome with the aid of Philip conquered Aetolia, restricted her League and forced her to abandon Delphi. Twenty years later Rome turned on Perseus, Philip's son, defeated him at the battle of Pydna (168) and divided Macedonia into four republics. The Aetolian League was dismembered; to insure loyalty Rome took many hostages, including 1,000 (with the historian Polybius) from the Achaean League alone. Hatred of Rome slowly rose to fever heat in Greece and the Achaean League became the rallying center of all patriots, chiefly the democratic masses. The propertied classes, for their part, favored Rome as the power best able to thwart the threat of social revolution. The issue was decided at Corinth in 146. The Roman consul, Mummius, razed the city to the ground, killed all the men and sold the women and children into slavery. The Achaean League was disbanded. A century was to pass before the formal incorporation of Greece into the Roman Empire as a province; meanwhile, only those leagues of purely religious significance continued to exist.

The Greeks satisfied so many yearnings of the mind and spirit that their inability to solve the problem of federation appears especially tragic. As we look back upon their experiments, we see that the unwillingness of the city-state to surrender sovereign powers, especially in the field of foreign relations, was more often than not the chief obstacle to union. A league which refused to expand beyond its narrow boundaries or to share its privileges with others, if it did expand, was doomed to failure from the start. On the other hand, the promise of success was bright if the members of a league were united by a community of interests. This implied not only a scrupulous respect on the part of the leading state for the rights of the other members, but also a vital corporate life based on a common citizenship and a primary Assembly.

The Peloponnesian League, which was remarkable for the supremacy of its Assembly, brought internal peace and a unified foreign policy for many generations to a large part of the Greek world, but the organs of government were not based on a common citizenship and in the last analysis the League was ruined by the provincial outlook and selfishness of Sparta. The League of Corinth had true representative government and, with more cooperation from its members and less interference from its hegemon (the Macedonian king), might have developed into a great Panhellenic union. It was the Aetolian League, however, which first held out high hope of success. With a tribal group as its core it was able to extend a common citizenship over a wide area, but sufficient care was not taken to make the primary Assembly and the Council effective instruments of government and vital forces in the lives of the individual members. The Achaean League possessed the advantages of the Aetolian, together with the enthusiastic loyalty of its members. Its federal officials, representative Council and primary Assembly were effective without, however, infringing on the rights of the constituent cities. In the final issue the Achaean League, and with it all hope of federation in ancient Greece, succumbed before the imperialistic struggles of more powerful states. Had not Rome intervened, however, the Greeks might ultimately have given the Mediterranean world not only a common culture, but also a form of government ensuring unity, freedom and permanence.

From the Cambridge Ancient History

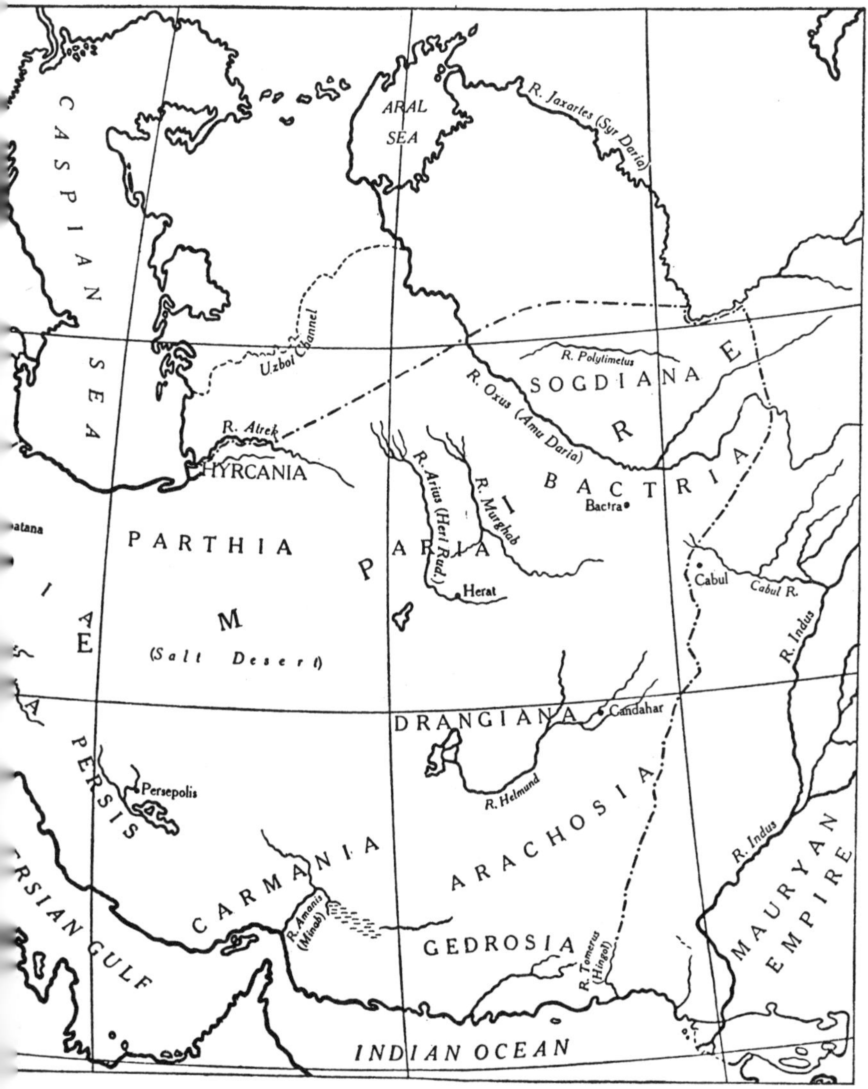
CASPIAN SEA
ARAL SEA
R. Jaxartes (Syr Daria)
Uzbol Channel
R. Polytimetus
SOGDIANA
R. Oxus (Amu Daria)
R. Atrek
HYRCANIA
BACTRIA
Bactra
ARIANE
R. Arius (Heri Rud)
R. Murghab
PARTHIA
ARIA
Herat
Cabul
Cabul R.
R. Indus
(Salt Desert)
DRANGIANA
Candahar
PERSIS
Persepolis
R. Helmund
ARACHOSIA
CARMANIA
R. Amanis (Minab)
GEDROSIA
R. Tomerus (Hingol)
MAURYAN EMPIRE
PERSIAN GULF
INDIAN OCEAN

VIII. ALEXANDER AND THE WORLD-STATE

BY O. W. REINMUTH

A SEARCH for the genesis of the idea of a world-state would in all likelihood lead to Alexander, for he was the first man in recorded history to attempt to consolidate widely divergent racial groups into a political unity on a basis other than military force. It is attested on good ancient authority that Alexander believed in the brotherhood of all men and the common fatherhood of God; indeed a recent study makes it seem very likely that Alexander originated the pregnant idea of the unity of mankind.[1] In what Alexander did may be seen evidence that he was striving to give political expression to his belief in the unity of man by laying the groundwork for a state to which Greeks and barbarians might give a common allegiance.[2] The presentation of this evidence is the purpose of this chapter.

What are the essential features of a world-state? Its necessary characteristic would seem to be the union of all races of men under one political organization, that is, unity of power and totality of extent. A union of this kind might be achieved and maintained by forcible imposition of and voluntary consent to political control on the part of a central authority. Voluntary consent of the governed to the exercise of political power over them depends in the final analysis upon the conviction that their interests can be served best

[1] W. W. Tarn, *Proceedings of the British Academy*, vol. XIX (1933), pp. 123-166.
[2] Tarn (for his contributions see the section of the Bibliography relating to this chapter) maintains that Alexander had no intention of forming a world-state. Kolbe and Wilcken (consult the Bibliography for their works) take the view which the author here presents. In addition to these scholars Endres, Kornemann and (again) Wilcken (whose monographs are listed in the Bibliography) treat particularly the authenticity of the plans, which (according to Diodorus, *Bibliotheca Historica*, XVIII. 4. 2-5) were found in Alexander's papers after his death and which among other things proposed an expedition westward and an interchange of peoples between Europe and Asia "to promote general concord and inter-racial friendship." Since Tarn has given some valid reasons for questioning the genuineness of these plans, I shall leave them aside, because they are not vital to the inquiry whether in what Alexander did the first steps were taken to the coordination of his empire along cosmopolitan lines.

by a given form of government. Such conviction is engendered by common ideals of value, common interests and a common way of life. How far did Alexander go along the road toward a world-state, so conceived, in the thirteen years of his active life?

Greek political theory and practice up to the time of Alexander had not gone beyond the point of the city-state combined in leagues. Plato and Aristotle saw the state as the organization through which the citizen may realize the moral life. This theory was formulated from the actual historical development of the *polis*, which was in fact a community with homogeneous racial, religious and cultural antecedents. Politically the polis had taken the form of an autonomous, autarchic state with a limited area and a small body of citizens. Citizenship was, in the main, restricted to sons of citizens and the mark of citizenship was the possession of political power. The need for expansion was not inherent in the structure of the polis, since it grew by founding other states in its own image, attached to it by race, religion, custom and trade, but politically independent. A larger unit than the polis could not be more, in fact it would be distinctly less, effective in assuring the participation of every citizen in the whole of its cultural life.

In the period preceding Alexander two forces were at work to destroy the polis: one internal, the other external. The belief that the state was the expression of the highest ethical principles was weakening. Increasing industrial production, communication and trade had followed colonization and had brought the city-states into the orbits of greater powers, thus threatening their autonomous existence. Indeed the grant of autonomy made by the Persian king in the Peace of Antalcidas (387/6) was freedom by sufferance; what the king had given, he might, if he pleased, wrest from them.

No one of these city-states alone could meet the threat which a large and aggressive state represented to the independence of all. The foreign relations of the state did not receive the same consideration from Plato and Aristotle which they devoted to the state's internal problems, but foreign relations were the chief concern of Isocrates' realistic philosophy. He saw that two problems might be helped to a solution by opening up Asia Minor to trade and colonization: the domestic problem of surplus population with resulting poverty and vagrancy and the foreign problem of Persia's threat to Greek freedom. Upon the basis of union this might be achieved; but only against a common enemy could *all* Greek states be united. There was hoary precedent for concerted action in the symmachy of the Hellenes against Troy and it was precisely along these lines that Isocrates in his *Panegyricus* of 380 proposed common action against Persia.

The strongest barrier to union among the Greeks was the value which they placed upon the small polis organization. Association with non-Greeks in a common citizenship was inconceivable, since citizenship was the political expression of race and culture. Blood was the necessary basis of culture and hence of citizenship. The sharp dichotomy made by Greek thinkers between Greeks and barbarians rested on the belief that the former were naturally endowed for citizenship in the polis, the latter, speaking by and large, were not. Plato felt that the barbarians were the natural enemies of Greeks and Aristotle agreed with him: they did not have the qualities of free men. The natives of Europe and of cold climates, wrote Aristotle, are full of courage but are wanting in intelligence, while the reverse is true of the inhabitants of Asia, "but the Hellenic race, which is situated between them, is likewise intermediate in character, being courageous and intelligent. Wherefore it continues free and continues to be the best governed and it could rule all men, if it were one polity."[3] Under the pressure of political necessity Isocrates made a tripartite division of mankind by considering the Macedonians (who, whether actually of Hellenic stock or not, were by the Greeks reckoned outside the Greek fold) worthy of participation and of leadership in Panhellenic action. In purely rhetorical fashion he had previously expressed the idea that culture without blood might be a common denominator, that "thanks to philosophy the name of Hellene will not designate race but temperament and those will be called Greek rather who share our culture than those who share our blood."[4]

The Greek political leagues were, for the most part, regional confederacies of states already loosely bound together by ethnic and religious ties. There was no strong central authority in the leagues

[3] *Politica*, 1327b29.   [4] *Panegyricus*, 50.

except for the conduct of foreign affairs; in none of them, whether based on sympolity or isopolity, was citizenship in the polis surrendered for common citizenship in the league and excepting in the Athenian Confederacy there is little evidence of a tendency toward the formation of a larger union by expansion, amalgamation or absorption.

Such was the political scene when Alexander appeared. When he was thirteen years old, his father, Philip, King of Macedonia, appointed Aristotle, then forty years of age and but a few years removed from his own studies under Plato, to be his tutor. It is significant that the contact occurred when neither the pattern of Aristotle's thought nor the mold of Alexander's action had been cast into sterilizing rigidity. That Alexander so often departed from Aristotle's theory, as we know it, does not mean that Aristotle did not influence him; it must rather be ascribed to the selective activity of an independent mind upon a broad and comprehensive presentation of political theory. Alexander's ideology was closer to Isocrates', because both dealt with the same problem—the international, rather than the internal, policies of the state.

When he succeeded his father in the kingship of Macedonia and the headship of the League of Greek States for War against Persia (336), Alexander was at once faced with the problem of political relationship to Greeks, Macedonians and barbarians. Isocrates had counselled Philip to act as a benefactor to the Greeks, a king to the Macedonians and a ruler to as many barbarians as possible. The advice of Aristotle to Alexander on this point was to treat the Greeks "as their *hegemon*, the barbarians as their despot, caring for the former as friends and kinsmen, behaving toward the latter as toward animals and plants."[5] Eratosthenes reports how Alexander interpreted Aristotle's dictum: he preferred to divide men into good and bad without consideration of race and to consider the good man the real Greek and the bad man the real barbarian and he thought that this was perhaps what Aristotle really meant.[6]

[5] *Frg.* 658 (Rose).
[6] Strabo, *Geographica*, 1. 4. 9 (p. 66); Plutarch, *De Alexandri Magni Fortuna aut Virtute*, 1. 6.

After his first victory Alexander showed that for him Isocrates' threefold division of peoples had shrunk to two, for the dedication on the panoplies sent to Athens read "Alexander and the Greeks except the Spartans." At the very outset of the campaign he demonstrated that he had no intention of imposing an undiscriminating and despotic rule upon the people who came under his power. Ruthless he was, if necessary, until his power was recognized; thereafter his policy was one of reconciliation. On the point of authority he would brook no quibbling, as is clear from his treatment of the Thebans and the Tyrians.

This attitude was clearly present in Alexander's personal relations. His associates in the Macedonian command were treated equitably and considerately, but they were not permitted to stand in the way of his policies. The attitude is, in fact, confirmed by the account of the differences between Alexander and two of his generals, Parmenio and Cleitus.

Parmenio was the ablest of Philip's generals and diplomats and was winning victories for him when Alexander was born. He had been faithful to Alexander from the day when Parmenio declared for him after the murder of Philip. After Alexander had become Great King of Persia, Parmenio's son, Philotas, commander of the Companions, had been found guilty of treason in a trial before the Macedonian army and had been executed. There seems to have been no evidence that Parmenio was involved. He was not present with the army, having been left behind in charge of communications, and was not brought to trial. Alexander had him put to death. Tarn would explain the act without justifying the crime by saying that Parmenio could not be left in command after his son's treason. Why not? Amyntas, the leader of the Phalanx, and others had been suspected of complicity, but after acquittal were allowed to hold their commands. The explanation must be sought elsewhere. Our sources plainly indicate that Parmenio and Philotas represented a conservative group in the Macedonian command, a group in sympathy neither with a continuance of the campaign beyond the defeat of Darius nor with Alexander's intentions, as they interpreted them, with regard to the conquered peoples. They were prepared to go along with him so long as he confined himself to the tasks which he had undertaken. But these had now been accomplished, the Greek cities had been liberated, the Persian king had been defeated, still Alexander continued. It is not likely that they objected to an extension of conquests as such, since war was their business; but they noticed that their king showed the same consideration for Persians as for Macedonians, appointing them as satraps, wearing some of their characteristic dress, following certain of their customs. They did not wish him to be what his actions declared him to be: the same kind of king for one race as for the other. By his counsel on several occasions Parmenio had made clear his conception of what Alexander ought to do in Asia: secure Asia Minor from the Persian king and return to Macedonia. Alexander's real motive for getting rid of Parmenio is to be found in the fact that he alone among the generals had the prestige to make effective the opposition which some of them felt toward Alexander's policies as they saw them.

At the bottom of the Cleitus episode, the accounts of which vary, lay dissatisfaction with the new order of things under Alexander. The drunken utterances of Cleitus (*in vino veritas*) reveal what really rankled in his heart: by elevating Persians to the status of Macedonians Alexander was degrading Macedonians; Alexander was no longer a king like Philip. After enduring his taunts for some time Alexander, who was also intoxicated, seized a weapon and killed him.

After Philotas, Parmenio and Cleitus were out of the way, the tendency to which they had objected was accelerated. Within a short time after the murder of Cleitus Alexander married Roxana, daughter of a Bactrian chieftain, employing Iranian marriage rites. Arrian represents it as a love match, which it obviously was not. Alexander was not given to the grand passion; Roxana had no child for four years and three years after this marriage he espoused another woman. The marriage with Roxana was not an attempt to win over the chieftains of Sogdiana. Roxana was captured when her father's stronghold was taken and, if marriage with her could reconcile the other leaders, Alexander missed a fine opportunity for reconciliation by not marrying Darius' daughter after Issus (333). The marriage with Roxana was the beginning of a new policy, perhaps already inchoate in Alexander's mind when he permitted himself to be adopted as the son of Ada, the former regent of Caria. In Greek theory and practice the state was a community of families of Greek race. By his example Alexander recognized a new family structure as the basis of the state and gave an earnest of his intention to form his state on an interracial basis.

Confirming this intention also is the fact that after his return from India Alexander celebrated his conquest of Asia by a mass wedding ceremony at which he and eighty of his officers took wives from among the Persian and Iranian aristocracy. But the mingling of races was not confined to the nobility, for the marriage relations into which a large number of Macedonian soldiers (Arrian says 10,000, but this may be an exaggeration because the whole Macedonian army eleven years earlier had numbered only 14,000) had entered with Asiatic women were legitimized. These women were taken from all the races with which the army had come in contact. It is significant that again native wedding rites were followed, indicating that a fusion of customs as well as of blood was to play a part in the integration of Macedonia and Asia. Furthermore, the children of these mixed marriages were treated as Macedonian subjects. When Alexander dismissed 10,000 Macedonians unfit for further service at Opis, he kept the children, promising to train them in Macedonian ways and to restore them to their fathers when he returned. That nothing came of this or of the marriages proves nothing, for Alexander died in the next year and many, perhaps the majority of his men, like Parmenio and his group, had scant understanding of or sympathy with his plans.

In the administration of conquered territories Alexander followed a policy of fusion in service. To political units and to individuals he allotted a share in the government proportional to their development and capacities. To the Greek cities of Asia Minor he restored autonomy, an expedient thing to do, since it made them his supporters when he needed support; but, as Tarn has pointed out, he did not revoke his action later when he might have done so. Some Greek cities, at first treated as subject cities, were put into the category of free cities after a short time, as in the case of Mallus and Soli. The Persians had ruled these cities through tyrants, by military force or by the support of one faction, and this was the method employed by Antipater, Alexander's regent in Greece. But Alexander insisted on a united city, contrary to Aristotle's theory that a king must keep opposing parties balanced.

In the appointment of governors for the various provinces of the Persian Empire Alexander made use of the two ruling races, speaking generally, Macedonians in the west, Persians in the east. Separate financial supervisors were appointed throughout the empire and in the eastern satrapies the military power was in the hands of the Macedonians, leaving the civil administration alone to Persian governors. Other monarchs had worked through national groups; it was a new thing to employ administrators from a conquered race on a large scale. It would be difficult to imagine Xerxes appointing Greek *strategoi* throughout Greece or to think of Romans giving power except in isolated cases to the aristocracy of a conquered race. The balance of real power throughout the empire, however, was with the Macedonians. Alexander's attempt to give the Persian nobility a small part in the government was not entirely successful. Native governors were in time replaced by Macedonians, until at his death only three Persian satraps were in office. His willingness to try this scheme demonstrated his idealistic intentions; his prompt recognition of its failure, his realistic action.

More successful were Alexander's efforts to use Macedonian and Asiatic elements in common military service. Upon setting out in Asia Minor (334) his army consisted of some 14,000 Macedonians and 21,000 Greek troops, partly allies, partly mercenaries. After Gaugamela (331) he dismissed the Greek allies. As early as 330, considerable bodies of troops from Lydia and Cilicia joined his forces and the 120,000 troops, which, according to Arrian, he led into India (possibly no more than 35,000 fighting men, the remainder camp followers), were largely composed of foreign contingents. The association of infantry from Syria, sailors from Phoenicia, cavalry from Iran, Turkestan and India, soldiers from Macedonia, Persia and "all sorts of Oriental tribes" in a common enterprise did something toward bringing the races closer together. But more effective in this direction was the training of the children of the soldiers and the presence of native wives with the army. From the changes which

Alexander made in the Macedonian army it is clear that he intended to decrease the influence of the Macedonian element and, as Kolbe puts it, to "denationalize" the army. When in 324 Alexander prepared to dismiss 10,000 Macedonians and enroll 30,000 native youths, who had been trained and equipped in complete Macedonian fashion, the whole army mutinied and was discharged. For two days Alexander waited for them to accept the new order of things. On the third day he began enrolling a barbarian army. Then the Macedonians broke and stated their grievance: Alexander had made the Persians his kinsmen. "But all of you I regard as my kinsmen" was Alexander's reply. He did not yield his position. The men of Asia were to be treated as Aristotle had advised him to treat the Greeks. Dismissing the 10,000 veterans, as he had planned, but restoring the remainder of his men to his service, he incorporated picked Persian and Iranian cavalrymen into the Companions' cavalry, originally composed of Macedonians from the upper classes, and made Persian noblemen members of his own Bodyguard on the same footing as their Macedonian companions-in-arms. The final step was taken in 323, when 20,000 native troops, who had rendered faithful service to Peucestas, were enrolled in the Macedonian phalanx. The army was composed of "real Greeks" according to Alexander's definition of that term.

Fewer than half of the seventy cities which Alexander is said to have founded are known. They were not designed as Hellenizing agencies any more than as centers of oriental influence. They were, in the first instance, links in a chain to bind the empire into an economic union by forming centers of trade and communication. Other acts of Alexander had this same end in view: the building of harbors and dry docks, opening the Tigris to navigation, the investigation of possible sea routes from east to west, the adoption of a uniform standard of coinage, the circulation of the sterile treasures of Darius as well as the granting of huge sums from his own purse in gifts and payments to his soldiers and others, the construction of buildings and public works. In the second instance, cities were established for military purposes, to secure conquered areas, as, for example, Alexandria in Arachosia and the Alexandria which was a refounding of Merv. All of these served as cultural melting pots. Most of these were founded at or near existing native settlements. Within and alongside organizations of natives with separate political status were planted Greek corporations. The Greek population was not large, consisting at first of Greek mercenaries and a few Macedonians, to which in the course of time might be added settlers from the cities and areas of the Greek world. The Greek mercenaries were largely drawn from men without fixed means of livelihood, who in times of comparative peace wandered from city to city seeking subsistence and in times of war sold their services singly or in groups to some military leader. There was a large contingent in the Persian army, many of whom re-enlisted under Alexander after Darius' defeat. In time a considerable part of the transient population, which constituted such a grave economic problem in Greece and in Asia Minor during the period preceding Alexander's campaign, was absorbed in Alexander's army. When their terms of enlistment expired, Alexander provided for these men by settling them in the newly founded cities. Although their numbers in the new cities were not large, they occupied a preferred position and their influence was proportionately strong.

But influence was not exerted alone by Greeks and Macedonians upon natives. The most conservative element of the population and that which exerted the strongest influence upon family life was the women who were almost entirely native. Native culture affected and changed Greek folkways. Alexander did not impose Greek culture upon the people under his rule. He established centers from which it might radiate. The customs, laws, religious practices, art, literature, the modes of thought and the way of life of Greece, imperfectly as they were represented by the oasis of Greek culture, were under the daily observation of the natives. Alexander doubtless hoped that in the battle of cultures Greek culture would predominate, but he was more concerned that by living together a common culture might result.

Such unity as Alexander's kingdom had rested in the final analysis upon military power and found its common attachment in his person. His power took various legal forms. He was King of Macedonia, hegemon of the Greek cities, feudal lord of some Iranian chieftains, over-rajah in the Punjab, Pharaoh and god in Egypt, controlling partner in an alliance with native rulers, absolute monarch wherever else his army had touched.

The retention of this political patchwork is not evidence against Alexander's intention of bringing about a closer amalgamation, for the simple reason that the arrangement remained only so long as he willed it and the power to change it was throughout his lifetime in his hands. The fact was that the world had hit upon no political form other than monarchy to join men of various races and of different stages of development into a unity—and it may be questioned whether it can. What was needed was a common denominator to form a rallying point for a common citizenship. One approach to this *desideratum* is a common culture with similar standards of value, but a common culture is a matter of slow growth. Until an approximation to this was achieved, a change in governmental form would have little meaning and might actually retard the *rapprochement* of cultures by its artificial nature. The Greeks possessed a common culture, but no political unity; the subjects of Persia had had a kind of external union, but no common way of life. Alexander attempted a synthesis of these two peoples by policies which promoted unity by a fusion of blood and a fusion of service in military and civic life. What Alexander meant to achieve by these measures was unmistakably expressed at the banquet of reconciliation after the mutiny at Opis, when he prayed for a like spirit and a joint commonwealth between Macedonians and Persians. These words were not translated into a constitutional right, but the intent to put Persians on the same basis as Macedonians in their relation to the unity of power, himself, is clear. The extension of this relation to other peoples, as they merited it, is indicated by the fact that outstanding members of other races participated in the ceremonies of reconciliation.

These policies concerned Macedonians and Persians. What about the Greeks? Common citizenship in a Panhellenic world of culture already existed, but a common citizenship bound to one source of political power was incompatible with the principle of the polis. Alexander approached this problem by transferring an idea at home in Greek thought, and to a very limited extent in practice, into actuality. In 324 he sent a request to the Greek cities that they recognize him as a god and all acceded. Living men had been deified before in Greece, but here for the first time *all* cities of Greece held the *same* man *uniformly* high in honor as a god. His divinity was thus unique, not only among men who, like Lysander and Clearchus, were recognized as gods by their own cities, but even among the gods themselves who were not held in uniformly high honor in all places. The way for this step had been prepared by the declaration of the oracle of Ammon that he was the son of Zeus and by the apparent confirmation of the oracles of Didyma and Erythrae as well as by the alleged obeisance of the sea waves to him. Aristotle had said that an individual of superior virtue and political capacity might be compared to a deity upon earth and that he should be a perpetual king in the state. Callisthenes, the nephew of Aristotle, in his history, a part of which had gone to the Greek public some time after 330 with Alexander's cognizance or approval, had represented Alexander as a god. A few years later Alexander had tried to introduce the custom of prostration before himself as king, but Callisthenes refused obedience and opposed the practice. For the Persians prostration before royalty was merely a ceremony; for the Greeks it was worship of a god. It does not, however, appear to have been so much a matter of religion as of politics in the mind of the Macedonians and of Alexander. Some of the Macedonians laughed at the practice and Alexander did not press its adoption ofter Callisthenes' opposition. A god is not balked by a mere man.

It has been customary to interpret Alexander's deification as a sanction for his political authority over the Greeks and specifically for his decree, issued at this time, commanding all cities to restore citizenship and property to their political exiles, a decree for which he had no authorization under the provisions of the Corinthian League. But that decree needed no sanction other than the enabling clause which empowered Antipater to use force in its execution.

The connection between this decree and his deification is of another sort. Tarn has shown[7] that the theory which makes it the chief business of the king to promote harmony among his subjects, of whatever race they might be, in all likelihood derived ultimately

[7] W. W. Tarn, *op. cit.*

from Alexander himself. He arrives at this conclusion without using the evidence of reliable tradition, which attributes an even more exalted ideal of kingship to Alexander. Alexander's prayer for harmony and association in rule between Macedonians and Persians has already been noted. In two passages, one from Eratosthenes, the other very likely from him,[8] we are told that Alexander felt that he had a divine mission to bring harmony and reconciliation to the world, that he was to mix men's lives and customs as in a loving cup, that he held that the good man was the real Greek and was to be treated as a kinsman and the bad man was the real barbarian and was to be considered a stranger. Plutarch attributes to him the intention of bringing peace and harmony to the world and of making one people of all races of men.[9] Plutarch relates too that Alexander accepted the teaching of an Egyptian philosopher that all mankind is under the kingship of God, but went beyond this himself in holding that God was the common father of all mankind and that "he makes peculiarly his own the noblest and best of them."[10]

In these ideas ascribed to Alexander there is no suggestion that the king who promotes harmony (*homonoia*) was a god. But in the first expression of opinion on this point which has come to us after Alexander, the king is represented as the Living Law, the counterpart on earth of God who brings order and harmony to the universe. This philosophy rests, according to Tarn's reasoning, upon Alexander's theory as to the duties of a king. The king-god idea, however, rests not upon his theory, but upon his practice. The king became a god *after* he had fulfilled his mission as king. By telescoping the sequence, subsequent philosophy made the ideal king a Living Law at the outset. Isocrates had outlined a dual program for Philip: promotion of homonoia among the Greeks and war against Persia. He had also said that Philip could do nothing else but become a god if he were successful in the second of these undertakings. Could a lesser honor come to the king who had done both? Alexander had eased the economic situation in Greece by absorbing the homeless wanderers into his army of mercenaries and settling them in his newly

---

[8] Strabo, *Geographica*, 1. 4. 9 (p. 66); Plutarch, *De Alexandri Magni Fortuna aut Virtute*, 1. 6.
[9] *De Alexandri Magni Fortuna aut Virtute*, 1. 8 (330d).   [10] *Vita Alexandri*, 27.

founded cities; by providing for the return of political refugees he proposed to put an end to party strife. These were precisely the measures advocated by Isocrates for bringing about homonoia. Alexander's deification was not a sanction of authority, but it was a recognition of what he *had* accomplished. Heracles had won his way to heaven by what he had done; thus Alexander was to become a god. That the apotheosis of living rulers later degenerated by a *hysteron proteron* into a sanction for *acta* before a ruler had demonstrated his genuine kingship does not alter the case.

Did Alexander intend to expand his empire into a world-state? Intentions not expressed must be ascertained by *probabilia ex vita* and by the direction in which actions tend. Prominent in Alexander's character were two qualities: passionate devotion to his heroic ideals, Heracles and Achilles, who had placed few limitations on their actions and whose trophies never allowed Alexander to rest, and a dynamic energy "that bids not sit nor stand, but go." In his conquest of Persia he could have stopped with glory at many points—after Issus, already past the river Halys which Isocrates had suggested to Philip as a possible limit; after Tyre, when Parmenio advised him to accept Darius's offer to cede all territory west of the Euphrates; after Gaugamela when he had put a definite end to Persian rule and, in recognition of that fact, had dismissed his Greek allies; before the invasion of India, which had not been a part of the empire of Darius II. When he turned back at Beas, it was because his men refused to go farther. Alexander wanted to move forward, even with reduced forces. Why? Because he thought that the ocean which marked the eastern limit of the inhabited world (*oekumene*) lay just a little way beyond. If we accept Arrian's account,[11] this is substantially what he told his men. At the same time he sketched the shape of things to come; their fleet would sail around Libya to the Pillars of Heracles (according to ancient concept, the western boundary of the oekumene) and "from the Pillars all Libya will become ours; and all Asia likewise and the boundaries of the empire in Asia, these boundaries which god set for the whole world." Could the descendant of Heracles stop before he had reached the Pillars named in honor of his ancestor? Arrian states that Alexander had them in

[11] *Anabasis Alexandri*, v. 26. 2.

mind as an objective, not of exploration, but of conquest; and all we know of his character compels us to accept that statement as genuine. In the same speech Alexander pointed out that a campaign against the unconquered Scythian tribes in the north still remained. He had earlier assured the king of the Chorasinians, who had offered his services for just such an expedition, that, although he was then engaged in subduing India, he would return to Greece, when he was master of Asia, and would make a campaign into the Pontus "with all his forces, navy and infantry alike."[12] When death came, Alexander was in the midst of preparations to circumnavigate Arabia, the remaining known area to the south.

Alexander's contribution to the world was the idea of world unity and the creation of some of the conditions under which in time, he thought, world unity might have been realized. He sought the basis of unity not in a dominant race, but in a dominant culture. Cautiously he applied the principle that the degree of participation in the state was to be determined by capacity for such treatment. To the "barbarian" part of his empire he made available the higher culture of Greece; he offered to the Greek part the formula of the god-king as a basis for political unity. The divergent cultures he held together in a firm but benevolent paternalism, the avowed object of which was to make one people of all races of men. No common political denominator was devised for Greeks and barbarians, because there was as yet no common cultural denominator. Political parity, he seems to have realized, without the cohesive force of a common way of life on the part of a predominant element in the state might be a factor in political disintegration, as it proved to be in the Roman Empire after Caracalla's indiscriminate grant of citizenship. Absolute power he had, and there is evidence that he planned to extend it to the bounds of the world as he knew them. He could not create common ideals or implant in the hearts of men the conviction that such ideals are desirable; what he could do, promote policies which might develop a common civilization, he did. How well and how poorly succeeding years have shown.

[12] *Op. cit.*, IV. 15. 5-6.

The weakness of his system is obvious. Alexander was the sole link between Greeks and barbarians until common culture should bring them closer together. Political advancement to a larger share in the state, until uniformity of status should be achieved, depended upon his good pleasure. His was the intention to bring about unity. His alone was the power to initiate and carry out policies. And Alexander was a man, not a god.

IX. THE ANTIGONIDS

BY JOHN V. A. FINE

AFTER the death of Alexander the Great in 323 his empire rapidly disintegrated. By 315 certain great generals, although outwardly pretending to be loyal to his young son by Roxana, in reality were engrossed in establishing their own kingdoms. Cassander was ruling Macedon almost as king and had control over much of Greece by means of garrisons and oligarchies devoted to his interests. Ptolemy had entrenched himself in Egypt and Lysimachus was consolidating his position in Thrace. Antigonus Monophthalmus, the founder of the Antigonid dynasty, had secured practically all Alexander's Asiatic empire. Confident in his ability and in the limitless resources at his disposal, he had conceived the ambition of winning Alexander's entire heritage for himself and his son Demetrius. The revelation of this ambition caused Ptolemy, Cassander, Lysimachus and Seleucus, who had fled from his satrapy of Babylonia in fear of Antigonus, to make a coalition against him.

Realizing that effective action against his widely scattered enemies was impossible while they—especially Ptolemy—controlled the sea, Antigonus immediately took steps which paved the way for his and his son's subsequent thalassocracy. Three great shipyards were established in Phoenicia and a fourth in Cilicia. Rhodes also agreed to build ships for him. To obtain the necessary harbors Antigonus wrested Joppa, Gaza and, after a long siege, Tyre from Ptolemy. Since his plans required uninterrupted communications with Greece, early in the war he persuaded many islands of the Aegean to form the League of the Islanders under his protection. Alliance with a powerful ruler afforded these communities welcome safety from the depredations of pirates and Antigonus in return acquired invaluable bases for his fleet.

In the first year of this war Antigonus circulated far and wide a proclamation declaring that all the Greeks should be free, ungarrisoned and autonomous. This championing of the Greeks, whereby

Antigonus adopted Alexander's policy of regarding them as free allies, remained a cardinal principle with him and Demetrius until the battle of Ipsus in 301. It was motivated by genuine admiration for Greek culture and also, naturally, by political considerations. Greece was still the center of civilization and the moral effect of conciliating Greek public opinion was immeasurable. Greece was also the home of redoubtable soldiers—a highly important consideration in view of the tremendous drain on Macedonian man power in recent years.

The war ended indecisively in 311. Antigonus' ambitions had been temporarily thwarted, but by rigid adherence to his proclamation of freedom he had secured the confidence of the Greeks. He increased his popularity with them by having their autonomy recognized in the peace treaty. Since he realized that Cassander would not relax his efforts to dominate Greece, he thereby provided himself with the opportunity to appear as champion again at the auspicious moment. In general, the peace maintained the status quo. Cassander was to be general in Europe until the young Alexander came of age. For Antigonus the most disastrous result of the war was Seleucus' recovery of Babylonia after Demetrius' defeat at Gaza in 312.

Cassander's murder of Roxana and her son in 310 left Alexander's empire without an heir and permitted each ruler to act openly in his own interests. Antigonus, a kinsman of the royal Argead family,[1] was strengthened in his resolve to become Alexander's successor. Once again the liberation of the Greeks was to be the war cry. Antigonus was convinced that the success of his policy in Greece depended on winning over Athens—the beacon tower of the world, as he called it. Consequently in 307 Demetrius in command of a large fleet delivered the city from Demetrius of Phalerum, who for ten years had been Cassander's governor there. The joy of the great majority of the Athenians was unbounded. In gratitude they heaped every conceivable honor—human and divine—upon Antigonus and his son and greeted them as kings—a title which none of the Successors had as yet dared to adopt.

[1] C. F. Edson, Jr., "The Antigonids, Heracles, and Beroea" in *Harvard Studies in Classical Philology*, vol. XLV (1934), pp. 213-246, seems to have proved definitely that the Antigonids were related to the Argeads.

THE ANTIGONIDS

Ptolemy's threat to Antigonus in Asia compelled Demetrius to sail eastward in 306. Off Salamis in Cyprus he annihilated Ptolemy's fleet in one of the greatest naval battles of antiquity. For twenty years his ships were to be supreme in the eastern Mediterranean. Antigonus and Demetrius now assumed the diadem, thereby claiming to be the heirs of Alexander. In their eyes Ptolemy, Lysimachus, Cassander and Seleucus were rebels and usurpers when shortly afterwards they declared themselves kings over their respective territories.

The next step was to crush Ptolemy in Egypt. After the failure of a joint land and sea attack, Antigonus and Demetrius decided to reduce him to impotence by severing his communications with Greece and Macedon on which he depended for soldiers and timber. The co-operation of Rhodes—the center of the trade route between Greece and Egypt—was essential for this purpose and when that island for commercial reasons refused to boycott Egypt Demetrius began his famous siege. Circumstances in Greece, however, forced him to abandon this undertaking after a year in which his invention of mighty siege-engines had earned him the name of Poliorcetes (the Besieger). The attack on Rhodes was a clear violation of the principle of the autonomy of the Greeks. As realistic statesmen, Antigonus and Demetrius would probably have justified their action on the basis of necessity. The weakening of Ptolemy was essential to the re-establishment of Alexander's empire. If Rhodes would not contribute to this end voluntarily, she must do so under compulsion.

Demetrius hastened to Greece and rapidly checked Cassander's aggressions. So successful was he that early in 302 he consummated his father's Hellenic policy by reviving the Hellenic League of Philip II and Alexander. Every constituent state swore eternal friendship and alliance with Antigonus, Demetrius and their descendants, and also with one another. Each member was to send delegates, probably in proportion to its population, to the federal Council (*synedrion*). In peace time this synedrion was to meet where and when the four great Panhellenic festivals were held, an excellent arrangement in view of the importance of these festivals in promoting a Panhellenic spirit. In war time sessions were to be called at the pleasure of the chairmen or of Demetrius. Since the delegates had full powers, the synedrion was a sovereign body. The various states owed military service, but apparently no regular system of tribute was imposed. Demetrius was elected leader of the federal forces in the war against Cassander. In time of war his powers were undoubtedly great, but there is no reason to believe that in forming this League he was seeking an instrument with which to tyrannize over the Greeks. His garrison in Acrocorinth was installed at the request of the Corinthians. If he and his father had been victorious at Ipsus, Greece might have enjoyed a successful form of federal government. Unfortunately the League was not universally popular with its members. Athens in particular was dissatisfied. Since the federal synedrion was a sovereign body, the independence of the individual members—at least as regards foreign policy—was restricted. Also Demetrius because of his power and prestige was bound to influence policies. The Athenian democrats, however, were desirous of making Athens once again the recognized leader of Hellenic affairs and they were loath to serve the ambitions of Demetrius on the same plane as any other Greek state.

Demetrius' success in Greece led to the inevitable result. Cassander and Lysimachus, realizing their imminent danger, combined their forces and persuaded Ptolemy and Seleucus to help crush the ambitions of Antigonus and his son. Demetrius was recalled to Asia Minor and at Ipsus in 301 the eighty-one year old Antigonus was slain at the head of his troops.

Ipsus was a bitter blow to Demetrius. Asia, save for a few coastal cities, fell to his enemies and much to his chagrin the Hellenic League renounced him. He retained his fleet, however, and with it the control of the League of the Islanders. For some years his real kingdom was the sea. Although circumstances forced him to become an opportunist, one unerring purpose was always before his mind: the recovery of his father's Asiatic realm. In 294 fortune turned in his favor. Internal troubles at Athens enabled him to become master of the city, which had so completely destroyed his hopes of uniting Greece under a benevolent hegemony. He treated the Athenians generously, but garrisoned strongly both the Piraeus and the city itself. Next, taking advantage of a quarrel between the sons of Cassander, who had recently died, he succeeded in having the Macedonian army declare him King of the Macedonians. Thus seven years after the disaster of Ipsus Demetrius was ruler of a powerful kingdom.

Preparations were now begun for the recovery of Asia. As Greek man power was essential, Demetrius proceeded to bring the majority of the states under his control. The failure of his Hellenic League had convinced him that only by force could he maintain his supremacy in the peninsula. Consequently he garrisoned many cities, but he tempered this policy of constraint by unusually lenient treatment of rebellious states and by appointing as his chief governors in Greece men of such integrity as the historian Hieronymus of Cardia and his own son Antigonus Gonatas.

If Demetrius had been satisfied with being King of the Macedonians, he, rather than his son, might have been the real founder of Antigonid rule in Macedon. To him, however, Macedon represented merely a means of regaining the Asiatic kingdom. He neglected shamefully the administration of the country and outraged the Macedonians, accustomed to a patriarchal type of kingship, by introducing the pomp of an oriental court. Consequently, when the fears aroused by his assembling of great land and sea forces had led in 288 to a coalition of Pyrrhus, Lysimachus, Ptolemy and Seleucus against him, the Macedonians deserted him. Driven from Macedon, Demetrius nevertheless sailed for Asia Minor, but with far fewer effectives than originally planned. The story of his campaign against Lysimachus' son, Agathocles, and Seleucus, in which he almost achieved the impossible, is one of the most thrilling and moving chapters in history. Finally he was captured by Seleucus and two years later (in 283) he died in captivity.

Antigonus and Demetrius were two of the ablest men the Greek world produced. When the impossibility of maintaining the integrity of Alexander's empire for his son became apparent, they alone of the Successors were inspired by the vision of securing the whole unwieldy structure for themselves. Asia became Antigonus' "spear-won" territory, but until Ipsus, true to their philhellenism, they strove tirelessly to achieve an honorable destiny for the Greeks. This, of course, was not unmixed altruism, for they hoped to profit by the resources and prestige of Greece, but even so the Hellenic League—a union of Greek states bound to one another and to them by mutual alliances—was a noble conception. Such a league would have spared the Greeks untold misery in the future, but city-state particularism doomed it to failure. Antigonus' policy toward the Greek cities of Asia Minor was complicated by the fact that they formed enclaves within his territory won by right of conquest. Although constantly emphasizing his championship of their autonomy, inevitably, as he consolidated his Asiatic kingdom, he encroached somewhat on their independence. For strategic or economic reasons he urged—or possibly commanded—certain synoecisms. In his letter to the people of Teos concerning their synoecism with Lebedos he threatened punishment for those who proposed unsuitable laws. In this seemingly despotic pronouncement he was undoubtedly following Alexander's policy of insisting that the Asiatic Greeks who became his allies should have democratic constitutions. His wish to supply the Greek cities with grain from his crown lands reveals an effort to link those cities and his conquered territory in a common economic system. He thereby could dispose of surplus grain with a minimum of difficulty and, if we can believe his statement, also prevent the Greeks from incurring too great debts. Circumstances of which we have no knowledge unquestionably necessitated many such measures and the numerous divine honors which he had received made them seem not unnatural. A god could interfere where a mortal could not. After Ipsus Demetrius' policy toward the cities of the Greek mainland became less generous. The collapse of the Hellenic League had taught him that idealism would not unite the Greeks. Despite the garrisons and taxation which he imposed and the military contingents which he exacted, however, Demetrius maintained his enlightened attitude toward Greek culture until the end.

When Demetrius sailed to Asia Minor in 287, he left his son, Antigonus Gonatas, as governor of his possessions in Greece. Gonatas, although passionately devoted to his father, was a very different type of man from Demetrius. Having spent most of his life in Greece and Macedon, he was impervious to the lure of the Orient. The friendship and teachings of such men as Menedemus of Eretria and Zeno of Citium had had, and continued to have, tremendous influence on him. His debt to Stoicism is beautifully exemplified by his admonition to his son that "our kingship is a noble servitude."

The decade following Demetrius' departure was a precarious period for Antigonus. Much of Demetrius' fleet and the protectorate over the League of the Islanders passed without a struggle to Ptolemy. Antigonus' kingdom was reduced to his garrisons in Greece and a general uprising against Antigonid control started by Areus of Sparta in 280 led to many defections. By 279 Gonatas' possessions were limited to Demetrias, the great city founded by his father at the head of the Pagasaean Gulf, Corinth and a few places in the Peloponnese. Meanwhile Macedon had fallen as prize in rapid succession to Pyrrhus, Lysimachus, Seleucus and Ptolemy Ceraunus. In 279 the unhappy country was ravaged by a horde of Celts, who advanced into central Greece before they were halted by the heroism of the Aetolians. Two years later Antigonus annihilated another detachment of Celts in open combat near Lysimachia. The prestige thus gained was so great that the harried Macedonians, who were sorely in need of a strong ruler, proclaimed him king.

Macedon in the plans of Antigonus I and Demetrius was to be only a part of the huge empire which they envisaged. Gonatas, abandoning these grandiose schemes which were no longer feasible, intended to be a national king of the Macedonians. Everything he did in his long and stormy life was aimed at promoting the welfare of Macedon. From the very beginning of his reign he was faced by appalling problems. His own country was exhausted by the steady drain on its man power, dating back to the start of Alexander's Asiatic expedition, and by the anarchy to which it had been exposed since Demetrius' expulsion in 288. On the north was the constant danger of barbarian invasion and to the west the restless Pyrrhus was always a troublesome neighbor. Greece, subject to nationalistic movements and to foreign intrigue, was as usual an uncertain quantity. Ptolemy II, master of Egypt and the Aegean, was a menacing opponent, especially after his marriage in 276 to his brilliant sister, Arsinoë, who was ambitious to secure the throne of Macedon for her son by Lysimachus, Ptolemaeus.

For Antigonus, who could not as yet depend on the loyalty of the Macedonians, peace on as many fronts as possible was a necessity. Already in 279, as a result of the Celtic invasion, he had made a treaty of friendship with Antiochus, Seleucus' son, who had succeeded to his father's kingdom in Asia Minor, Syria and the Orient. This alliance was subsequently sealed by Antigonus' marriage to Phila, the half-sister of Antiochus. Henceforth for three quarters of a century, with only occasional lapses, good relations existed between the Antigonids and the Seleucids. In 276 Antigonus, probably employing only mercenaries, recovered Thessaly which had recently broken away from Macedon. A few years later he reached an important understanding with the Aetolians based on non-interference in each other's interests.

Antigonus' plans for restoring order to Macedon were rudely shattered in 274. In the preceding year Pyrrhus had returned from his Italian and Sicilian fiasco. He was angry with Antigonus, who had refused to contribute troops for his expedition, and he also thought that he had a claim to the Macedonian throne. He now, probably subsidized by Egypt, invaded Macedon and Antigonus, who had not yet secured the firm allegiance of the Macedonians, was forced to flee from his kingdom. Pyrrhus, as usual, was too impatient to consolidate his conquests. In 272 he invaded the Peloponnese, liberated the cities still subject to Antigonus, except Corinth, and then attacked Sparta. Since the time of Philip II Sparta had been bitterly hostile to Macedon, but, realizing that Pyrrhus must be stopped, Antigonus rushed troops from Corinth to the defence of the famous city. Foiled in this undertaking, Pyrrhus turned against Argos where, fortunately for the peace of the world, he was killed.

Antigonus had already regained Macedon and he was now in a position to dominate the Peloponnese if he so wanted. He had no desire for conquests in that region, however. He was satisfied when his partisans seized control in Megalopolis and Argos, for these cities could act as a check on their old enemy Sparta. He then directed his attention to his communications with Corinth. Free access to this city was essential, for by his possession of that strategic site he hoped to prevent the Greeks from uniting against Macedon. Land connections were impossible and those by sea were jeopardized by Egypt's naval supremacy. Consequently he subdued Euboea (*ca.* 270), where he garrisoned Eretria and Chalcis, and about the same time he took Megara, where he garrisoned Nisaea. His loyal half-brother, Craterus, governed Euboea and Corinth for him and kept watch on Peloponnesian affairs. In Corinth, Chalcis and Demetrias Antigonus possessed the famous "fetters" of Greece. He also recovered the Piraeus and installed a garrison there. Dearly as he loved Athens, he considered this restraint necessary to prevent the glorious city from falling under the influence or into the hands of Ptolemy.

It was not until 267 that Antigonus' arrangements in Greece were again seriously challenged. In that year Sparta with numerous Peloponnesian allies, instigated by Ptolemaic intrigue and money, initiated a movement to liberate Greece from Macedonian influence. Athens on the motion of Chremonides threw in her lot with the Peloponnesians and Egypt. In this Chremonidean War Antigonus was completely victorious. The Spartans were thoroughly defeated, their allies melted away and by 262 an isolated Athens had to capitulate. To prevent the recurrence of an Athenian uprising Antigonus put the city entirely under his control. In addition to the garrison at the Piraeus he installed troops in Athens itself and in the various Attic forts. Magistrates of his own appointment replaced the existing ones and a governor was set over the city. Henceforth Athens ceased to count as a political force in the Greek world.

Once again Antigonus could have made conquests in the Peloponnese, but once again he refrained. If Egypt had not shown such interest in fomenting trouble in Greece for Macedon, he might well have been content to ignore the Peloponnesians. Egyptian intrigues, however, and Spartan hostility, which afforded an excellent entering wedge for Ptolemaic interference, forced him to take cognizance of the problem. It was imperative to keep guard on Sparta and for this purpose Megalopolis and Argos were invaluable. In the decade following the conclusion of the Chremonidean War Aristodemus and Aristomachus made themselves tyrants in Megalopolis and Argos respectively. Both were excellent rulers and Antigonus offered them support when necessary. In the ensuing years tyrants appeared in a few other Peloponnesian cities, but there is no good evidence that

Antigonus installed them nor is it true that every tyrant was pro-Macedonian.

The whole question of Antigonus' "system" of tyrants in the Peloponnese is very obscure. It must never be forgotten that our scanty information on the subject goes back to bitterly anti-Macedonian sources. Antigonus' policy can probably be stated as follows. Because of the menace from Egypt and Sparta he considered it necessary to exert some influence in the Peloponnese. Garrisons would have been expensive and also would have aroused much hatred. The failure of Demetrius' Hellenic League did not encourage him to repeat the experiment and also that League had been formed with the purpose of attacking Macedon. Consequently when tyrants from the pro-Macedonian party seized power in certain cities, Antigonus was glad to support them. Dealings with individual rulers simplified matters. He knew that the institution of tyranny was repugnant to many Greeks, but there seemed to be no better way to prevent the Peloponnese from becoming a source of danger to Macedon.

Antigonus realized that as long as the Ptolemies controlled the sea Greece would be exposed to their interference. Like his father, he decided to crush their naval power. Unfortunately very little is definitely known about his maritime policy. He defeated Ptolemy's fleet off Cos in a battle which may have terminated the Chremonidean War or may have been fought some four years later. Unquestionably this victory weakened Egypt and increased his influence in the Aegean, but there is insufficient evidence to say that he won control of the sea and of the League of the Islanders. Within a few years his prestige suffered a severe blow. Alexander, Craterus' son, who had succeeded his father as governor of Corinth and Euboea, revolted—probably at Ptolemy's instigation—and established himself as king in his little realm. About 245, however, Antigonus managed to recover Corinth and apparently Euboea from Alexander's widow Nicaea. He also struck again at Ptolemy, for the Sophron whom he defeated off Andros must have been a Ptolemaic admiral. The results of Andros are as uncertain as those of Cos. All that can safely be said is that henceforth the Egyptian protectorate over the Island League was relaxed and the Antigonids were able to exert influence in some of the Cyclades.[2]

Despite many vicissitudes Antigonus' policies seemed finally to have achieved permanent success. He had secured the unswerving loyalty of the Macedonians for himself and his descendants. He had restored Thessaly and Paeonia to the Macedonian fold and his authority in Greece seemed well established. Egypt had been weakened at sea and in consequence Antigonus had deemed it safe to remove his governor from Athens and to withdraw almost all the Attic garrisons save the one at the Piraeus. The expansion of the Aetolian League in central Greece must have given him pause at times, but the success of his plans elsewhere apparently justified his policy of nonintervention in Aetolian ambitions.

In the Peloponnese, however, his "system" of tyrants, however benevolent, outraged many patriotic Greeks and a powerful rival was soon to appear in the federal movement. In 251 Aratus of Sicyon freed his native city from its tyrant Nicocles—a man who had no connection with Antigonus—and united Sicyon to the little Achaean League. Heretofore this League had formed a homogeneous ethnic group, but, once Sicyon had been admitted, there was no reason to exclude any Greek city which might wish, or which might be persuaded, to join. Aratus was consumed with a fanatical hatred for the institution of tyranny and, since some of the Peloponnesian tyrants were supported by Antigonus, a conflict between the two men was ultimately inevitable. Like most fanatics, Aratus was unscrupulous in his methods. In 243, although the Achaean League and Antigonus were at peace, by a daring stratagem he drove the Macedonian garrison from Acrocorinth. Corinth, freed from an Antigonid garrison for the first time since 303, was persuaded to join the Achaean League. The loss of Corinth, Antigonus knew, spelled the collapse of his Peloponnesian system. At first he made some preparations for the recovery of the city, but, realizing

---

[2] E. Bikerman, *Revue des études anciennes*, vol. XL (1938), pp. 369-383, has given a recent and conservative discussion of Antigonid and Ptolemaic influence in the Aegean. He emphasizes the danger of inferring a Macedonian protectorate from the highly unsatisfactory evidence.

the difficulty of the task, the aged king soon decided to accept the disaster as a *fait accompli*. In 239 he died.

The death of Antigonus Gonatas gave a great impulse to the federal movement in Greece. The Achaean and Aetolian Leagues, seeing in Macedon the chief obstacle to their expansion, formed an alliance against his son, Demetrius II. Demetrius' attempt to maintain his father's system in the Peloponnese inevitably led to a conflict with Aratus, who was determined to overthrow all tyrants and enlarge the Achaean League. Circumstances favored Aratus, for Demetrius, fully occupied in central Greece and lacking Corinth, could not effectively aid his friends. When the various tyrants realized this, they abdicated. By 228 all Macedonian influence had been eradicated from the Peloponnese.

The agreement between the Aetolians and Gonatas had ended with his death and almost at once the policies of the two strongest states in Greece clashed. The immediate cause of the rupture was the fact that by marrying the Epirote princess, Phthia, *ca.* 239 Demetrius pledged himself to aid Epirus against the current Aetolian aggressions. It was an important step. Henceforth the Macedonians and Aetolians were always enemies—an enmity which was to prove disastrous for Greece. On the other hand, the bad relations between Epirus and Macedon, which had characterized the reigns of Pyrrhus and his son Alexander, were now changed to friendly ones and with slight interruptions remained so for many years. The course of Demetrius' war with the Aetolians is practically unknown, but its final phase was significant for the future history of Greece. In 231 Demetrius, unable himself to assist his friends the Acarnanians, who were hard pressed by the Aetolians, persuaded the Illyrians to rescue them. Acarnania was saved and within a year she and the new Epirote republic allied themselves with the Illyrians. All were in close relations with Macedon. Since Rome was about to appear on the scene, the Macedonian interests along the eastern coast of the Adriatic cannot be overemphasized. Before the emergence of the Roman threat, however, Demetrius died after sustaining a serious defeat at the hands of the invading Dardanians (229).

Since Demetrius' son was still a child, the Macedonian army assembly appointed his kinsman, Antigonus Doson, regent and subsequently king, to cope with the critical situation. Doson was unable to prevent the collapse of the last vestiges of Macedonian authority in the Peloponnese or the winning of complete independence by Athens, but by vigorous action in 229 and 228 he expelled the invading Dardanians and recovered most of Thessaly which had revolted at Aetolian instigation. In the west, however, he was powerless to forestall events which heralded a new chapter in Greek and Macedonian history.

For years the Illyrians had practised piracy on Greek and Italian shipping in the Adriatic. The Romans had shown complete indifference to such enterprises until 230, when they sent envoys to the Illyrian queen, Teuta, to protest. Receiving no satisfaction, they crushed the Illyrians in 229 and 228 and established a protectorate over about 120 miles of the coast from Lissus southward to the neighborhood of Phoenice in Epirus. Before returning home the Romans sent envoys to the Achaean and Aetolian Leagues and shortly thereafter to Athens and Corinth. The prevailing view is that in this First Illyrian War Rome was acting solely to protect Italian merchants and that she had no imperialistic motives. It is none the less true, however, that by planting herself on the eastern Adriatic coast—a region in which Macedon had been interested for generations—Rome was pursuing a course which to the Macedonians seemed menacing. It was hardly by mere chance that the Romans endured Illyrian piracy without complaint until a time when Macedon was almost overwhelmed by disasters and that after the formation of the protectorate they sent envoys to four states which were all hostile to Macedon. To say the least, Rome was treating Macedon in a singularly cavalier fashion and it is hard to escape the conclusion that she was adopting her usual policy of fomenting trouble for a powerful neighbor.

The difficulties of Demetrius II and Antigonus Doson had been the opportunities of Aratus. Under his leadership the Achaean League had expanded greatly. His goal was to include the whole Peloponnese in the League. Such an ambition inevitably led to conflict with Sparta, where the able and energetic Cleomenes was now ruling. In 227 Cleomenes overthrew the hopelessly decadent oligarchical regime in Sparta by an almost bloodless social revolution. With the enthusiastic backing of his people he then turned his thoughts to regaining for Sparta her ancient hegemony in the Peloponnese. Thus monarchical and federal principles struggled for supremacy in the peninsula. Cleomenes carried all before him, for Aratus was no match for him as a soldier. Also, since the constitution of the Achaean League decidedly favored the upper classes, the common people of the Achaeans felt little enthusiasm for the contest. In despair Aratus realized that outside help was imperative to prevent the collapse of the Achaean League. Ptolemy had recently transferred his financial support from the Achaeans to Cleomenes, thinking that Sparta would prove a more effective check on Macedon. Consequently the world witnessed the amazing spectacle of Aratus appealing to Doson. In Aratus' eyes partial subordination to Macedon was preferable to submission to Cleomenes, exposure to the possible spread of social revolution and personal eclipse by the Spartan king.

Once again the perennial quarrels of the Greeks had given an opening to an outside power. After Acrocorinth had been promised to him, Doson came south and at Sellasia in 222 the so-called Cleomenic War ended with the total defeat of Cleomenes. It now looked as if a new order might prevail in Greece. During the war Doson had gathered his various allies into an Hellenic League. The new organization revealed how widespread the federal movement had been in the third century, for it was a League of Leagues and not almost exclusively of cities as had been that of Demetrius I. The membership comprised the Leagues of the Achaeans, Boeotians, Phocians (possibly the Locrians and Euboeans), Acarnanians, Epirotes, Thessalians and Macedonians. It is significant of the tendency of the times that even the Macedonians can be spoken of as constituting a League. About this period there is a reference to the Commonwealth of the Macedonians and in official language the Macedonians are mentioned side by side with the king. Externally, therefore, Greek influence and possibly the progressive urbanization of Macedon had altered the government, but there is no evidence that *de facto* the powers of the king were in the least diminished.

The new Hellenic League was a loose alliance under the presidency of the King of the Macedonians. In war time he was the supreme commander. There was the usual synedrion of delegates from the various member Leagues, but in contrast to Demetrius' League this synedrion was not a sovereign body, for its declaration of a war required the consent of the government of each constituent League. Thus Doson made concessions to the fiercely autonomous spirit of the constituent Leagues at the risk of failing to achieve concerted action. Constraint was applied sparingly. Sparta was forced to join the symmachy—the only member which was not a League—and Macedonian garrisons were kept in Acrocorinth, Orchomenus and Heraea. Doson naturally did not feel complete confidence in the Achaeans who, he knew, had appealed to him only in desperation. He also commissioned a trusted general to keep watch on Peloponnesian affairs. It should be emphasized that this Hellenic League was not Panhellenic. Athens and the powerful Aetolian League with its allies, Elis and Messenia, were not included and Sparta was a member only under duress.

Doson hastened home immediately after Sellasia to defend Macedon against another barbarian invasion. He died soon after routing the invaders and was succeeded by the young son of Demetrius II, Philip V (221-179). All seemed to augur well for the new reign, for Doson had left Macedon in a prosperous condition and had won much good will among his allies. Greece, however, was divided into two hostile camps and within a year the conflicting ambitions of the Aetolians and various members of the Hellenic League—particularly the Achaeans—led to the outbreak of the so-called Social War (220-217). Philip fought loyally in behalf of his allies, achieving numerous successes for them, but, since the Aetolians were practically unconquerable once they retired to their native mountains, the war achieved very little. Philip soon learned that the Achaeans expected the Macedonians to bear the brunt of the fighting. Consequently, when other matters demanded his attention, he made peace on terms favorable to his allies.

To understand Philip's desire for peace with the Aetolians it is necessary to trace events in the west since 228. At that time the

Romans had placed Demetrius of Pharos, who had revolted from Teuta to them, in charge of certain parts of Illyria north of their protectorate. Subservience to Rome and curtailment of piratical opportunities, however, were distasteful to Demetrius. Thinking that the Romans were fully occupied with the Gauls in northern Italy, he entered into close relations with Antigonus Doson, who naturally was anxious to reaffirm Macedonian influence among the Illyrians. Demetrius aided the Macedonians at Sellasia. In 220, throwing discretion to the winds, he raided Roman Illyria. In the following year he paid the penalty for his rashness, for the Romans sent an expedition across the Adriatic, re-established their position in Illyria and forced Demetrius to flee. He sought refuge with Philip.

If one considers the Illyrian situation from the Macedonian point of view rather than from the Roman, as is usually done, it is obvious that the Roman protectorate was fraught with great danger to Macedon. By her possession of Atintania and the passes of the Aoüs Rome controlled the western gateway to Macedon. Consequently Macedon could never be secure unless Illyria were liberated from foreign domination. The time for action seemed to have arrived in 217. After hearing of the Roman defeat at Lake Trasimene Philip, as stated above, made peace with the Aetolians. In 216 he made his first hostile gesture against Rome. With an improvised fleet he attempted to attack Illyria, but fear of the great Roman squadron, which was hovering around southern Italy and Sicily, brought this expedition to naught. His lack of a real navy now caused Philip to take a momentous step. In 215 he formed an alliance with Hannibal. The agreement probably was that a Carthaginian fleet would help Philip conquer Roman Illyria and that then the Carthaginians would transport Macedonians to Italy to take part in the struggle there. Acquisition of territory in Italy by Philip played no part in the bargain. His one objective was the expulsion of the Romans from Illyria.

The utter inability of the Greeks and Macedonians to co-operate toward a common end was perfectly revealed in the ensuing years. Philip knew that as soon as he became actively engaged in Illyria—or later in Italy—the Aetolians would cause trouble in his rear. Since his allies, the Achaeans, were incapable of restraining them, he wished to take control of the strategic fortress of Mt. Ithome in Messenia, which had joined the Hellenic League in 220. Thereby he could block communications between Aetolia's allies, Sparta, which had left the Hellenic League at the beginning of the Social War, and Elis. Such a plan, however, was vigorously opposed by Aratus and the Achaean aristocrats, who, despite Macedon's many recent services for them, were anxious to diminish her influence in the Peloponnese. Philip at first yielded to Aratus, but subsequently, exasperated by the refusal of the Achaean upper classes to co-operate in his campaign against the Romans, he sent Demetrius of Pharos to seize Messene. When Demetrius was killed in the attempt, Philip in a rage plundered the countryside. As a result, Messenia abandoned the Hellenic League and joined Aetolia and relations between the Achaeans and Philip were badly strained. Philip may well have been unduly arbitrary and harsh, but it is a sad commentary on the selfishness and shortsightedness of the Greeks that none of his allies assisted him in his effort to expel the Roman threat from the Balkan peninsula.

By 212 Philip had achieved considerable success in Illyria and had reached the sea by capturing Lissus. Since Hannibal had simultaneously seized Tarentum, it was now possible for the Carthaginian fleet to transport Macedonians to Italy, if it could elude the Roman ships on guard in the Adriatic. Aware of the danger, Rome acted quickly. She easily persuaded the Aetolians to take up arms against Philip and his allies on the terms that all booty, human and material, should fall to the Romans, whereas all territory conquered should belong to the Aetolians and those of their allies who entered the fray. The Aetolians were joined by the Eleans, the Messenians, the Spartans and Attalus of Pergamum. This monarch now saw an excellent opportunity to acquire influence in the Aegean at the expense of Macedon. The Romans received useful support from the Illyrian Scerdilaidas and his son, Pleuratus, who had been their tools since 217.

Thus the First Macedonian War was transformed into an Hellenic War, for, considering the belligerents, it was inevitable that the fighting would occur in Greece proper. By kindling this struggle the Romans achieved their purpose, since Philip, forced to devote all his energies to the defence of his almost helpless allies, had to abandon all thought of co-operation with Hannibal. Having succeeded in confining Philip to Greece, the Romans left his opponents to bear the brunt of the war. Consequently the Aetolians and their allies were glad to accept peace in 206 and a year later the Romans, now having the Hannibalic War well under control, came to terms with Philip. By the peace of Phoenice the Romans kept the coastal districts of Illyria, but Philip retained numerous conquests which he had made in the interior of that region.

Although the war had ended honorably for Philip, his position was unsatisfactory. His allies were bound to feel some gratitude for his recent valiant efforts in their behalf, but the upper classes, especially among the Achaeans, considered him responsible for unleashing the Roman scourge and they were also sullenly hostile because of his leanings towards the masses. Philip, in fact, disgusted with the selfishness of the well-to-do, had begun to seek favor with the underprivileged, thus reversing Doson's policy of supporting the conservatives. The Aetolians, of course, were as irreconcilable as ever. In the west the Romans still held the Illyrian coast and Philip had no desire to arouse their ire again. In the east conditions were particularly alarming. Antiochus III had returned in 205 from his *anabasis*, during which he had re-established Seleucid authority as far as the Indus. His prestige was enormous. He clearly wished to take vengeance on Egypt for his previous defeat at Raphia and to recover the former Seleucid possessions in Syria, Asia Minor and Thrace which were now in Ptolemaic hands. Egypt, weakened by the lax rule of Philopator and by native uprisings, seemed to be at his mercy. Such a situation boded ill for Macedon. If the Ptolemaic empire were to disappear, the balance of power in the eastern Mediterranean would be gone. Flanked on the east by a victorious Antiochus and on the west by the ruthless Romans, how was Macedon to retain her status as a great power? Her hold over Greece would become precarious and, restricted to the position which she had held before Philip II, she would be an easy prey for any ambitious power.

Philip, apparently deciding that a strong offence was the best defence, reverted to the policy of his ancestors and in the years 205-200 attempted to become dominant in the Aegean. His aggressive actions against numerous free cities naturally raised a storm of protest. Aetolia was enraged by his seizure of certain of her allies, Rhodes felt her commercial supremacy menaced and Attalus saw the ruin of his hopes to dominate the Aegean. In 201, although they had not been directly attacked, Attalus and Rhodes combined their fleets and defeated Philip off Chios. Shortly afterwards Philip won a victory over the Rhodians at Lade and raided Pergamum. Then fearing Philip's power, Attalus and the Rhodians sent envoys to Rome to beg for help.

These envoys, knowing that Philip had scrupulously abided by the peace of Phoenice and that their countries had no claim on Roman protection, tried to convince the Senate that Italy was threatened. They told of a compact between Philip and Antiochus to divide the empire of the new child-king of Egypt and argued that the ultimate purpose of the two monarchs was to attack Italy. Although totally devoid of truth,[8] such statements as these, undoubtedly garnished with plausible Hellenic rhetoric, galvanized the Senate into action. It had heard of the prowess of Antiochus and the latent hostility of Philip to Rome was not to be questioned. It immediately decided that the best policy for Rome was to crush Philip, while Antiochus was still engaged in wresting Syria from Ptolemy, and, by playing the role of champion of Greek liberty, to prevent Antiochus from obtaining a foothold in Greece, which he might use as a point of departure against Italy. An excuse for attacking Philip was easily found. The Senate sent an ultimatum ordering him to make restitution to Attalus (despite the fact that Attalus had been the aggressor) and forbidding him to make war on any Greek state. When Philip naturally scorned this insulting ultimatum, the Romans with clear consciences declared war on him.

Thus, much against his will, Philip was forced to fight Rome again. His enemies straightway grasped the opportunity of employing foreign aid to wreak vengeance on him. From the beginning of the war in 200 Rome could count on the services of the Illyrians under Pleuratus, the Dardanians, the Athamanians, Rhodes, Pergamum, and Athens, which had outraged Philip's allies, the Acarnanians, and subsequently had felt the severity of his wrath. Later the Aetolians,

[8] David Magie, *Journal of Roman Studies*, vol. XXIX (1939), pp. 32-44, has shown conclusively that in reality there was no agreement between Philip and Antiochus.

the Epirotes, the Achaeans, under pressure from the dominant upper classes, and even Nabis of Sparta joined the Romans. Internal dissension and fear of opposing Rome led to the complete collapse of the Hellenic League. Philip resolutely faced this formidable array of enemies, but the task was hopeless. The decisive battle was fought in 197 at Cynoscephalae in Thessaly and the victory lay with the Roman legions and the Aetolians.

The peace granted Philip was severe, but honorable. The Romans, fearing Antiochus, did not wish to drive Philip to desperation. He had to abandon all his extra-Macedonian possessions, but Macedon itself remained independent. In Greece, much to the anger of the Aetolians, the Romans managed matters as if they had been the sole victors. At the Isthmian Games in 196 Flamininus, amid frenzied excitement, proclaimed the liberty of the Greeks. This freedom, however, was largely illusory, for Rome did not intend to have her arrangements altered and naturally many states were dissatisfied with the static condition which Rome desired to create for Greece.

Cynoscephalae marked the end of the great days of the Antigonids. Henceforth Macedon was always at the mercy of Rome. The Romans made a treaty of alliance with Philip, but the weaker member of such a compact was always the tool of the stronger. Philip abided loyally by the alliance. When war broke out between the Romans and Antiochus, who was supported by many disaffected Greeks, Philip gave his ally invaluable assistance. The Romans, in gratitude and to insure his loyalty, restored his youngest son, Demetrius, who had been taken as a hostage in 197. They also assured him that when he conquered cities which had voluntarily joined Antiochus he could retain them. After the war, however, when the supposed menace from Antiochus had disappeared, the Romans found it more expedient to remember their proclamation of Greek liberty than their promises to Philip. He was compelled to relinquish the cities which he had taken. Subsequently he tried to extend his kingdom eastward into Thrace, but on the complaint of Eumenes of Pergamum the Romans ordered him to abandon this project. Hoping to reach better relations with the Senate, Philip sent his son Demetrius to Rome. Demetrius was popular with the Romans and the Senate, realizing that it would be advantageous to have a pro-

Roman on the Macedonian throne, hinted that it would help him to succeed his father in place of his eldest brother, Perseus. Thus the Senate incited the young man to treason and drove Philip to the tragic necessity of having his son executed. Convinced that he was merely Rome's pawn, Philip devoted his last years to strengthening his kingdom. He increased taxes and the output of the mines, transported numerous Thracians into Macedon for economic and military reasons and attempted conquests among the barbarians to the north. Such measures were purely defensive. He wanted his kingdom to be prepared in case Rome should strike again. The Senate, however, professed to see unfriendly and aggressive acts in everything which he undertook.

In 179 Perseus succeeded to the hopeless task of keeping peace with Rome and simultaneously maintaining the integrity of Macedon. He was loyally supported by the Macedonians and was popular in Greece with the common people, who were being oppressed by the wealthy classes preferred by Rome as rulers of the various states. Such popularity the Romans interpreted as a threat. Eumenes, always the enemy of Philip and Perseus, increased their suspicions by endless accusations concerning Perseus' ambitions. Once again Rome took up arms and at Pydna in 168 Perseus went down in defeat before Aemilius Paullus. Taken prisoner, the last of the Antigonids graced the triumph of his conqueror and died in Italy after two years of barbarous imprisonment. Macedon was divided into four republics, but after the people had rallied around Andriscus, who claimed to be a son of Perseus, the Romans crushed the pretender and in 148 organized Macedon as a Roman province.

The Antigonids can justly be called one of the ablest and most energetic dynasties in history. Despite this undoubted ability the reign of each of the seven kings was marked by great and sometimes fatal disasters. The magnificent ambition of Antigonus I and his son proved impossible of fulfilment. The later rulers could not find a satisfactory solution for the age-old ills of Greece and they were powerless to stem the onward march of Rome. They cannot in fairness be blamed for these failures. The Greeks themselves had never been able to regulate their own affairs. How could the Macedonians

—barbarians as the Greeks insisted on naming them—succeed where Greek genius had so dismally failed? The Romans, it is true, achieved comparative peace and order for the Greeks by destroying all that had made Greece great, but the Macedonians had neither the power nor the desire to make of Greece a spiritual desert. The Macedonian stand against Rome belongs to the most heroic annals of Greek history, but Roman might, aided by the subservience of many of the Greeks, was irresistible. The Antigonids had performed many services for the Greeks by reducing the number of their suicidal wars and above all by saving them time and again from the horrors of invasion by northern barbarians. In the critical years of the Macedonian struggles with Rome, however, the Greeks forgot such services and thought only of their anger at the influence which the Antigonids tried to exert in the peninsula. The destiny of the Greeks under Roman domination was tragic, but impartial judgment must term it deserved.

X. PTOLEMAIC EGYPT: A PLANNED ECONOMY

BY SHERMAN LEROY WALLACE

ALEXANDER THE GREAT in 332 invaded Egypt because of military necessity. The Egyptians welcomed him as their liberator from the Persian yoke; they could not foresee that the Macedonian would bring Egypt under a rule stronger and more lasting than that of the Persians. Since he stayed in Egypt less than a year, Alexander did not have time to devise an elaborate organization of the country. He did found the city of Alexandria, which was to have a profound effect upon the future economy of Egypt—it was to become one of the great ports of the Mediterranean Sea and the most brilliant capital of the Hellenistic world.

Arrian tells us that Alexander "is said to have divided the government of Egypt into many hands, because he was surprised at the nature and strength of the country, so that he did not consider it safe to let one man undertake the sole charge of it." Alexander's system of elaborate checks among the officials left behind in Egypt soon became inoperative, for Cleomenes of Naucratis, one of the civil governors, gathered the control of the country into his own hands. Cleomenes had been ordered to receive the taxes from the native officials and it is not unlikely that he used his financial control to wrest other power for himself. Since he had no assurance that the power which he had usurped would be permanently his, he sought immediate wealth, which he obtained by cornering the grain market in a time of famine, by extorting huge sums from the capital of the priests and wealthy merchants and, again, by fixing the price of grain and monopolizing its sale.

After the death of Alexander in 323 one of his able generals, Ptolemy son of Lagus, was appointed satrap of Egypt. Ptolemy soon rid himself of Cleomenes and then moved to consolidate his new satrapy. He conquered the adjacent territory of Cyrene, Syria south of Lebanon, Cyprus, the ports of Phoenicia and the Cyclades Islands in the Aegean Sea. He was attempting to get military and naval bases, but he was also trying to obtain sources of timber and minerals which the land of Egypt could not supply. He wished also to provide ports for a new Egyptian commerce and to control the caravan routes through southern Arabia by which luxury products were carried from the Orient. The ancient Pharaohs had generally left commerce to the Phoenicians and, later, to the Greeks and were satisfied to enjoy the fruits of the phenomenal fertility of Egypt and to exploit the resources of quarries and mines. But Ptolemy, who saw from the successes of Cleomenes what could be accomplished by throwing the monopolized products of Egypt upon the Aegean market, determined to expand the commerce of Egypt to the greatest possible extent. The prosperity of the Aegean world renewed by the conquests of Alexander offered an opportunity for free and oecumenic commerce never before realized in the ancient world. In furtherance of his commercial designs Ptolemy introduced into Egypt for the first time a system of coinage in order to promote trade and commerce.

Although he lost many of the new external provinces during the great struggles among the successors of Alexander, Ptolemy made himself king of Egypt in the year 305. He could then look forward to permanent rule and he devoted himself to the recovery of the external provinces. The sea-power which he had once lost was regained and he was able to hand over to his successor, Ptolemy II Philadelphus, an Egypt whose internal economy, developed along traditional lines, was essentially sound and an empire supported by an adequate fleet.

Philadelphus continued and developed the political and economic policies of his father. Unaware that a vast excess of exports over imports might be dangerous, he sought for his kingdom self-sufficiency based on the utmost development of its economic resources and he sought to secure for its products the largest possible market, especially in the Aegean. By right of conquest the Ptolemies regarded the entire country of Egypt as a huge estate to be worked for the profit of its owner the king. Philadelphus, therefore, felt free to plan its economy as he desired and he planned for his own profit rather than for the benefit of his subjects. Since his able generals relieved him from the necessity of conducting military campaigns, he could devote his attention to the formulation of a systematic plan for the development and the exploitation of the resources of the country. In this project he was most ably assisted by his minister of finance, Apollonius, whose minute regulations have been preserved in part in the famous *Revenue Laws*.

The greatest resource of Egypt is its ever-fertile soil. The Nile River rises in the mountains of east central Africa and flows northward emptying its waters into the Mediterranean through several mouths in the broad Delta. Egypt is the long and narrow valley from two to thirty miles wide which follows the northern portion of the river's course. On either side of the valley lie vast deserts. Each year, from June to December, the waters of the Nile gradually rise and flood the valley. As the river recedes, it leaves behind a deposit of mud which maintains the fertility of the soil. The area which could be cultivated was about 10,000 square miles (about the size of Maryland), but in the Ptolemaic period the country supported a population between seven and eight millions. From the time of the early Pharaohs a network of dikes and canals on either bank of the Nile had been developed to assure and extend the blessings of the yearly inundation. The system of irrigation demanded constant care. It had probably suffered during the Persian regime and the Ptolemies set to work to reconstruct and improve it, seeking especially to reclaim additional land.

The ancient Pharaohs had released parts of their land to the temples and to the military nobility, retaining a large part to be directly managed by themselves. The Ptolemies found this arrangement suited to their own purpose, especially since the native nobility had disappeared during the previous regime and could be replaced with Macedonian and Greek military colonists. The priesthood because of its superior organization had retained its share of the land in spite of the Persian occupation and was left in possession of it by the Ptolemies. The different districts in the Delta and the valley of the Nile, each with its own chief town, had been independent settlements before their union into the realm of the Pharaohs. They retained their distinct existence under the Pharaohs and were preserved by the Ptolemies in the organization of their own administration. These districts were called nomes. Conditions differed in the various nomes, and a fundamental principle of administration inherited by the Ptolemies was that agriculture and industry and the system of taxes levied thereon be closely adapted to the varying conditions in the nomes.

The Royal Land the king cultivated directly through his officials. The actual work on this land was done by Royal Cultivators, mostly native peasants. The land was divided into small plots and the right to cultivate each plot was leased by officials to the highest bidder or association of bidders for a period of years. Rents varied according to the productive capacity of the land. The government specified what crop was to be sown and supplied the seed; the cultivator undertook to deliver in return at harvesttime a specified number of measures of grain as rent, to return the seed-loan with interest (usually 50 per cent.) and to make certain minor payments in grain to cover the costs of transport, storage and supervision of the king's grain.

The Sacred Land was left in the possession of the temples, but a tax had to be paid to the king. The government, moreover, undertook the administration of these lands, offering the priests subventions to compensate them for their loss of control.

Allotments were granted by the king to military colonists upon condition that certain fixed dues were to be paid to the state. The amount of land ceded and the terms of the cession depended not upon the value of the land but upon the rank of the individual colonists. Such land was not alienable, at least not at first. It was to make room for these military colonists that the first Ptolemies hurried the reclamation of additional lands by great drainage works in the Fayûm.

Private ownership of land was not unknown in Egypt before the coming of the Ptolemies and it was a familiar concept to the Greeks. But such privately owned land seems to have been rare in Ptolemaic Egypt and to have consisted largely of vineyards and orchards. Taxes were collected on private land, but the rate and kind of taxation were determined by the type of land.

Large estates were conveyed "in gift" by the king to eminent officials and courtiers. Such estates reproduced in miniature the feverish development and exploitation of the whole country by the king. Apollonius, the finance minister of Philadelphus, held the best known of these estates which was in the newly reclaimed land of the Fayûm. Such "gift" estates, including the improvements made upon them, reverted to the crown, when the usefulness of the holders to the king had ended.

An annual ordinance determined the areas in each nome which were to be sown in wheat, barley and other grains, in flax and in oleaginous plants. The centralized control of the Royal Land was absolute, as was that of the Sacred Land in the third century. It is probable that the holders of Allotted Land and of the estates followed the suggestions of the central government, but it is difficult to determine how rigid was the state's control over these lands. After the sowing the officials carefully watched over the growing crops; the effects of irrigation were closely observed, since insufficient inundation lessened the yield of the land and compelled a modification of the rents. Detailed reports of the state of the sowing and of the inundation as well as estimates of the yield had to be compiled by local officials and sent to the capital of the nome, thence to be forwarded to Alexandria. At the harvest the grain was brought to the public threshing floors. There the officials measured out the rent or taxes, before the farmer was entitled to remove his share of the crop. This sequestration of the crop was a guarantee of the revenue of the king and insuring of revenues was a fundamental policy of the Ptolemies. The state provided granaries for the storage of its revenues in grain. Donkeys and their drivers were requisitioned for transport of grain to central granaries; payment for these services was fixed by the state. The transport of grain to Alexandria by canal and river boats was controlled by the government. Privately owned boats were used, but the king also owned boats which were employed in this service.

The rent from a parcel of Royal Land combined with the numerous supplementary charges apparently totalled a little more than one-half the yield. The various taxes on Sacred Land and on Allotted Land probably equalled rather less than half the yield. In addition to rents and taxes received in kind the king purchased grain. Some of this purchase was foreseen in options in the leases of Royal Land, but the king probably resorted to requisition when necessary to complete the desired amount. Such purchases had the advantage of circulating coinage in country districts which had before used only barter. From the great granaries in Alexandria the grain was released for the use of that populous city. The surplus was available for export and sale to foreign markets; this surplus has been estimated at a third of the entire yield. Export of grain was one of the most lucrative business activities of the king; it could also be used for magnificent gifts to friendly cities—and such gifts were employed by the Ptolemies in international politics.

The planting of vineyards and orchards was encouraged by the Ptolemies as a part of their policy of self-sufficiency. No immediate return could be expected from land newly planted in vines or in fruit and olive trees, so that it was necessary to allow such land to pass into private ownership. Royal Land already planted with vines paid a rent, probably of one-half or one-third the yield, the "portion," which was a tax of one-sixth devoted to the divine cults, and probably other minor dues. The private vineyards and orchards paid a variety of taxes: the "portion," the acreage tax, a surveying tax, the dike tax and other dues. The yield was estimated and the harvest controlled by the government. The taxes were originally assessed in kind, but, as the use of the new currency increased, commutation of the payments into money was allowed and eventually this became the ordinary way of paying these taxes. Rents, too, were set in money instead of in kind.

Egypt was most deficient in timber and one of the constant concerns of the king was the import of this product. Philadelphus ordered the planting of trees on Royal Land and encouraged it on the great "gift" estates. Later, at the end of the second century, the priests who held the Sacred Land were ordered to plant trees. New varieties were introduced for experimental planting and every effort was made to increase the available supply of timber. No one could cut down a tree without official permission. On trees felled and sold a tax was collected.

Not only were vegetable products obtained from the land of Egypt, but also live-stock was reared: cattle, sheep, swine, geese for food, sheep for wool, oxen and donkeys for transport, horses for war, various animals for sacrifice. The king possessed large herds and flocks kept by Royal Herdsmen who paid a rent in kind from the yield of the herd; later this rent was commuted to a payment in money. Private owners of large and small cattle paid a licence tax at a fixed rate per head of cattle, which entitled their beasts to the use of the common range, and often they paid an additional tax to provide official guards against theft. Furthermore, the king owned areas of pastureland which he leased to the highest bidder.

The king also owned swarms of bees and flocks of pigeons from which he received a rent. Private owners of bees paid a tax of one-fourth of their profits; this was in Ptolemaic Egypt an important industry, for honey took the place of sugar and there were many uses for beeswax. Private owners of pigeons paid a tax of one-third of the increase of their flocks or a tax upon the area of their pigeon-cotes.

The king exercised a sovereign right over hunting and over certain fisheries. The king had his own huntsmen, who brought in game, and he himself engaged in the traditional lion-hunts. The pursuit of elephants in the interior of Africa was undertaken by military expeditions. But the king also leased hunting rights to companies of men, who paid for the concessions in the districts surrounding the villages. Similarly varied were the methods of exploiting the fisheries —a very important source of food in Egypt.

The king controlled the revenues from mines and quarries. Stone fit for building and for sculpture was one of the great resources of Egypt, but it was not easy to work the quarries situated in the desert. Quarrying was entrusted to entrepreneurs who bid for the privilege. They assured the presence of labor which was the principal problem in working the quarries. Skilled quarrymen were well-paid, but the cheap labor of prisoners was also used where possible. Gold, lead and some other minerals were mined in the territory of Egypt. Emeralds, turquoises and other semi-precious stones could be found in districts near Egypt proper. The method of exploitation was similar to that employed in the quarries. Silver was rare and iron was lacking, as was tin; these were necessities of life in the Hellenistic period and they were purchased outside the country.

When the Ptolemies succeeded to the throne of Egypt, their "spear-won" property included many places for manufacture and sale of various commodities. The profits from production and distribution of these goods belonged to their owner, the king of Egypt, and were a source of no little revenue for his treasury. To secure the maximum profit from such enterprises, moreover, the first Ptolemies developed state monopolies of the manufacture, import and sale of certain products. By strict regulation of the production of such monopolized commodities and by a prohibitive tariff against their importation by private traders the Ptolemies were able to set an artificially high price, whether wholesale or retail, and so to secure an increased revenue for their treasury.

The king had a complete or partial monopoly of the production of oil (regulated minutely in the *Revenue Laws*) and of certain textiles which were an important article in foreign trade, of the coinage of money, of banking, of the sale of salt and alum, of brewing and the sale of beer, of leather, of Arabian incense and other aromatic herbs and perfumes and of papyrus, which (produced only in Egypt) was one of the most important and lucrative objects of export. There were probably other monopolies as well. But to protect themselves against possible loss the Ptolemies farmed out state monopolies to the highest bidders. The successful bidders had to be closely watched to protect the treasury from fraud and the public from extortion—and this required officials to supervise the farmers of the monopolies. At best the regulation and supervision was often a complicated problem and an onerous task. Consequently the officials charged with the financial administration made little effort to maintain a complete monopoly of an industry, where unfavorable local conditions made it unprofitable. As a result full monopoly, leased monopoly and taxes on free industry were all used by the financial administration of Egypt and indeed were often combined in the treatment of a single industry.

Trades taxes were paid by bleachers of linen, dyers and fullers. Butchers, bakers, grocers and other merchants were obliged to pay a sales tax, a familiar rate was one-fourth—whether of profits or of gross sales is not known. A tax of one-third was collected from the owners of public baths. The king owned public bathing establishments which he leased probably at a higher rent.

Upon sales of real property and of slaves a tax was assessed. The rate varied from 5 to 10 per cent. Various supplementary charges also were collected upon the sale. Official registration of transfers of property was necessary, if the ownership was to be protected in litigation. From the fees collected for this service and from the writing bureaus, where the multitudinous documents were prepared, the state may have drawn some profit.

Internal customs were collected at the boundaries of the districts of Egypt, but more important in the Ptolemaic period were the external customs dues collected at the ports. In the third century duties on goods received at Pelusium for transfer to Alexandria were assessed at rates of 20, 25, 33 1/3, and 50 per cent. (and in addition there were small charges due the local authorities). As far as is known, these rates are much higher than those found elsewhere in the ancient Mediterranean world. And if these rates did not suffice to protect national industry, the Ptolemies resorted to the establishment of import quotas. Since Egypt enjoyed a monopoly of the export of papyrus, fine linen and certain luxury products, the king collected dues upon exports as well as upon imports.

Not only the soil, the industry and the commerce of Egypt were liable to taxation, but the population itself was considered subject to taxation. Some time during the Ptolemaic regime the poll tax was introduced into Egypt. The time of its establishment, the rate or rates, the methods of assessment are not certainly known. The principle of *per capita* taxation was known in very early Ptolemaic times, but such assessments seem to have been confined to limited groups of the population and to have been levied for the maintenance of specific services. The populace was also expected to supply labor to build public works and to maintain the system of dikes and canals and to perform other unremunerated services. In addition the Ptolemies required the native Egyptians to provide lodging for the military colonists. Even the inhabitants of Alexandria, who enjoyed special privileges in regard to taxation, had to provide quarters for troops. Furthermore, the king, queen, their guests and functionaries of high and low rank had to be entertained on their progress through the country.

Gifts were made to the king, especially by the receivers of his bounty, the holders of "gift" estates and the military colonists. Unscrupulous officials often had an unhappy tendency to convert these gifts into annual exactions. The military colonists were also obliged to pay special taxes for the fleet's maintenance and for the support of a public health officer and of various other functionaries.

The priests, too, contributed to the revenues of the king. Some had to purchase from him their office with its perquisites. A fee was paid for entry into the priesthood, its rate varying according to the importance of the office, and other taxes paid by the priests are known.

Taxation was not uniform, but was diversified and nicely adjusted to the varying capacities of the different nomes. Provision was made for exemptions or for lower rates for Greeks and Macedonians. In order to manage this elaborate system of leased and ceded land and industry and in order to collect the rents and taxes a veritable army of officials was required. The minister of finance was the most important of these and, since the financial administration of the country was the chief concern of the Ptolemies, he ranked next to the king himself. He was called the Manager of Economic Affairs. Sub-managers assisted him in his management of the king's estate, namely the kingdom. His immediate subordinate was a Chief Accountant, whose business was to check the endless reports and accounts. Under him were local Accountants throughout the country.

In the nomes the bureaucracy extended into every division, subdivision and finally into every village. All these officials were directly concerned with the administration of the finances of the kingdom. From their hands passed the estimates and reports to be forwarded to the central administration at Alexandria. In addition there were collectors of taxes in kind and of taxes paid in money and also various guards and police and superintendents to ensure the safe passage of the revenues.

The Ptolemies brought with them the Greek practice of the farming of taxes. In a country which had had no coinage there was no point in farming revenue in kind, since its collection could be assured by sequestration. With the introduction of coinage the Ptolemies encouraged the payment of taxes in money and found the farming of taxes useful. But the Ptolemies did not allow the tax farmers to collect taxes. The tax farmers merely guaranteed the payment of a specified amount of taxes. If collections fell behind, they had to make up the difference or it was exacted from their sureties. The tax farmers drew little profit from their activities, for the officials of the financial administration took care that bids should not be low enough to yield them much profit.

In addition the royal officials were held responsible for the collections which they were to make. Thus the Ptolemies sought in every way to ensure the full payment of the estimated taxes and to protect the treasury if for any reason they could not be collected.

In spite of the terrifying elaboration and heavy incidence of taxation the success of the system was immediate and sensational. After the irrigation system was revamped and new land reclaimed, the improvements in agricultural science introduced by the Greeks restored the productivity of Egyptian fields. Greek advances in the techniques of industry were employed and almost the whole of Egypt was one great factory which produced enormous quantities of grain, oils, textiles, papyrus and various other goods, for sale both inside and outside Egypt. As Philadelphus exploited every resource of Egypt, his wealth increased with incredible rapidity. Stories of his fabulous riches were common in antiquity and excited the envy of his rivals. His revenues enabled him to meet the huge expenses of administration with ease. The army, the fleet, the endless number of bureaucratic officials, the cults of the gods, the public works and the royal court with its famous scientific institute and library were all supported and a huge surplus enabled Philadelphus to engage in a diplomacy of financial subventions. Egypt became the richest state among the Hellenistic kingdoms. Immigration increased, because much of the king's wealth was allowed to filter down to faithful Greeks in his service. Possibly the whole population of Egypt enjoyed a degree of prosperity unknown before. Alexandria became the great clearing house for the commerce of the eastern Mediterranean and its influence was felt in distant Pontus and in the western Mediterranean at Carthage and in Sicily and at Rome. A strong navy enabled Philadelphus to protect this commerce from pirates.

This great prosperity Egypt shared in the early third century with the other Hellenistic kingdoms and with the mainland of Greece. But such universal prosperity was not destined to continue long. The ambition of the Ptolemies, shared by the rulers of other Hellenistic kingdoms, to make their domain self-sufficient soon affected their foreign trade. Egypt no longer needed to import Greek wine, olive oil and industrial products. Since the Seleucid Empire, too, was gaining self-sufficiency, prices in Greece began to fall and Greece was presently unable to buy so much Egyptian wheat and other exports.

The diminution of its foreign trade did not at once affect Egypt too adversely. The decline was cushioned by the great accumulated wealth of Philadelphus, for whose enrichment the whole economy of Egypt had been planned. Furthermore his successor, Ptolemy III Euergetes, made a successful raid into Syria and Mesopotamia and brought back an immense booty of 40,000 talents of silver which was nearly the equivalent of three years' revenues in money from Egypt itself. With that treasure Euergetes satisfied his subjects who had revolted in his absence. He also undertook a great and costly building program, which was especially gratifying to the Egyptian priests, who began more and more to make their influence felt.

After Euergetes, however, the history of Egypt is one of decline. Attacks by the Seleucids, even when successfully resisted, sapped the financial resources of Egypt. The external provinces were lost one by one, until the once proud empire was reduced to little more than Egypt proper. In relinquishing her provinces Egypt lost a regular supply of cheap raw materials as well as exclusive markets for her own exports. The caravan trade, too, was largely lost to Syria. In fact, only the intervention of Rome prevented Egypt itself from being incorporated into the Seleucid Empire.

Not only was the external empire lost, but the king's income from Egypt itself was decreasing and during native revolts and dynastic crises could be only irregularly collected. The planned economy, which had proved so successful in the days of Philadelphus, failed in the second century. The very fact of its former success, which was in no small part dependent upon the stimulus of foreign trade, was its undoing. Industries could not be maintained on the old scale and as a result local capacity to buy decreased. The dikes and canals were injured during the natives' revolts, so that grain production as well as industry declined. Rents and taxes set at too high a figure could be collected only through ruthless exploitation of the people by the host of crown officials and tax farmers who were held responsible for the collection. Strikes became common in the second century. The peasants fled to the temples for asylum or hid in the swamps. Sometimes the desperate officials and tax farmers threatened to join them in flight.

The government tried various devices to break the resistance of the populace. Compulsion and repressive measures were employed in vain, because the right of asylum had to be granted to increasing numbers of temples in order to retain the friendship of the priests. Amnesties were granted, but these weakened the authority of the government. The king in his decrees repeatedly promised to stop the abuses of the corrupt bureaucracy, but at the same time the treasury was threatening officials and seizing the sureties of tax farmers, where the taxes were not collected in full. Depreciation of the coinage was tried and once begun it was not halted, although the depreciated silver coinage was viewed with suspicion in foreign trade. In transactions within Egypt itself copper coinage replaced silver, but the value of the copper coins could not be supported and the ratio of silver to copper coins was determined by the values of the metals upon the market. Good silver, of course, disappeared from circulation.

Finally Ptolemy VIII Euergetes II recovered the authority of the throne and attempted to restore order to the kingdom. His decree of the year 118 provided amnesties and remission of taxes, regularized tenure of property, corrected abuses by the bureaucracy and granted special privileges for those employed in agriculture or industry for the king. An attempt was made to give some satisfaction to every class in Egypt, but it was done at the expense of the wealth and authority of the king.

The reforms of Euergetes II brought order to Egypt and a degree of productivity was restored. The center of commercial activity, however, had shifted toward Rome and an ambitious foreign commerce was no longer possible for Egypt. Therefore the internal economy of Egypt as restored by Euergetes II was less dependent upon foreign trade. The wonderful fertility of Egypt was again ready to produce great revenues in grain and the productive capacity of its industry was sufficient to make Euergetes II and the Egyptian kings of the first century men of great wealth. Rome found it advisable to detach the province of Cyrene from Egypt to prevent the kingdom from too great recovery of its prosperity and the covetous eyes of Roman politicians were constantly turned to the wealth of Egypt until in 48 Julius Caesar occupied Alexandria. A few years later the enormous booty taken from Cleopatra by Octavian enabled him to finance the organization of his empire and the Roman emperors found that the system of taxation devised by the Ptolemies required but slight adaptation to make Egypt, restored to order under iron rule, their greatest source of wealth.

The planned economy of Ptolemaic Egypt combined two methods of appropriating property income. The king owned a large part of the land and industry; the rest he controlled through regulation and taxation. After a relatively high degree of self-sufficiency had been reached, the surplus value of production of the whole economy of Egypt was expended by kings whose interests and ambitions during 300 years were not restricted to military affairs. It is interesting to note that modern totalitarian states accomplish the same end—controlling property income for the state—by one or the other of the two methods. In Soviet Russia the state owns real property and industry: wages are paid to all who work for the state and the surplus value of production is the income of the Soviet government, to be expended according to the best judgment of Stalin and his commissars. Nazi Germany and Fascist Italy accomplish similar results, but without resorting to general expropriation of private property, by rigid regulation of industry and agriculture and by complete control of labor: prices are fixed, consumer's goods are rationed, investment and distribution of earnings are subject to strict supervision and through the exaction of crushing taxes and "voluntary" contributions most of the surplus value of production becomes state income. In Russia, Germany and Italy during the past few years most of the surplus value of production has been devoted to attaining self-sufficiency and to armaments.

The production of Egypt under the planned economy of the Ptolemies seems generally to have been equal to the internal demands put upon it. Egypt was rich in natural resources of agriculture and industry, the lack of which has frequently embarrassed modern totalitarian states. But production alone did not solve the diplomatic, political and social problems which faced Ptolemaic Egypt. When the vigorous policy of imperialistic expansion ceased in the reign of the second Ptolemy, Egypt lost many of its foreign markets during the depression in international commerce which followed wars and the efforts of all the Hellenistic monarchies to become self-sufficient. The Syrian raid of Ptolemy III Euergetes brought booty which relieved the distress of the Egyptian populace, but, since the territory could not be consolidated, there was no permanent gain to Egyptian economy. The elite Macedonians and Greeks, in return for special privileges and benefits in the royal economy, were to render military service to the king; but after long residence in Egypt the third and fourth generations were merely an incompetent militia and Ptolemy IV Philopator was obliged to hire mercenary Greek troops and to arm the native Egyptians in order to check the invasion of Antiochus III.

The financial strain of that war resulted in native insurrections, in defection of the Jews and in most of the external provinces being stripped from the empire. This entailed the loss of supplies of timbers for ship building and thereafter the cost of maintaining an adequate fleet was prohibitive (until at the end the financial and territorial resources of Cleopatra and Antony were combined). During most of the second century Egypt exhibited all the political evils of an hereditary monarchy. The restoration of order in Egypt by the reforms of Euergetes II toward the end of the century showed, however, that the productive power of the country had not been essentially impaired. But the enormous expenses of the royal court, the bureaucracy and the priesthood did not leave enough revenue for the support of a great mercenary army and without military might Egypt was not a power but a pawn in international politics. The kings of the first century were content with that status. The power of Rome was overwhelming and the last Ptolemies fearfully sought by huge bribes to curry favor with powerful Romans in order to retain the rich prize of the kingship. Only Cleopatra had any higher ambition: from her treasures she supplied Antony with the sinews of war, but all the planned economy of Egypt could not furnish him with the men and military genius necessary to win at Actium.

XI. THE SELEUCIDS: THE THEORY OF MONARCHY

BY GLANVILLE DOWNEY

WHEN the realm of Seleucus Nicator finally emerged from the fighting which filled the years following Alexander's death, the new king's immediate problem was to hold the territory which he had won and to organize it in some way which would enable him and his heirs to continue to hold it. All the Successors of Alexander faced this same problem, but in the case of the Seleucids it was peculiarly difficult. Seleucus Nicator eventually ruled Syria, Mesopotamia, Iran and most of Asia Minor and, even though parts of this territory were later lost, the domain at all times embraced a multitude and variety of peoples such as no other Greek state ever included. The Greeks had never before encountered the problem of organizing and holding together such a conglomeration of diverse nations. The way in which the Seleucids undertook the task is an instructive demonstration of the interplay which by choice or by necessity marked the operation of various phases of Greek political theory and political practice.

Seleucus and the other Successors of Alexander had at first to rely on force to maintain themselves. This meant that Graeco-Macedonian troops formed the principal source of strength in each of the new states. In the beginning, at least, the new rulers would likewise have to depend on their Greek and Macedonian subjects as agents of their programs and as their chief sources of domestic support. Hellenization would have to wait on security and the brotherhood of man would have to give place for the time being to the consolidation of the foreigners. In such circumstances a ruler like Seleucus Nicator depended naturally on the personal devotion of his army, of his circle of advisers and higher officials, of the Greeks and Macedonians who were scattered through the empire. To them the practical basis of the king's power was personal. He ruled because of his personal supremacy and personal qualities and he was assured of

THE SELEUCIDS: THE THEORY OF MONARCHY 163

loyalty and support so long as he showed himself worthy of his position.

For the existence of such an empire as the Seleucids undertook to maintain the essential problem was that of the means by which such a mass of peoples might be held together. There was no common native speech, no common culture, no common citizenship. There was no possibility that all the peoples within the empire could feel that they all shared in the conduct of their government. What, then, was to be done, or what could be done, to give some semblance of unity, and if possible some real basis for common strength, to such a fortuitous grouping of nations? The urgency of the problem allowed no time for preparation and gave no opportunity for prior experiment.

A complication arose from the existence of Greek cities and colonies throughout the realm. Of these some had existed before Alexander's time, others had been established by him, still others were founded by the Seleucids, who meant them to be the backbone and the nervous system of their empire. How could a king who was in addition an absolute ruler govern Greek communities which by all tradition were free political bodies?

The problem which faced the new Successor states was really the creation of a new political world order to meet the changed needs of the Greeks, now spread so far from their original territory. A new order was indeed made, but it was one which was based upon the idolatrous worship of the republican city-state as a political institution. Whether the rulers found it to their interest to preserve this form of local sovereignty or the political habits and instincts of the Greeks really made it impossible to do otherwise is a question which is beyond the scope of this chapter. The essential point is that the city-state, which was actually dwarfed in the new world, was not only kept alive, but also new city-states were created.

The way in which both parties, the rulers and the ruled, reacted to the situation in which they found themselves is of capital importance, not only because of the light which it throws on Greek political habits and modes of thought, but because out of this reaction there arose (not only in the Seleucid Empire but in the other Hellehistic states as well) a theory of monarchical government which was subsequently adopted in its essential features by the Romans and by them was transmitted to the states of Europe, where until recently it formed the principal mode of political life.[1]

The ruler himself had a more than academic interest in anything that offered a possibility of founding his power on some kind of transcendental basis. From a purely practical point of view his absolutism would last only so long as he had enough money and troops and so long as his personal success continued; and if accidents or reverses occurred, it would be well for him if he could fall back upon a source of power and a principle of statecraft which were not dependent solely upon the strength of his army and the prosperity of his Greek and Macedonian subjects. He must find some means of persuading his people that he was fit to rule them and that they were being ruled for their own good.

Moreover, it was urgently necessary to establish some sort of satisfactory relation with the Greeks in the empire. A people to whom political activity was a major interest in life would have to find, or would have to be given, some means by which they could continue to live under an absolute monarchy. If the Seleucids did not wish to abandon or suppress the habits of the republican city-state or if they were unable to do so, the presence of Greek cities and colonies seemed the only way to maintain foreign rule in such an empire as they had acquired. The Seleucid king's relations to the free city-states, which had existed before the founding of the Successor states, thus presented a characteristic problem. These cities were bound to the king by alliance; but, since each party here possessed a certain amount of power which was indispensable to the other, there were inevitably occasions when one or the other had to make concessions, so that in actual practice the king's relations to these cities varied all the way from that of autocrat to that of suppliant.

There is no means of determining how extensively or how publicly such questions were discussed when the Seleucid Empire came into

[1] The subjects treated in this chapter have already been discussed in such convenient form that it would be pointless to attempt here a comprehensive review of Seleucid administration. Instead an effort will be made to point out some of the questions which are suggested by the major problems of the Seleucid state. Readers who wish to pursue the subjects can consult the studies (upon which the present treatment is principally based) listed in the section of the Bibliography pertaining to this chapter.

being. Anyone who thought of such things at the time would probably have examined two concepts familiar to Greek experience and political thought which had some bearing on the new situation.

One of these was the idea of deification of the ruler. This had been employed as a political device to legalize absolutism even before the time of Alexander. Its value lay in the fact that it permitted an independent political body like a city-state to submit to an outside authority which had a *de facto* existence but possessed no other basis for its power. The deification of Alexander himself had brought the institution home to the whole Greek world. At the same time the philosophic trends of the time were rationalizing the old Greek theology and making it easier for men to admit such new deities into their array of gods. A world which had many gods (and no longer believed seriously that they had supernatural powers) had no difficulty in accepting a new one.

At the same time, however, the mere exaltation of a ruler into a god would not have been enough to turn him into an established and fully equipped political power. It was at this point that the second concept, a philosophical analysis of the nature of monarchy, was joined to the religious sanction of deification. Philosophers had long been speculating on the nature of monarchy and of the ideal monarch. To trace the origin and development of this speculation, its growth among the Pythagoreans and the influence on it of the Persian conception of kingship, as well as the teaching of Plato and of Aristotle, Alexander's tutor, is beyond the purpose of this chapter. What is of primary importance here is the form in which this philosophic teaching circulated in Seleucid times. One of the first clues is to be found in the epithets which were officially applied to the Seleucid kings, such as Savior, God Manifest, Benefactor and (with special reference to cities) Creator.

The ideal ruler of the Greek thinkers was one who was endowed by nature with virtues and political capacities superior to those of his fellow men. If a person appeared who was so equipped, he ought to be a ruler; and it was axiomatic in Greek political theory that such a man of genius should be above the law. To the Greeks any extraordinary endowment partook of the supernatural; and hence it was inevitable that anyone with extraordinary political gifts could justly be regarded only as a god among men. This had been the teaching of Aristotle (*Politics*, 1284a3) and it was indeed the logical outcome of Greek thought on the subject.

Thus, when philosophers in the Hellenistic period speculated on the nature of monarchy, they attributed to the ruler certain qualities and virtues which men would expect or hope to find in the ideal sovereign, qualities and virtues which expressed themselves in certain activities the results of which were reflected by the epithets Savior, Benefactor and Creator. Because of the presence of such characteristics in the ruler he would naturally come to represent the source of all good things: the fount of all wisdom, justice and law. He came, in fact, to stand for the law itself; and then logically the king himself came to be regarded as Animate Law, the creative law of the universe and the animate constitution of his realm. As Savior, for example, he represented military protection and security to his subjects. He could be Creator of a city or of his country, even though the city or country had existed long before him, simply because, as Animate Law, he was the State itself. Thus the philosophers pictured the relations of the god-king to his Greek and Macedonian subjects.

In the eyes of his oriental peoples, whom he had inherited from his Persian predecessors, the Seleucid king possessed a sanction which was quite as important and quite as effective, for he was to them the heir of the Persian rulers, who had been, quite simply, the vicegerents of God on earth. Thus the Seleucid king was, so to speak, a dual personality—one thing to the Greeks, another to the orientals. His godhood was official, not personal.

In the thought of the ancients, therefore, there was no Seleucid Empire as such. The way in which they speak, for example, of "King Antiochus and his subjects" shows this very plainly. There was only the Seleucid ruler, plus the territory—embracing divers cities, peoples and tribes—which was ruled by a Seleucid king. This territory formed the Seleucid domain only because a Seleucid king controlled it; and the various cities and countries which comprised the territory existed as parts of it only because they were all individually controlled by the king. Clearly it was only the existence of the king, and his official personality, which could hold all these parts together. Indeed all there was to the empire was a king, an army and a bureaucracy—and the army and the bureaucracy were entirely in the hands of the king.

There is no direct record of the views of Seleucus Nicator himself on the theoretical basis of his power. Appian, however, quotes (*Syrian Wars*, 61) a speech which Seleucus is reported to have made to his army on the occasion of his son's marriage, in which the king said: "I shall not impose on you the customs of the Persians and other peoples, but a law common to all, by which that is always just which is decreed by the king." This speech is probably spurious, but the expression which Appian puts into Seleucus' mouth may well represent the way in which the king viewed the situation. At any rate, it soon came to be generally accepted that Seleucus was divinely descended from Apollo. Thus the Greek cities, which by their nature and tradition could not accept subjection to a monarch, were enabled to establish on their own initiative a cult of the king, whose absolute power could be justified by his divine descent. In this way there finally came into existence not only local cults of the deceased kings and of the reigning sovereign, maintained by individual cities, but also an official state cult with a priesthood and fixed ceremonies.

While the stages of development are not as clearly marked in the Seleucid Empire, they evidently were much the same as those which took place under the Ptolemies in Egypt. Ptolemy I, probably when he became king in 305, certainly before 289, ordained an official state cult of Alexander. When Ptolemy I and his queen died, they were deified by their son, Ptolemy II. This ruler and Arsinoë, his sister-wife and consort, who were already elevated above mortals by being descended from Ptolemy I and his wife (the "Savior Gods"), took the final step about 273-270. By their own decree they were to share a temple with Alexander in the worship which had been instituted by the first Ptolemy. In this way the living ruler became the divine object of worship by his people, representing a source of law which stood above them and constituted the power in the whole kingdom. In Egypt and still more in the Seleucid domain (where the diversity of races was so much greater) this concept provided a basis for uniting all subjects, of whatever race or religion, in one common loyalty and at the same time served to place the king himself above all his subjects in such a way that he was at once superior to all of them and represented the same thing to all of them.

The importance of these sanctions lies not only in the fact that they were adopted, but in the method by which they were introduced. Detailed knowledge of this process has not come down to us and one can only conjecture upon the various factors involved. The chief point is that the process was slow and gradual and that the theoretical basis upon which the Seleucid Empire was governed did not exist fully developed, when the empire came into being. Nor did it, so far as is now known, appear immediately when the state was organized. It has been pointed out that both the Greek cities and the king himself would have a vital interest in the establishment of such sanctions. The gradualness of the process of their establishment is of course characteristic of the tentative and rather experimental way in which both the rulers and the ruled approached the novel and unaccustomed political problems which arose in the Hellenistic states. Evidently here the theory had to wait on the establishment of the fact.

We do not know which side took the initiative—the king or his subjects. Each would have had good reason to act, but again each would have seen advantages in letting the other take the lead. Nor do we know whether the philosophers offered their services spontaneously or were called upon to furnish a formula. The philosophers could have won favor for themselves by offering the solution on their own initiative, but on the other hand the rulers might have found it politic to arrange that the suggestion should seem to come from the philosophers rather than from themselves.

One wonders what lay behind the slowness with which, even in an unsettled world, the new sanctions for the king's authority were introduced. Why this seeming reluctance, when both parties had such good reason to take the initiative at once? It might at first appear more likely that the subjects themselves would play the principal part. Certainly the matter concerned them intimately and Greek communities would respond to such a need in a characteristic way. This supposition might seem especially plausible in view of

THE SELEUCIDS: THE THEORY OF MONARCHY 169

the fact that the new rulers were Macedonians, not Greeks, and soldiers rather than men educated for civic and political life. Yet these Macedonian soldiers had had a thorough training in affairs under Alexander, an experience which should have made them quick to see how the Greeks lived and how they had to be handled. In the upheaval and uncertainty of the changing world order the rulers would certainly perceive the value and necessity of the new sanctions as readily as their subjects; and it seems not unlikely that the sovereigns would decide to bide their time and let the initiative come entirely from the people, who would no doubt be more satisfied with the solution, if they thought that it was their own invention rather than a device imposed on them from above. One wonders, again, whether people thought of these sanctions as an ultimate solution, whether these political devices were regarded as a comprehensive formula which would cover all contingencies, or whether some may have viewed such a formula as at best only an expedient which would be convenient for a number of purposes, but could hardly be expected to solve by its own virtue all present and future problems. The practical situation was after all of far more immediate importance than the device with which one hoped to meet it.

Study of the king's actual position and of his relations to the cities could be extended in detail. In the present place it seems more profitable to confine attention to one matter, namely the privilege of asylum, especially since the full significance of this institution has only lately been suggested.

The way in which religious sanctuaries enjoyed the right of asylum is well known. The Seleucid kings of course had to grant this traditional privilege to certain sanctuaries within their territories, thereby probably renouncing the extradition of suppliants who took refuge there. This was purely an administrative measure on the part of the king. But there was another type of asylum, having in common with the first only the religious basis. By this arrangement certain sanctuaries and also cities had their right of asylum recognized by oracles and by foreign states. The states which entered into these conventions undertook to spare the sanctuary or the city from acts of piracy or to defend it against pirates or to take religious sanctions against any power which carried out such arbitrary acts against it. They might also renounce any claims to seize hostages or to carry off persons or goods from the consecrated territory. The significance of such conventions appears at once, when it is realized that the cities in the Seleucid Empire enjoying this privilege were maritime cities or places which would be exposed to pirates.

The cities obtained these conventions by diplomatic action of their own, sending embassies to ask other powers to recognize their right of asylum. The king himself had nothing to do with these proceedings. He did, however, control the matter ultimately, in a characteristic way. Before a city could enjoy asylum, it had to be consecrated to a god, so that any arbitrary act against it would be considered to be directed not only against the inhabitants but also against the god himself. This was the essential religious basis of the convention. And it is significant that the cities could not consecrate themselves, but that this act was reserved for the kings who thus determined which cities should enjoy the status. By consecrating a city the king lost the revenue from it, which under the new arrangement had to go to the local treasury of the deity who now possessed the city.

The introduction of this device could have a number of implications with regard to the extent of the king's actual power and one immediately wonders what compelled the cities to seek and the rulers to permit this rather curious status. Apparently the king was willing to sacrifice the revenue from a city in order to gain protection for it. How much income was thus lost is not known (and this is one of the major difficulties), but the difference to the royal treasury must have been considerable. Perhaps it was calculated that this drop in income would be compensated by the relief from the necessity of maintaining troops and naval forces to protect the cities concerned. Again, one asks whether the king was forced to adopt or to permit this device because his strength was so uncertain that he could not protect his cities. Did he actually prefer to lose the money if he could be relieved of responsibility? Did the cities feel themselves driven to arrange for their own protection in this way because they could not rely on their sovereign? Use of this convention was not, of course, allowed to get wholly out of the ruler's

THE SELEUCIDS: THE THEORY OF MONARCHY

control, for by reserving the right of consecration he could determine which cities should enjoy the privilege and incidentally how much revenue he should lose. In this way he was able to prevent cities which did not really need the protection from adopting it in order to remove themselves from his control and to divert their income from the royal revenues. However, it is conceivable that the king's control of the arrangement was only an apparent reservation of authority and that he may actually have been glad to grant the privilege to any who asked for it.

In any case, the privilege of asylum seems a rather strange device. It meant that a ruler, who was in theory the supreme power and the supreme source of law in his state, the creator of cities and father of his people, could leave them to arrange for their own protection and could renounce part of his revenues in return for being relieved of an important responsibility. Certainly the cities seem to have retained or recovered a certain amount of independence by this means and to have felt responsible for their own protection—possibly because they did not trust too much to their Savior and Benefactor. The sole vestige of the king's absolute power here was his exercise of the right of consecration. And whether this device of asylum was fostered by the king or was forced upon him, the exercise of the right of consecration appears to represent an adaptation of the ruler's theoretically supreme power to meet a practical need which was more or less beyond his control.

The essence of the problem was the need for compromise, for the adaptation of theory to reality. But behind this need for compromise lies a further question: whether the philosophical and religious conception of kingship was not something which could be turned on and off like a tap. The theory itself was admirable in its simplicity and in the flexibility which enabled it to be adapted and applied to a variety of actual conditions. The ultimate question is whether a strong and lasting state could have been manufactured on any theoretical basis with such materials as the Seleucids had to use and with political forms which they determined to follow or were compelled to follow. Their empire came into being by violence and they fought almost continually with their neighbors—

often in senseless and costly struggles from which no great profit could reasonably be expected. The Seleucid kings had no precedents to fall back upon and no previous experience upon which to draw. They could and did take over the administrative machinery of their Persian predecessors and imitate the constitutional innovations of their colleagues the Ptolemies. Yet if they ever embarked on a policy or plan with regard to the "natives," they must often have wondered what the outcome of it would be. Polybius (v. 83) has left us a description of one of the Seleucid monarchs on the eve of a great battle exhorting his troops—through his interpreters. The picture is unobtrusive, but it brings home to us very vividly the problem which must have haunted every Seleucid king. The dynasty managed to maintain itself, but the land and the people on it never changed. They had lived there under the Persians and they continued to live there under the Seleucids, as they would later under the Romans. The Greeks and the Macedonians were unable to take to the land themselves. Instead they maintained themselves by various devices, chief among them a theory of monarchy, which, fostered by circumstances, was to live a long life in the world. Like other great empires, the Seleucid realm could not maintain itself without a constitutional fiction; yet a fiction alone could not make such a state live or keep it alive.

This empire, which was "the bridal chamber in which the Hellenic and Syriac civilizations were married," fell when its internal weaknesses, inherent and inescapable as they were, encountered pressure from the other Hellenistic states and from Rome. The collision with Rome in the war of 192-188 was the beginning of the end for the Seleucids, but it was only one of the series of blows which between 220 and 168 the new Power in the west dealt to all the other Great Powers of the day. The economic and military weakness of Syria increased, gradually and inevitably, until at last among petty bickerings the dynasty disappeared. The spectacle of the last kinglets quarreling among themselves, while Rome waited for the proper moment to occupy Syria, calls to mind the words which Herodotus (1. 32) puts into the mouth of Solon speaking to Croesus: "In every matter it is needful to mark the end: for oftentimes God gives men a glimpse of happiness and then plunges them into ruin."

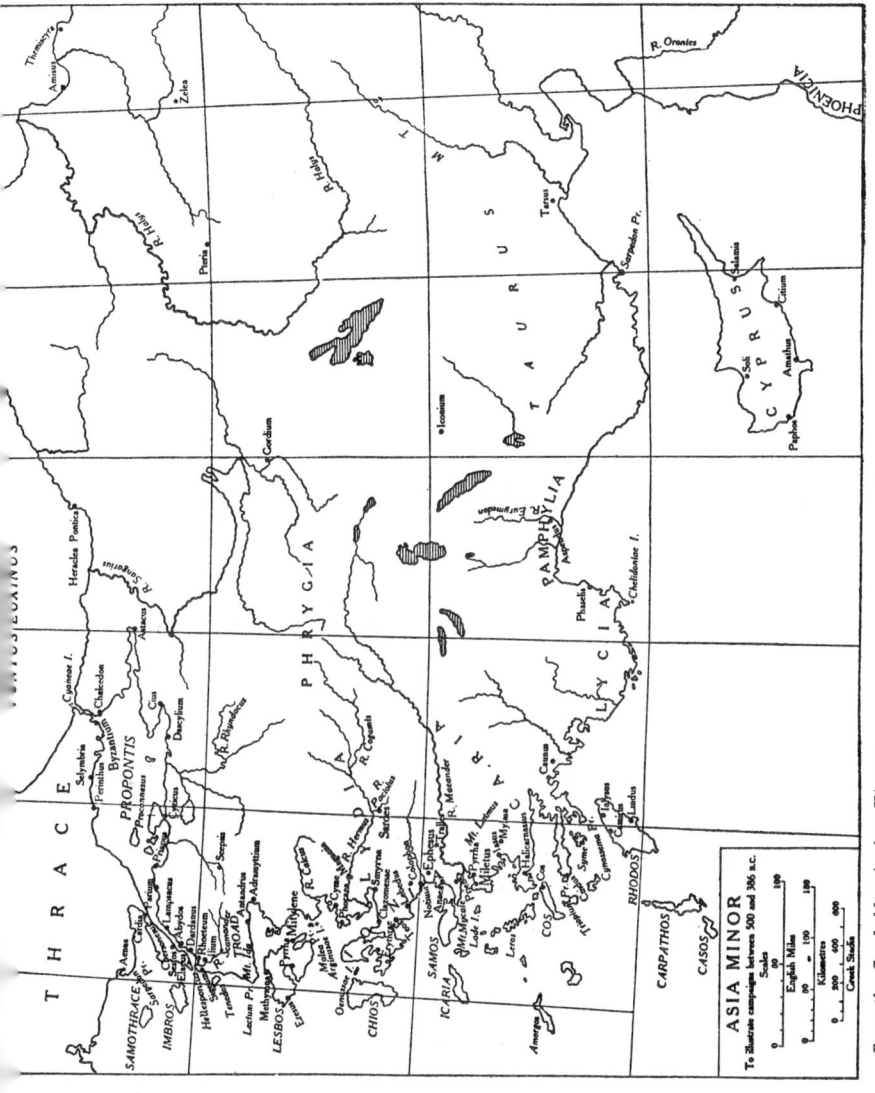

From the Cambridge Ancient History

XII. THE POLITICAL STATUS OF THE INDEPENDENT CITIES OF ASIA MINOR IN THE HELLENISTIC PERIOD

BY DAVID MAGIE

IN the early third century before Christ the western seaboard of Asia Minor, from the Propontis on the north to the Strait of Mermeris on the south, was fringed with a long line of Greek city-states approximating forty in number. Save for a few, which lay a short distance back from the Aegean, they were all seaports, some situated on islands, but most of them on the many bays which indent the coast.

In the fifth century the communities of this coastal region and the adjacent islands, then numbering (large and small) about 150, had been members of the so-called "alliance" which was formed, with Athens as the "leader" in all military operations, to defend the Greek world against the Persians. For this purpose a very few communities furnished ships for a common navy, but the overwhelming majority paid fixed yearly "contributions" to a common fund administered by the Athenians. After the fall of its "leader" from power, however, this coalition collapsed and in the spring of 386 the Spartan envoy Antalcidas signed a treaty with King Artaxerxes II, by the terms of which all the Greek cities on the mainland of Asia Minor became directly subject to the Persian monarch.

Fifty-two years after this act of betrayal the Asianic Greeks were liberated from alien rule by the victory of Alexander the Great on the bank of the river Granicus. Sending his representatives to the Hellenic cities, the Macedonian king announced that the Greeks of Asia were henceforth free. The old communities, as the result either of amalgamation or of natural decline, were now greatly reduced in number, but those which were of sufficient size and importance were organized as independent *poleis*, the condition being imposed that the local tyrannies and oligarchies, which had been the instruments of Persian domination, should be overthrown and the traditional forms of democracy re-established. Even the island cities, such as Chios, Mytilene, Samos and Cos, which the treaty of Antalcidas had not deprived of independence, were commanded to set up a similar form of government and to restore to their civic rights all political exiles, *i.e.*, those who in times past had been supporters of the "people's rule." By this regulation the principle was laid down that liberty and democracy were inseparable.

These city-states were, in almost every instance, communities whose civic existence long antedated the Persian supremacy. In any discussion of their status with regard to the Hellenistic rulers they must be distinguished not only from those communities which, originally subject to the Persians and, later, to the Hellenistic monarchs, were reorganized and then made autonomous, but also from those which, after being founded by these monarchs, received civic rights modelled on the constitution of a Greek *polis*. Whatever the loss of independence suffered from time to time by individual cities which were forced to submit to the more ambitious among the rulers, the ancient poleis as re-created by Alexander were "free and autonomous," *i.e.*, independent, republics. Each had the usual administration of a Greek city, consisting of a Council, a popular Assembly and magistrates charged with divers functions, and each had a territory which provided revenues and, in part, sustenance for the citizens. In appearance at least, these cities had all the rights commonly enjoyed by independent states. How far, during the period which followed their liberation by Alexander, this appearance corresponded with fact is the question to be treated in this discussion.

It is evident that in his program for the restoration of Hellenic freedom in Asia Minor Alexander acted on the theory that those Greeks who had been held in subjection should again enjoy the independence which they rightfully possessed but had lost through the treaty negotiated by Antalcidas. The view has sometimes been held that the status of freedom which the cities now received was founded on the conqueror's right to make whatever disposition he wished of territory "won by the spear" and that their existence as "free and autonomous" city-states was a grant dependent on a unilateral act of the monarch and so revocable at his pleasure. While

THE INDEPENDENT CITIES OF ASIA MINOR

this view, it is true, applies to those ancient cities which had always been subject and to those new communities founded by the kings, which had no claim to freedom except through the monarch's grace, it does not apply to cities which had previously existed as political entities and which had wrongfully been deprived of their rights. This view, too, fails to take into consideration the fact that Alexander, whose professed purpose was the deliverance of the Greeks from the Persians, was bound by that profession to recognize Hellenic cities as independent. Their territory was not "won by the spear" but freed from subjection to an alien rule.

The doctrine that a Greek city had an inherent right to freedom received a new importance from the policy adopted by Antigonus "the One-eyed," who after seven years of nearly continuous warfare made himself supreme in the Asianic portion of Alexander's empire. As a means of securing support against his rivals, who in spite of his success were still formidable (in particular, against Cassander, the master of Macedonia), Antigonus made himself champion of the cities' liberty by issuing a proclamation which declared that all Greeks were "free, autonomous and ungarrisoned." He retained this "freedom" as a useful political watchword and when concluding treaties with his rivals in 311 he inserted clauses which not only declared the Greek cities autonomous but also provided that they should join in taking an oath to aid one another in preserving their independence. Thus the cities, designated as Antigonus' "allies," became parties to the monarch's agreements with his fellow-rulers and thereby received practical recognition as independent political powers.

In practice Antigonus appears to have acted on the assumption that the cities' liberty had been granted by Alexander. Thus he seems to have recognized the independence of the Ionian communities of Erythrae and Colophon as a right already in existence and he confirmed the freedom and autonomy of Miletus, restoring the "democracy" which had been overthrown by an associate of his rivals. But in the execution of a policy which was evidently opportunistic, it was presumably difficult to be wholly consistent. In spite of the guarantee contained in the treaties of 311, the communities of the Troad seem to have found it necessary to send envoys to Antigonus "in behalf of their liberty and autonomy." In a plan for the union of the decayed cities of Teos and Lebedos—possibly a project of his own, but in form, at least, an "answer" to delegations sent by the two communities—he reserved for himself the right to punish those who framed any laws for the united city that were "not for the best." Also, in founding the new Alexandria Troas he brought together, presumably by compulsion, the inhabitants of several smaller communities—one of them that very Scepsis which in 311 he had requested to take the oath to maintain the cities' independence. Nevertheless, retaining this independence as a political expedient, in 302, the year before his defeat and death, he caused his son, Demetrius, to convene at Corinth a congress of the "free and autonomous" cities of Greece for the purpose of concluding a general treaty of friendship and alliance, in which the various representatives took an oath both to one another and to their "leaders," Antigonus and Demetrius, for the common defence, an action which was the culmination of the old ruler's policy of giving the Hellenic polis a definite status in international affairs.

The policy of Lysimachus, who in 301 defeated and killed Antigonus in battle, was in certain instances, at least, a reversal of that of his predecessor. While ready to recognize the free status of communities willing to support him, as, for example, Lampsacus and Parium which submitted to him voluntarily, he did not hesitate to use repressive measures against those which offered opposition. The cities of Ionia, which during the early years of his power had supported his enemy, Demetrius, he reduced by force, plundering their territory. Later, placing them under the command of a military governor, he brought them into a condition of virtual subjection. In the case of Miletus, which received Demetrius a second time (in 286), he punished the citizens by the imposition of an indemnity. It is true that when a city, as did Priene, obeyed his governor "with readiness," he was willing to grant favors, but even then his attitude was that of a superior rather than of a political equal.

On the overthrow of Lysimachus in 281 and the advent to power of the victorious Seleucus I the cities found themselves in a difficult situation. They had no assurance that the new ruler would confirm the position which they had held under Alexander and Antigonus and regard them as independent city-states rather than as territory won by conquest. They hastened, therefore, in various ways to confer honors on Seleucus and on his son Antiochus, hoping thereby to win the royal favor and so obtain a recognition of their former status.

Seleucus, however, was assassinated seven months after his victory and the determination of the cities' status devolved upon Antiochus. The new ruler, beset by enemies on every side and forced to make friends wherever possible, was willing enough to gain the support of the Greek communities by recognizing their independence. The assurance of the support of the coastal cities and the use of their harbors and their ships was an important consideration, especially in view of the fact that Antiochus' most dangerous opponent was King Ptolemy II of Egypt, the owner of a powerful navy, with whom he himself and his son, the second of the name, during the thirty-five years of their combined reigns waged two—perhaps three—wars.

In accordance with this policy Antiochus recognized the Ionian cities as independent democracies. They in gratitude requited his action by establishing in his honor a festival modelled on that which they celebrated in memory of Alexander, and by proposing to build a sanctuary for his worship. The envoys sent to announce the bestowal of these honors were charged also to exhort the king to "take all care for the Ionian cities, to the end that in the future, being free and under the people's rule, they may be governed in accordance with their ancestral laws." The implied comparison of Antiochus to Alexander seems to show that the monarch was regarded (and regarded himself) as carrying out the policy of the Liberator and confirming the action taken by him and by Antigonus. That the precedent established by these two rulers was still considered valid appears in a decision of "King Antiochus" (either of the two rulers of the name may be meant), who, in response to a plea that under Alexander and Antigonus Erythrae had been autonomous and exempt from tribute, promised envoys from the city that he would "join in maintaining its autonomy and grant it exemption from all other charges as well as from contributions to the Galatian fund."

As in the case of Antigonus, the relationship of the monarch to the city-state took the form of a military "alliance," the parties to which, according to the meaning of the Greek word, were "fellow fighters." This was the arrangement both under Antiochus I, who in an official order referred to the cities of the Troad as those "in the alliance," and under Ptolemy II, who formed a relationship of "friendship and alliance" not only with Miletus (which, after conferring an honorary office on Antiochus, seems to have been won over by a gift of land from the Egyptian king), but with the island of Cos and apparently also with Samos and the Carian communities Halicarnassus, Myndus and Caunus. By this system of alliances the coastal cities were divided into two spheres of influence, each of the two rival monarchs being desirous of securing as many "allies" as possible.

As an alliance, this relationship perhaps had to be renewed at the accession of each monarch. This is not to say, however, with certain modern scholars, that the cities' status of freedom, as dependent on the ruler's favor, had also to be recognized afresh at the beginning of each new reign. This view was based in part on the resolution of the Ionian cities, already cited, in honor of Antiochus I and in part on the action of his grandson, Seleucus II, with regard to Smyrna. In the first case, the proponents of this theory failed to take account of the fact that the document in question was not a petition for a grant of freedom but the announcement of the bestowal of honors, with a request to the king to co-operate in maintaining freedom as an already existing status. It was presented, moreover, not at the time of Antiochus' advent to power but after he had been on the throne for at least thirteen years. In the second case, while it is true that the "freedom" of Smyrna depended on Seleucus' grant, no argument may be derived from this action of the monarch, for Smyrna, which in Alexander's time existed only as a group of villages, did not become a polis until it was refounded in a new (its present) site by Antigonus. Consequently, unlike the other cities of the seaboard, it had no inherent right to independence and its freedom could, indeed, be obtained only as an act of the king's grace.

While in the lack of any documentary evidence for the actual terms of the "alliances" between the cities and the monarchs of the dynasties of Seleucus and Ptolemy it is not clear whether the relationship depended on formal treaties or on agreements of greater or less elasticity which might be interpreted according to the wishes of the stronger partner, it may be assumed that as "fellow fighters" the allies were bound to furnish aid in time of war. Alexander had called upon Chios to supply twenty triremes fully manned to accompany the Hellenic fleet and during the third century the allied cities were doubtless in a position to contribute warships or fighting men. Thus a papyrus document of 257 mentions a "trierarch" from Halicarnassus, who commanded (or equipped) a ship furnished by the city for the Egyptian navy, and the Smyrniots boasted of having defended amid "great dangers" the interests of Seleucus II against some enemy troops, probably Egyptians.

As had regularly been the case in the "alliance" organized by Athens against the Persians, the rendering of aid could be commuted into a money-payment. This was evidently the "contribution" which Alexander remitted to Priene and it was probably also the payment "to the Galatian fund," from which, as well as from all other charges, the first or second Antiochus declared Erythrae exempt. On the other hand, Alexander abolished the annual payments of a definitely fixed sum of money (the so-called *phoros*), which had been made—perhaps as ground rental—to the Persian kings, and his declaration that henceforth the cities were not only autonomous but also exempt from phoros shows his intention that no such payments should be made in the future. This principle was adopted also by Antigonus, who in his letter concerning the union of Teos and Lebedos distinguished between the cities and the territory on which a phoros was levied, as well as by Antiochus and Seleucus II who, respectively, referred to Erythrae and Smyrna as "exempt from phoros."

Nevertheless, the view has sometimes been held that the status of freedom did not in itself include exemption from the payment of a definitely fixed tribute and that in the cases of Erythrae and Smyrna this exemption was a special grant on the part of the monarch. It is true that "golden wreaths" and actual gifts of gold were presented by the cities to the kings and that in the almost continuous warfare waged by Antiochus I, his son and his grandson the war "contributions" may have been so frequent as to seem to be a regular phoros. There is no evidence, however, that the Seleucid rulers exacted any fixed annual payments from the independent communities or departed from the principle established by Alexander that a free city should not pay tribute. Even the kings of Egypt who, as will be pointed out, were less observant of the cities' rights, even to the extent of establishing financial officials in certain places, cannot be definitely shown to have made such exactions. The sum of 3,000 drachmae which was raised by Halicarnassus for Ptolemy II was given to the king in the form—real or fictitious—of a "golden wreath" and, whereas the mention of money, grain or other *phoroi* from Lesbos, which appears in a papyrus, probably of 218/17, suggests the payment of tribute, the document may refer to income from royal estates on the island. From what definite evidence is available it would appear that the monarchs, in the exaction of fixed payments at least, adhered to the principle which in 220 was expressed in the promise made by the allied states of Greece, that those communities which had been compelled by force to join the Aetolian League should, on acceptance of the terms offered, be "restored to their ancestral form of government, having full possession of their lands and cities, without garrisons, exempt from tribute and free, using the constitutions and the laws of their fathers."

It cannot, indeed, be maintained that all the rights enumerated in this particular promise were respected by all the monarchs in their dealings with the Asianic cities. Under Ptolemy II, who introduced into Asia the centralizing method of administration used by his dynasty in Egypt, we read of a military governor and a royal comptroller in Caria, who, since the interior of the district was not subject to Egypt, must have wielded authority over the cities of the coast. At Halicarnassus there seems to have been a representative of the king's treasury, while at Calynda and at Soli in Cilicia Egyptian garrisons were maintained, the soldiers of which appear to have been billeted on the citizens. The Egyptian government even interfered in the conduct of the courts, for Miletus together with Halicarnassus and Myndus received orders from a royal official to furnish judges to Samos and likewise Cos was commanded to send similar officers for trying cases at Naxos. Finally, under Ptolemy III, who for a short time extended his rule over southern Ionia, Ephesus was held by an Egyptian garrison and a royal commandant is mentioned in an inscription from Priene.

During the third century all the known acts of aggression against the cities' rights were committed by the kings of Egypt; there is no record of any similar infringement on the part of the Seleucid monarchs. At the beginning of the second century, however, a definite move was made by the energetic and ambitious Antiochus III to force the city-states of Asia Minor into a position of virtual subjection. The step was due to a desire to restore the power and prestige of the Seleucid dynasty, which had greatly declined as the result partly of the war between Seleucus II and his brother and partly of the revolt of the king's own general, Achaeus. A third factor in this decline was the rise of Attalus I of Pergamum. This shrewd ruler had taken advantage of the dissension among the Seleucids to build up his power by forming alliances with several of the city-states, including Ilium and the great ports of the Troad, Lampsacus and Alexandria Troas, as well as Smyrna and the cities of southern Aeolis and northern Ionia. By this means Attalus had created for himself a position with regard to the cities which did not differ greatly from that of the earlier Seleucids.

This situation Antiochus sought to remedy by a policy of active aggression. Having strengthened his power in Caria a few years previously by granting privileges to various communities, he occupied Ephesus with an armed force. Here, in the spring of 196, he came forth with a definite program—"to restore all the city-states of Asia to their place in his empire." What was meant thereby was soon apparent. Sending envoys to Smyrna and Lampsacus, he offered to recognize their independence—on condition, of course, that they would become his "allies"—an offer which was so palpably a ruse for reducing them to the position of subjects that both cities rejected the proposal. Their refusal revealed the king's true intentions, for he at once sent troops to attack Smyrna and threatened to use force against Lampsacus. The two cities, needing a more powerful champion than Attalus, turned to Rome for protection: the Lampsacenes presented a petition to be included as signatories of the treaty about to be made with King Philip V of Macedonia, thereby receiving recognition as allies of Rome; the Smyrniots established the worship of the deified Roma as an official cult of their city.

Rome had, in fact, already taken the position of protector of the city-states of the Hellenic world. Having entered the war against Philip of Macedonia in the name of Greek freedom, the Senate, after concluding peace with the king, caused its commissioners to have the proclamation made at the Isthmian festival in 196 that "All the Greeks, those who dwell both in Asia and in Europe, are free, ungarrisoned, exempt from tribute and governed by their own laws." In conformity with the principle thus adopted the commissioners who were sent to negotiate with Antiochus upheld the appeal for protection made by Lampsacus and Smyrna. Inviting the representatives of the two cities to attend a conference between themselves and the king, the Romans rejected Antiochus' claim that it was only by an act of grace on his part that the Greek cities of Asia might receive their independence. Even the monarch's offer to compromise by submitting the question to the arbitration of the Rhodians met with a refusal.

The opposition of the two cities to the claim put forth by Antiochus and the Romans' support of this opposition seem to disprove the contention of those modern scholars who have maintained that the cities' independence rested on the monarch's will. The negotiations show clearly that the king's assertion that the cities belonged to him, because they had formerly been subject to the rulers of Asia, and that only he was competent to pronounce upon their status was nothing more than sheer aggression, with no more basis of legality than the action of the Egyptian monarchs in subjecting their "allies" to the rule of royal governors and in otherwise trespassing on their rights.

Both during the sixty years which elapsed between the Romans' victory over Antiochus III and their acquisition of the kingdom of Pergamum and during the forty years' interval between the forma-

THE INDEPENDENT CITIES OF ASIA MINOR 183

tion of the new province of Asia and the invasion of King Mithridates of Pontus (when the majority of the Greek communities in Asia by opening their gates to the invader broke faith with their Roman ally and thereby forfeited their rights), the relationship maintained by the cities with Rome corresponded closely to that which they had had with the Seleucid monarchs. In the war against King Perseus of Macedonia the Romans were aided by ships from Samos, Chalcedon on the Bosporus and Heracleia on the Euxine; envoys from Miletus promised to carry out whatever commands the Senate might enjoin and representatives from Lampsacus brought a "golden wreath" to Jupiter Capitolinus. During the years immediately following this struggle Rome adopted the policy of admitting the cities of Asia into formal alliances. Beginning with Lampsacus and Rhodes, the Roman Senate before 135 also gave the title of "Friend and Ally" to Samos, Priene, Magnesia-on-Maeander and Methymna in Lesbos and, it may be presumed, to more important cities as well. Even communities which had no Greek tradition, such as Tabae in Caria and Cibyra on the high plateau between Caria and the mountains of Pisidia, were admitted to the same relationship.

In certain cases of which we have definite knowledge this relationship was strengthened by the conclusion of a formal treaty, which each of the contracting parties swore to observe. Whatever be the truth of an historian's statement that a treaty of this kind was made with the Pontic city of Heracleia soon after the defeat of Antiochus, we know from the actual documents that during the second and first centuries duly sworn treaties were concluded with several communities: with Cibyra probably before 167, with Methymna probably before 154, with an unknown Asianic city (perhaps Pergamum) soon after 130, with the island city of Astypalaea in 105, with Cnidus on the coast of Caria about 45 and with Mytilene in 25. As there is no reason to believe that these treaties, which chance has preserved, were the only ones concluded with Asianic cities, it is a mistake to suppose, as has recently been done, that the Romans neglected to regularize their relations with the city-states of the Orient.

These treaties, though varying slightly in their wording, contain the same provisions, whereby each of the two contracting parties bound itself (a) to deny passage through its territory or that of its allies or subjects to the enemies of the other, as well as to refuse to supply those enemies with arms, money or ships; and (b) to come to the help of the other in a defensive war. The relationship thus established is described as "friendship and alliance both on land and on sea." By the terms of such an alliance the city-states were bound to furnish aid—as they did in the war against Perseus—when Rome was attacked (or allegedly attacked) by another Power. While it is not improbable that this aid might be commuted into a payment of money, there is no evidence that the city-states were commanded to make such a commutation or that fixed payments at regular stated intervals were imposed during this period on free city-states bound to Rome by treaties of alliance.

In concluding such a treaty both parties acted on a footing of equality. While it was inevitable that the difference in strength made Rome appear by far the more important of the contracting parties, there is nothing in the terms of any of the extant treaties to suggest any difference in status between the two Powers. This equality becomes all the more apparent from the terms of a treaty concluded, probably in the second century, between Termessus in Pisidia and another, evidently a neighboring, city, in which each agreed to send aid to the other, if attacked, within ten days' time. In this arrangement—a close parallel to the treaties made by Rome with her allies—neither city was placed in a position of inferiority or sacrificed any of the rights which made it an independent state.

The knowledge concerning the status of the cities which we derive from the treaties of the second century is supplemented by two documents to be dated, respectively, about 71 and in 42. The first of these is an enactment of the Plebeian Assembly guaranteeing to the people of Termessus in Pisidia the "use of their own laws," full ownership of all property, public and private, exemption from the quartering of Roman troops (save by special order of the Senate) and the right to impose customs duties (save on produce belonging to Roman tax-farmers). The second is a senatorial decree confirming the grant of freedom made by Julius Caesar (and apparently ratified by a sworn treaty) to the united communities of Aphrodisias and Plarasa in Caria; it also contains a guarantee of full ownership of all properties belonging to the two communities at the time when they became "friends" of Rome and it, furthermore, defines the previous recognition of freedom and autonomy as including exemption from all money payments, as enjoyed by the most favored state (*civitas optimo iure optimaque lege*) possessing friendship and alliance with Rome. Neither Termessus nor Aphrodisias, it is true, was an ancient Greek city-state; and the question may be raised whether the rights accorded to them were enjoyed by the city-states which became allies of Rome in the second century. The enactment concerning Termessus, however, is evidently a standard form, for, although Termessus was far inland, there is mention of islands and maritime customs duties such as would appear in a document dealing with a city situated on the coast. One may suppose, therefore, that the form in which the document is couched was intended to apply to the city-states on the Asianic seaboard and that their "freedom" as recognized by Rome prior to the formation of an alliance included a guarantee of rights similar to those assured to Termessus.

According to the evidence obtained from documents of the third century and confirmed and amplified by what we learn from the practice of the Romans, an Asianic city-state, recognized, whether by the Seleucid monarchs or by Rome, as "free and independent," enjoyed the status which Alexander had established as the heritage of the Hellenic polis and which Antigonus had "preserved" as an existing right. As far as these independent city-states are concerned, the knowledge derived from our sources does not bear out a view recently expressed to the effect that in the concept of "freedom" held both by the monarchs and by Rome a free city was not an independent sovereign state, but a state subject to suzerainty and enjoying certain privileges only by the suzerain's grace—that "freedom was, it would seem, to the Roman government what it was to the Hellenistic kings, a privileged status granted by itself to cities under its dominion."

Far from such a condition of subjection, however privileged, either to the monarchs or to Rome, the status of those Greek communities which were formerly recognized as free and allied city-states was one of *de jure* independence. It included freedom from control by any outside Power, the right to enact legislation and exercise jurisdiction, a guarantee of full ownership of all landed property within the city's territory, power to manage the public finances, including the imposition of taxes, and the assurance that no regular payment of fixed tribute would be demanded or a garrison or troops of another Power stationed in the city or on its lands. The cities, moreover, could raise and maintain military forces, wage wars with each other, as did Miletus and Magnesia in 196, or serve as mediators, as did eight Asianic communities, acting in conjunction with the Achaean League, Athens and Rhodes, in the effort to end this struggle. The relationship between the city-state and the monarch or, later, with Rome was that of an "alliance" for mutual assistance in the event of an attack by a third Power, an arrangement rendered advisable, if not necessary, by the geographical position of the cities with regard to the dominions of the monarch or, after the Romans succeeded the Seleucids as the dominant Power east of the Aegean, to the new province of Asia.

XIII. THE IDEAL STATES OF PLATO AND ARISTOTLE

BY WHITNEY J. OATES

MR. GEORGE BERNARD SHAW, in the last speech of *Saint Joan*, has his heroine say, "O God that madest this beautiful earth, when will it be ready to receive Thy saints? How long, O Lord, how long?" The implication of these words is obviously relevant to any consideration of ideal states or "Utopian" literature in general, for if ever the world were, strictly speaking, ready to receive the saints of God, either all writing would be "Utopian" necessarily or because of the millennial state of the world Utopian writing by its very nature would be supererogatory. Or, to put the case differently, if the prayer of Shaw's Saint Joan were ever answered, the world of good and evil as we know it would be so radically altered that many of our current views as to its nature and structure would possess only the slightest intelligibility. Clearly, from the point of view of human beings, the most distinctive feature of our world and that which finally determines the milieu of morality is the real and ghastly fact of evil.

Perhaps one can therefore interpret the literal meaning of Utopia, *viz.*, "no place," to signify "nowhere on this earth," because, theoretically at least, evil has been eliminated from the scene. But evil cannot be completely removed even from a Utopian account of man and his human relationships without loss of intelligibility or meaning, as is indicated by a passage early in Plato's *Republic*. Socrates has outlined for his interlocutors, Glaucon and Adeimantus, what he conceives to be the basic nature of a political community. By enunciating the principle of the division of labor, he contends that the bare minimum of a state must be determined on economic grounds and should consist of the farmer, the builder, the maker of clothes, the herdsman, the merchant and the like. Socrates then describes the idyllic life of such a community, when Glaucon scornfully refers to it as a "city of pigs." Thereupon Socrates responds that they must consider not the origin of *a* city, but rather the origin of a *luxurious* city, and adds, "The true state I believe to be the one we have described—the healthy state, as it were. But if it is your pleasure that we contemplate also a fevered state, there is nothing to hinder" (372e).[1] It is then in terms of this "fevered state" that the discussion is carried on throughout the remainder of the *Republic* and so the ideal state of the dialogue is not strictly speaking a genuine ideal state at all, but sufficiently corrupted to be intelligible to men. It must—and does—have enough of injustice or of the element of evil in it to show how that evil can be reduced to a minimum. Consequently there seems to be a kind of lurking paradox in Utopian literature. The "nowhere" must be made sufficiently like the various "somewheres" that men know, by a forthright recognition of the presence of evil in the world. One can argue that precisely this situation makes the hardheaded and realistic Aristotle say in caution, when he undertakes to describe an ideal or perfect state, "We must presuppose many purely imaginary conditions, but nothing impossible" (1325b38). It is not unreasonable to contend that the only fundamental impossibility would be to conjure up an ideal state completely devoid of evil.

The delineation of an ideal state, as well as all other political theorizing, because it is basically concerned with the problem of evil, must be an essentially philosophical enterprise. This ultimate fact has often been disastrously neglected by self-styled political theorists. They tend perhaps to be blinded to the philosophical character of their undertaking, because, as a general rule, factual history, or specifically the factual history of political institutions, gives them the data for their speculations. And yet the political theorist, however closely concerned he may be with the events and records of history, must work primarily with abstractions, such as the Individual, State, Society, Nation, Government, Power, Force, Consent and the like. It goes without saying that only by means of philosophical inquiry can one invest these terms with adequate

[1] The following translations have been used in this essay: *Plato, The Republic*, with an English translation by P. Shorey (2 vols.) in the Loeb Classical Library (London, 1930-1935); *The Laws of Plato*, translated into English by A. E. Taylor (London, 1934); Aristotle's *Ethica Nicomachea*, translated by W. D. Ross (Oxford, 1925); Aristotle's *Politica*, translated by B. Jowett, revised edition (Oxford, 1921). I have slightly modified Jowett's rendering in the following instances: 1253a14, 1282b15, 1287b4, 1327b28, 1334b15.

significance. Furthermore, a brief review of the persistent problems facing the political theorist demonstrates beyond a doubt that he must first and foremost be a philosopher. How else can he fruitfully investigate such questions as the nature of the individual or the relation of the individual to the corporate groups of the family, village, city or nation? Only through philosophy can he hope to make progress, when he attempts to determine the legitimate functions of government, the distinction between the state and society, the means of acquiring and maintaining political power or the balance which must obtain between force and consent in any stable society.

If the contention is correct that political theory is essentially a subdivision of philosophy, then any political theorist will be forced to advance his conclusions in terms of some general metaphysical interpretation of the universe. Thus any convictions which he may hold concerning man's nature or purpose or place in the world and the relationship of man to man will be functions of the total metaphysic which he has espoused. Surely it is the political theorist's deepest obligation to have explored fully his own metaphysical assumptions and to have achieved the greatest possible awareness of all their implications. If he does not adopt this procedure, either he merely describes the various types of political institutions as they have emerged in the course of history (and here he may defend himself by misapplying the name of "science" to his activity) or he becomes a *philosophe sans le savoir* in the worst sense, thinking in a realm of unrealized major and minor premises unconsciously suppressed.

The first great contributions to political thought in Western European civilization were made by Plato and Aristotle, each of whom fully realized the deep interrelation of central metaphysical speculation and political theory. Obviously in order to achieve an intelligent understanding of their positions, one must know at least something of their lives and of their historical epoch.

Plato was born of an aristocratic Athenian family four or five years after the commencement of the Peloponnesian War and consequently his youthful years witnessed the decline and catastrophe of the Athenian state. We are told that, after some study with the

Heraclitean philosopher Cratylus, Plato became at the age of about twenty the devoted pupil and disciple of Socrates, from whom he was virtually inseparable until the latter's execution in 399. No single event in the life of Plato had such a profound influence upon him as this cruel judicial murder of the sage, whom he describes in the *Phaedo* as "the wisest and justest and best" of all the men whom he knew. Beyond doubt this action of the perverted Athenian democracy accounts for Plato's outright and continued antipathy for the corrupted "rule of the many." Perhaps it was in a spirit of revulsion that at this time the young philosopher left Athens to write and travel abroad. He returned to his native city about 386, when he founded the Academy, rightly known as the first university of Europe. Here he remained for the rest of his life, devoting himself to writing and teaching until his death about 346. These forty years were interrupted by two visits to Syracuse, where he engaged in an abortive attempt to establish a sound government for the youthful but unstable Dionysius II. This whole episode was bitterly disappointing to the philosopher; and we are fortunate in possessing the presumably genuine *Seventh Epistle*, which gives Plato's own version of the unhappy venture.

The early fourth century does not present a very heartening picture to the historian. Sparta was never able to establish any domination over the Greek world comparable to that held by Athens in the previous century. As a result, these years are marked by petty struggles of the various city-states, each striving for leadership. Thebes was moderately successful for a decade, but it became increasingly clear that the particularistic squabbles would end as they did—with a power from without imposing a political unity upon the Greek states. Such indeed was the case, when the battle of Chaeronea in 338 left Philip of Macedon the undisputed master of the Greek world.

Into this confused epoch Aristotle was born in 384 at Stageira, a small community of Thrace. At seventeen he entered Plato's Academy in Athens, where he remained for twenty years as a student and associate of the elder philosopher. Upon Plato's death, however, Aristotle left Athens to dwell in Assos, where he lectured on philosophy until called by Philip to assume the tutorship of the young Alexander. He probably left Macedon before the death of Philip, but it was not until 334, when Alexander set out on his eastward expedition, that Aristotle returned to Athens to establish his own school, the famous Lyceum. He lectured there for the following eleven years, but on the death of Alexander in 323 he was compelled to leave Athens under the pressure of the anti-Macedonian sentiment which was leveled against him. His ancient biographer records that he departed from the city because he was unwilling to let the Athenians "sin twice against philosophy." The following year saw his death at Chalcis in Euboea.

The philosophical association of Plato and Aristotle provides one of the most fascinating subjects in the history of European thought. Although Aristotle's indebtedness to Plato is that of a great pupil to a great master and therefore almost immeasurably large, there is every evidence to suppose that early in their association the student developed a central philosophy which was radically opposed to his teacher's position. Aristotle could not accept Plato's central Doctrine of Ideas. A metaphysic asserting that there are two modes of being, the realm of Ideas and the realm of phenomena, the former being eternal, immutable and unchanging, the latter transient, mutable and fraught with change, was completely uncongenial to Aristotle. While Plato held that reality in its purest sense is to be found in the non-spatial and non-temporal realm of Ideas, which operate mysteriously as sources of being and norms of value, Aristotle in sharp opposition maintained that the individual particular thing, the *tode ti*, as he called it, is ultimately real. He could see no satisfactory way in which the Platonic Idea could be related to entities in the phenomenal world of becoming and he dismissed as mere metaphorical verbiage Plato's contention that the particular "participates in" or "imitates" the Idea. To Aristotle Plato's hypothesis of a realm of Ideas was completely gratuitous and served only to multiply unnecessarily the material which a philosopher must seek to interpret and explain. To be sure, Aristotle developed a doctrine of Universals, which, he insisted, inhered in the individual particular and did not exist "apart." Though the doctrine of Universals provided him with an adequate base for his investigations in logic, his system nevertheless suffered in another aspect. Apparently he had no element in it to serve in the field of value theory as the Ideas served Plato in their normative role. If this analysis has accurately epitomized the fundamental metaphysical opposition between Plato and Aristotle, then it can be no surprise that the political thinking of the former is generally appraised as "idealistic" in the conventional sense, whereas critics call that of the latter "realistic" or "practical."

Because their central positions are basically divergent, one should not conclude that there are no points of agreement between the two philosophers. For our purposes, since we are primarily interested in them as political theorists, it is most significant that Plato and Aristotle both held a teleological view of man and of his place in the universe. A further point, even more important here, is that neither of them conceived of ethics and politics as dissociated, but rather as two aspects of the same subdivision of philosophy. Aristotle presents this view explicitly at the close of his *Nicomachean Ethics*: "We should ... in general study the question of the constitution, in order to complete to the best of our ability our philosophy of human nature" (1181b13). The same attitude is surely implicit in his famous statement that "man is by nature a political animal" (1253a3). When Sir Ernest Barker interprets this line to signify, "Apart from the State, man has no meaning,"[2] he does not intend to accent the "totalitarian" implications of the doctrine. He is simply insisting that one cannot deal with the ethical problems of man without considering him in his political context, any more than one can consider man as a member of a state without being concerned with man's individual ethical predicament. That Plato held the same view concerning the virtual identity of ethics and politics needs no lengthy demonstration. The *Republic* as a whole provides adequate support for this conclusion, particularly since the balance of the argument is carried on in terms of the famous analogy, introduced in the second book, of the state as the individual writ large. One cannot overemphasize the importance of this attitude toward the relation of ethics and politics in the thought of Plato and Aristotle.

As is well known, Plato incorporates his political theory primarily in the *Republic* and the *Laws*, while, of course, Aristotle treats the subject in his *Politics*. It is obvious that it is impossible here to

[2] *The Political Thought of Plato and Aristotle* (New York, 1906), p. 225.

analyze exhaustively these complex documents. One can merely attempt to select for special treatment those doctrines which have an abiding significance in political theory and relevance for the desperate confusion of our contemporary world. The present chaos has arisen in large measure either through a lack of faith in human freedom and dignity or through a failure to articulate positively the spiritual and intellectual values by which man lives. However, in recent years many men have come to realize that among available political systems democracy alone makes fully possible the development and preservation of man's most precious human possessions. Also these men are increasingly conscious that they must become capable of expressing in comprehensible and positive terms the goals or objectives of democracy. Consequently, an examination of the political theories of Plato and Aristotle takes on a peculiar importance, if they can be shown to have developed doctrines basically democratic in character. A knowledge of such doctrines not only will help us to understand democracy, but also will aid materially in the formulation of its principles. The ensuing account, therefore, will endeavor to demonstrate that Plato and Aristotle believed fundamentally in the essence of democracy. Though this thesis may not be universally accepted, nevertheless the argument in its favor may help to correct the widespread misconception that Plato and Aristotle were themselves "totalitarian" and therefore in some sense the ancient progenitors of all such political systems.

The *Republic* opens with a quest for a definition of *dikaiosyne*, justice or "justness." After preliminary efforts fail, Plato enlarges the scope of the dialogue, when he introduces the analogy between the state and the individual. After postulating a tripartite division of the individual soul into the rational, the spirited and the concupiscent elements, he constructs a *polis* or city-state, with classes analogous to the parts of the soul. In this state the philosopher-rulers correspond to the rational element, the guardians or military protectors to the spirited element, the mass of the population to the concupiscent. Plato next invokes the principle of the division of labor, already enunciated, and arrives at a working formula, though not a final definition, for the meaning of dikaiosyne. The words of the formula, *to ta hautou prattein,* signify the proper performance by each part of its specific function and the harmonious working together of the several parts for the general well-being of the whole. In terms of the analogy the definition can be applied equally well both to the state and to the individual and from it naturally emerges the important doctrine that the state should not be so organized as to provide for the happiness or well-being of one class at the expense of the rest of the community. In fact, Plato takes pains to be absolutely unequivocal on this point. While describing the type of life that the rulers and guardians should live, Socrates advances his so-called "communism" by insisting that the members of these upper two classes should have no private property and should live lives of almost ascetic austerity. The interlocutor, Adeimantus, interrupts by suggesting that some persons would undoubtedly regard these men's lives as not very happy. Whereupon Socrates replies, "While it would not surprise us if these men thus living prove to be the most happy, yet the object on which we fixed our eyes in the establishment of our state was not the exceptional happiness of any one class but the greatest possible happiness of the whole" (420b).

Such, then, in barest outline is the structure of the "ideal" state of the *Republic.* Its true character, however, does not really emerge until Plato develops his theory of education. He outlines a lower and a higher course, the former being given to the class of the military guardians or auxiliaries (as he later calls them), the latter to those qualified to become philosopher-rulers by having survived a rigorous series of preliminary tests. The lower education consists of gymnastic and "music," which to the Greek included not only music but also belles-lettres or (as we might say) humanistic studies. The object of this training is to inculcate in the guardians those moral virtues which are requisite for a true "watchdog" of the state.

Plato reserves consideration of the higher education until he has elaborated the implications of his famous dictum, "Unless either philosophers become kings in our states or those whom we now call kings and rulers take to the pursuit of philosophy seriously and adequately, and there is a conjunction of these two things, political power and philosophic intelligence, while the motley horde of the natures who at present pursue either apart from the other are compulsorily excluded, there can be no cessation of troubles for our states, nor, I fancy, for the human race either" (473c). In this context Plato proceeds to expound the metaphysical doctrine which will determine the type of education appropriate for the potential philosophic rulers. Through the two powerful images of the Divided Line and the Cave, Plato makes clear his views as to the nature of the eternal realm of the Ideas, dominated by the Idea of the Good, and the relation of the world of phenomena to this Ideal realm. The higher education is so designed that the ruler may come to know, to the greatest limit of human ability, this Ideal realm in which resides all truth, reality and the good. Because mathematics or the "science of number" by its very nature forces an individual to think in abstractions or, as Plato says, "tends to draw the mind to *ousia*, *i.e.*, essence and reality" (523a), he argues that this discipline is the necessary propaedeutic to the entire program of advanced training.

So Plato continues to describe the ascending degrees of the course, which includes in order geometry, stereometry, astronomy, harmony and, finally, dialectic, which he regards as the "coping stone" of the sciences (534e). The fact that Plato gives primacy to dialectic has important implications. By dialectic he means the best available method wherewith an individual can test his own prior assumptions or presuppositions, for these, after all, determine the individual's pattern of life and form his interpretation of the universe. Plato therefore insists that men must continually endeavor by dialectic to improve the character and validity of their presuppositions. And though dialectic depends heavily upon the right use of "reason," it is not altogether through "reason" that the philosophic ruler achieves awareness of the transcendental realm of the Ideas, but it is rather through quasi-mystical flashes of insight or vision. And here it is important to note that ultimately Plato never grants to his philosophic ruler a greater "knowledge" or awareness of the Ideas than is possible for a devout Christian to achieve in his comprehension of God.

If the rulers of the "perfect" state possess an adequate understanding of the nature and structure of all reality and if they face the various problems of politics in appropriate perspective, then Plato is justified in believing that such a state would be the very best attainable by man. In books VIII and IX of the *Republic* he describes how the "perfect" state may become corrupted and he follows the course of its deterioration through the degrees of timocracy, oligarchy, so-called "democracy,"[3] to the worst of all, tyranny. In terms of the analogy that the state is the individual writ large Plato accompanies the account of the several states with a description of the individuals whose souls are comparably organized. At the end of the analysis he argues that, since the tyranny and the tyrannical man are palpably most miserable, the "perfect" state and its corresponding individual must be the happiest. It is quite logical, then, that Plato should conclude his treatise with his great Myth of Er, which has a specific orientation towards the individual and stresses the fact of his moral responsibility. Such emphasis upon the individual at the close of the *Republic* reveals again that Plato saw no real distinction between politics and ethics.

Platonic criticism abounds in comparisons and contrasts between the doctrines of the *Republic* and the teachings of the later and lesser known *Laws*. Scholars tend to stress the more generally practical character of the latter work, which is cast in the form of a discussion between three "elder statesmen," who are considering what recommendations they would make for the supposedly actual founding of a city-state in Crete. For example, much is made of the fact that Plato modified his views concerning the community of wives and children, which he enjoined upon the guardian classes in the *Republic* along with the communism of property. It is true that in the *Laws* Plato, a trifle reluctantly it must be admitted, rehabilitates the family as a fundamental unit in his state and sanctions the possession of private property, though he still insists that its use be common. Furthermore, he specifies that citizens who own the carefully distributed allotments of land should hold them as inalienable. Likewise, Plato recognizes the institution of slavery in the *Laws* and adheres to a very strict limitation of citizenship, whereas in the *Republic*, though he pays scanty attention to the third or artisan class, he treats its members as part of the citizen body, whose interest

---

[3] I have placed quotation marks on democracy when it means the perverted form of that political system which both Plato and Aristotle attacked.

and well-being the ruling classes are obliged to ensure. The recognition of slavery, of course, makes the community of the *Laws* resemble much more closely the actual political and economic structures in the Greek world of Plato's time.

The Cretan state, according to Plato, is to consist of approximately 5,000 citizens classified, not as in the *Republic*, but rather according to the amount of their private property. Ownership is to be so regulated that the fourth or highest class can possess only four times the minimum assigned to the lowest. No citizen is permitted to engage in husbandry, the trades or crafts, which would by their nature tend to degrade him. All such activities are to be prosecuted either by slaves or resident aliens. There is no separate military caste, but all citizens are liable for military service between the ages of twenty and sixty. The same general equality of the sexes as is outlined in the *Republic* is to be maintained. Offices, whether civil, political, economic, military or judicial, are to be granted to those elected by the citizens, according to various ingenious methods devised to secure the choice of those best qualified to perform the functions in question. Plato adds to the regulations already noticed many more too numerous to mention and he elaborates them in great detail. The theory may therefore be correct that he incorporates in the *Laws* some of the specific recommendations which he had drawn up for the benefit of the younger Dionysius in Syracuse, but which, of course, were never used.

This study is concerned here less with these somewhat minor and external aspects of the state in the *Laws* than with the larger metaphysical and religious frame in terms of which Plato formulates his last words on political theory. In the first place, the state of the *Laws* is conceived as a theocracy. And here one notes another contrast with the *Republic*, where Plato tends to suppress the religious aspect of his thought and to work almost exclusively from the metaphysic of the Ideas. In the *Laws* there can be no doubt as to the ultimacy of God or the Godhead or the divine element, however one may wish to label this powerful monotheistic conception of Plato. In the great theodicy of the tenth book he makes clear the importance of right belief in God, even to the extent of imposing severe penalties upon those citizens who do not heed the persuasions to proper belief offered by the older and wiser religious heads in the state. God and an appropriate set of corollary religious conceptions become in a sense the criteria for all judgments with regard to the problems of political theory. For example, at one point Plato refers to the traditional story of the age of Cronus and its perfect bliss and adds, "The story . . . teaches us truly that when a community is ruled not by God but by man, its members have no refuge from evil and misery" (713e). Or again, the Athenian Stranger, who serves in the dialogue as spokesman for Plato's own views, imagines himself speaking to the prospective inhabitants of the new Cretan community and says, "My friends, God, who . . . holds in his hands beginning, end, and middle of all that is, moves through the cycle of nature, straight to his end, and ever at his side walks Right, the justicer of them that forsake God's law. He that would be happy follows close in her train . . . , but whoso is lifted up with vanity . . . is left alone, forsaken of God. In his abandonment he takes to him others like himself, and works general confusion by his frantic career" (715e).

Many other distinctive features of the state in the *Laws* derive from this theocratic core. Hence Plato assigns a prominent place to the laws themselves, for in them he sees the concrete embodiment of all that the divine organization of the universe has ordained to be the good for man. So he can say that the purpose of his dialogue is "to learn how a society is best administered and how a man will best conduct his personal life" (702a). Plato can therefore have a certain predilection for monarchy, but only if the monarch be a man completely blessed with all wisdom and all temperance, for such a man would easily produce the best constitution and the best laws. But the extreme unlikelihood that such a man will ever appear makes Plato evolve a constitutional system according to the principle of the mean. He argues that "there are two matrices . . . of constitutions from which all others may be truly said to be derived; the proper name of the one is monarchy, of the other 'democracy' " (693d).[4] He sees in Persia at its best the most excellent example of the former, while in Athens the latter has come closest to its perfection. By a fusion of these two extreme forms in a mean, one arrives at the constitutional system possessing both indispensable ingredients:

[4] Single quotation marks on democracy are mine.

IDEAL STATES OF PLATO AND ARISTOTLE 199

"where there is to be the combination of liberty and amity with wisdom" (693d). He never qualifies his insistence that a society "must have freedom, must have amity with itself, must have understanding" (701d).[5] A state, then, must be constructed with a proper measure of freedom and a proper measure of control and its laws must be so composed that they accord with belief in the primacy of God and the soul.

In political theorizing of this sort the conception of the moral function of the state and its laws comes increasingly to the fore. Plato had always held more or less to this view: we find him as early as the *Gorgias* advocating that the statesman is obligated to make his citizens good men. In fact, in that dialogue he refuses to call Pericles a great political leader because he failed to improve the Athenians under his regime. The doctrine is present in considerable measure in the *Republic*, underlying, for example, the strict censorship of all parts of poetry which might prove to be morally deleterious to the young guardians in their education. But in the *Laws* the moral agency of the state receives its fullest expression. Education (which the state, of course, supplies) is defined as "that schooling from boyhood in goodness which inspires the recipient with passionate and ardent desire to become a perfect citizen, knowing both how to wield and how to submit to righteous rule" (643e). The post of "minister of education" is to be given to the very best of all the citizens in the state and it is he who will assume practically the duties of a "prime minister." Since the highest purpose of the law is to make the citizens "truly excellent in the virtues of soul proper to human character" (770d), Plato regards his polity as "a dramatization of a noble and a perfect life,—the most real of tragedies" (817b) and hence to be studied in preference to any tragedy of the poets. He is even more explicit in another passage where he says, "There is, in

[5] Professor A. T. Masón of Princeton University has called my attention to the following quotation from *The Federalist* which reflects the same central attitude toward the problem of government as we find in these passages from the *Laws*: "If men were angels, no government would be necessary. If angels were to govern men, neither external nor internal controls on government would be necessary. In framing a government which is to be administered by men over men, the great difficulty lies in this: you must first enable the government to control the governed; and in the next place oblige it to control itself." *The Federalist* (E. M. Earle's ed.; Washington, 1937), No. 51 by either Hamilton or Madison, p. 337.

truth, no study whatsoever so potent as this of law, if the law be what it should be, to make a better man of its student—else 'twould be for nothing that the law which so stirs our worship and wonder bears a name so cognate with that of understanding [*nous, nomos*]" (957c).

No consideration of the *Laws* is complete without some mention of the so-called Nocturnal Council and in the present context it is particularly important. The Council is the body which has final control over the state and is composed of the elders who are qualified through experience and wisdom for their high position. Certain younger men who show the greatest promise of future development are also co-opted into membership. Plato makes clear that this body is to be trained fully in dialectic and is to be finally responsible for directing the state toward its goal of virtue as well as the individual citizens toward their aim of perfect goodness. So far as one can gather, the Nocturnal Council is the exact counterpart of the philosopher-rulers of the *Republic* and, because of the superior attainments of its members and their awareness of the central truths of metaphysics, morality and religion, they can be trusted to guide, control and ultimately be the salvation of the state and the laws.

If one passes directly from the *Laws* to Aristotle's *Politics*, one is impressed by the extensive influence which the former work exerted upon the latter. When the opening pages of the *Politics* insist that the state aims at the highest good, that it exists as a *natural* entity for the sake of the good life, we are meeting in essence a restatement of the doctrine of the *Laws,* particularly with respect to the theory that the state should be an agent to inculcate moral goodness. Aristotle attempts to establish this point in characteristic fashion by indicating that of the animals man alone possesses the power of speech; "mere voice," he says, is shared by all animals and is capable of expressing reactions of pleasure and pain, whereas "the power of speech [*logos*] is intended to set forth the advantageous and disadvantageous, and therefore likewise the just and the unjust. And it is characteristic of man that he alone has any sense of good and evil, of just and unjust, and the like, and the association of living beings who have this sense makes a family and a state" (1253a14).

Aristotle's opening book is concerned chiefly with the view that the family is the fundamental social unit. Within its structure he can see the prototypes of the three basic forms of the relation between ruler and ruled, *viz.*, between master and slave, husband and wife, father and children. Though this is the central emphasis of the book, Aristotle digresses into a somewhat lengthy attempt to establish slavery as an institution sanctioned by "nature." In the next book he criticizes at length the writings of his predecessors in political theory. Of course, he devotes most of his attention to Plato; and often one is conscious that Aristotle's strictures are not always scrupulously fair. In the third book, which in a sense concludes his introduction to the study of politics, after defining a citizen as one who has a share "in the administration of justice and in offices" (1275a22), Aristotle repeats certain doctrines which he has inherited from Plato. For example, he holds that no mechanic or laborer can be a citizen, for the lives of such men preclude the practice of virtue. Or again, he defines the virtues of the good citizen, to the end that "he should know how to govern like a freeman, and how to obey like a freeman" (1277b13).

Furthermore, any reader of Plato's *Politicus* or *Laws* can see readily Aristotle's obligation in his famous theory of the six types of government. Three of these are "true" forms and three are perverted. Since government can be in the hands of one man or of the few or of the many, there will be three "true" forms, *viz.*, kingship, aristocracy, polity, each of which must exist with the common interest in view. The "true" types become perverted when the state is organized for the private interest of the governing element and not for the common good of the whole. So kingship becomes tyranny which exists for the benefit of the tyrant; aristocracy becomes oligarchy and exists for the benefit of the wealthy; and polity turns into "democracy," which is constituted for the advantage of the poor.

Aristotle sounds what in many ways is the keynote of his political thinking in a passage following shortly after his analysis of the types of states. Here he concludes that "political society exists for the sake of noble actions, and not of mere companionship. Hence they who contribute most to such a society have a greater share in it than those who have the same or a greater freedom or nobility of birth but are inferior to them in political virtue; or than those who exceed them in wealth but are surpassed by them in virtue" (1281a4). This is, of course, only an expanded restatement of the principles announced early in his treatise, but it appears here with far more force because of the extensive theoretical analysis which he has already presented.

Now he can attempt to determine specifically how a political society can best be organized "for the sake of noble actions." After arguing that the combined judgment of the many is superior, he asserts unequivocally that "laws, when good, should be supreme" (1282b2). The magistrate or governing force in the state therefore controls only those problems which are not covered precisely by the laws; and there are bound to be instances of this sort, because it is inherently impossible to construct a universal principle or law which will comprehend accurately all particulars. Aristotle then makes more explicit the end or goal of political science, when he says, "In all sciences and arts the end is a good, and the greatest good and in the highest degree a good in the most authoritative of all—this is the political art of which the good is justice, in other words, the common interest" (1282b15). Hence, if Aristotle is thinking of "the political art" in these terms and if he regards law as supreme in the state, it is no wonder that he speaks of law with special regard to its moral or ethical implications. Such is unmistakably his attitude when he says, "He who bids the law rule may be deemed to bid God and Reason [nous] alone rule, but he who bids man rule adds an element of the beast; for desire is a wild beast, and passion perverts the minds of rulers, even when they are the best of men. The law is reason unaffected by desire" (1287a29).

Before discussing the important doctrines of books IV to VI of the *Politics*, it is necessary first to glance at a few points which Aristotle advances in books VII and VIII, which are in all probability earlier in origin than the preceding three. As Werner Jaeger has convincingly argued, VII and VIII, containing a full-length sketch of Aristotle's "ideal" state, probably followed III in an earlier version of his course on politics. Books IV to VI form a fairly coherent whole and contain apparently the results of close observation of the empirical data of politics. In other words, here Aristotle is probably using the material from which he or his associates compiled the famous studies of Greek constitutions. In the series the political systems of 158 states were completely analyzed and it is unfortunate that of the entire group only the *Constitution of Athens* has survived.

In the sketch of his "ideal" state Aristotle rephrases and expands upon a number of principles already expressed either in the first three books of the *Politics* or in the *Nicomachean Ethics*. The teleological tone continues strong. He argues, for example, that one cannot determine the best type of state unless one has considered first the most desirable kind of life. He repeats again his favorite doctrine that the happy man needs all three classes of goods, *viz.*, external goods, goods of the body and goods of the soul, and that all goods are for the sake of the soul. He succinctly relates happiness to virtue and wisdom when he says, "Let us acknowledge then that each one of us has just so much happiness as he has of virtue and wisdom, and of virtuous and wise action" (1323b21). He conceives that the true lawgiver is obligated to provide the opportunity for states, communities and men to achieve the good life and the maximum of happiness. In thoroughly characteristic vein he stresses "activity" and insists that happiness is "virtuous *activity*" and that "the active life will be the best both for every city collectively, and for individuals" (1325b14). And, of course, he goes on to point out that activity connotes more than its conventional meaning and includes the highest of all activities, contemplation.

With these presuppositions he turns to the "ideal" state itself and to such problems as its organization and limits. Arguing from the premise that good law is good order (*eutaxia*) and that a vast number cannot be well ordered, he concludes: "Beauty is realized in number and magnitude, and the state which combines magnitude with good order must necessarily be the most beautiful" (1326a33). The size of the state is therefore fixed by the criterion of self-sufficiency and the extent of its territory by "such as would enable the inhabitants to live at once temperately and liberally in the enjoyment of leisure" (1326b31). Aristotle next gives his reasons for concluding, among other things, that property is required by the state but is actually not a part of it, that mechanics, tradesfolk and husbandmen are not qualified for citizenship, that land should belong to the citizens, but that its use should be common, that common meals should be instituted. But he soon returns to the heart of his political doctrine by contending that "happiness is the realization and perfect exercise of virtue, and this not conditional but absolute" (1332a8). Nature (*physis*), habit (*ethos*) and rational principle or reason (*logos*) are singled out as the three grounds or means whereby men become good and virtuous and, therefore, as a corollary he emphasizes again his view that the legislator must work for the moral improvement of the citizens. Near the end of book vii and as an introduction to book viii (which includes Aristotle's account of education whose details need not concern us) he demonstrates the complete and final importance of education. The essence of the argument emerges when he says, "In men rational principle or reason [logos] and mind [nous] are the end toward which nature strives, so that the birth and moral discipline of the citizens ought to be ordered with a view to them" (1334b15). This must apply not only to the rational but also to the irrational part of the soul and consequently education must begin with the training of those manifestations of the irrational part, like anger and desire, which appear at the very moment of birth.

The closing sentence of the eighth book reads, "Thus it is clear that education should be based upon three principles: the mean [*meson*], the possible [*dynaton*], the becoming [*prepon*], these three" (1342b33). Though the text here is imperfect and though the book ends with unusual abruptness, there seems to be no reason to accept the theory of certain scholars that these concluding sections of the book are spurious. Aristotle has been discussing music and musical education and is evidently supporting his views by adducing three general principles of education. It is the first of these, the mean, which we must now examine, for its scope is not limited specifically to education, as anyone familiar with Aristotle's ethical theory well knows. Furthermore, the principle is all the more important for us, because we see it operating with increasing power in the development of Plato's thought in the *Laws*. Certainly in the remaining three books of the *Politics* the principle of the mean is highly significant; and we must therefore call attention to two crucial references in these five earlier books in addition to the passage in which the mean appears as a cardinal base in education.

The first of these occurs in the seventh book, where Aristotle is contrasting the people who live in the cold climate of northern Europe with the inhabitants of Asia. The former, though spirited, are lacking in intelligence, whereas the inhabitants of the East are "intelligent and inventive, but they are wanting in spirit, and therefore they are always in a state of subjection and slavery. But the Hellenic race, which is situated between them, is likewise intermediate (or in the mean) in character, being high-spirited and also intelligent. Hence it continues free, and is the best governed of any nation, and, if it could be formed into one state, would be able to rule the world" (1327b28). Here Aristotle clearly asserts the supremacy of the Hellenes by invoking the principle of the mean as a criterion of high value. Furthermore, the passage indicates by implication the true nature of genuine mediation, in that the mean absorbs, so to speak, the positive values of the extremes and in their fusion or combination there appears a value from which the weaknesses of either extreme have been eliminated. Therefore, Aristotle can contend that the mean which combines spirit and intelligence really operates as a source of freedom and of good government.

The other crucial passage in question illuminates his conception of law. We have already seen the importance which Aristotle attaches to the law and have noted that all three of the good or unperverted types of state are those in which the ruler or the ruling body governs in accordance with the laws for the interest and well-being of the whole state. So for our purposes, when we are attempting to understand the function of the mean in Aristotle's political thinking, it is most noteworthy that he says in the third book, "Hence it is evident that in seeking for justice men seek for the mean, for the law is the mean" (1287b4).

These three quotations show beyond any doubt that even in the earlier part of the *Politics* Aristotle is using, in the larger context of political theory, the principle of the mean, so important for him in his more strictly ethical thinking. But in the latest three books (IV-VI) he develops more fully the political implications of the mean—and, it must be noted, very much after the manner of Plato's treatment in the *Laws*. The three books set out ostensibly to describe the characteristic diseases of existing states and constitutions, in order finally to recommend various expedients whereby these diseases may be reduced to a minimum. On the whole, Aristotle fulfills this purpose, but as he moves through his discussion he by no means neglects to keep before the reader the fundamental bases of his political theory. Hence, even though these books are often regarded as a handbook for practical statesmanship, still in many ways they contain Aristotle's maturest theoretical views on the problems of politics. For example, he continues to assert the supremacy of law, as when he says, "Hence there are two parts of good government; one is the actual obedience of citizens to the laws, the other part is the goodness of the laws which they obey" (1294a5). Or again, one finds that he has not varied an iota in his thought on the crucial importance of education, as is clear in these words, "But of all the things which I have mentioned, that which most contributes to the permanence of constitutions is the adaptation of education to the form of government, and yet in our own day this principle is universally neglected" (1310a13).

A clue to Aristotle's attitude toward the mean in these later books appears in a somewhat casual remark inserted in his discussion of those forces which make for either the preservation or the destruction of states. He says, "Neither should we forget the mean, which at the present day is lost sight of in perverted forms of government" (1309b18). As this passage associates the mean with the "true" types of state, so also the mean is the principle distinguishing the "true" type of state which Aristotle finally prefers, *viz.*, the polity or commonwealth, as the Greek term *politeia* is sometimes rendered.

His argument in favor of the polity should be examined in some detail. First of all, he sees the polity as a fusion of oligarchy and "democracy" in a mean. Next, having established the polity as a mean, he supports his preference for that form of state in an extended passage which must be quoted in full. "For if what was said in the *Ethics* is true, that the happy life is the life according to virtue lived without impediment, and that virtue is a mean, then the life which is in a mean, and in a mean attainable by every one, must be the best. And the same principles of virtue and vice are characteristic of cities and of constitutions; for the constitution is in figure the life of the city. Now in all states there are three elements: one class is very rich, another very poor, and a third in a mean. It is admitted that moderation and the mean are best, and therefore it will clearly be best to possess the gifts of fortune in moderation; for in that condition men are most ready to follow rational principle or reason [logos]" (1295a35). The polity is thus a "middling" or a "mean" state and it looks for its strength to the middle or "mean" class, for that group will be best able to adhere to the dictates of reason, will be "least likely to shrink from rule, or to be over-ambitious for it" (1295b12) and will provide the best guarantee that equality and justice shall prevail in the state. There is every justification, therefore, to conclude that the principle of the mean is really the very essence of Aristotle's political thinking and that he uses it consistently as a criterion of the highest possible value.

Though it should be clear that a number of differences obtain between the Platonic and the Aristotelian political positions, yet they are sufficiently alike in certain respects to permit simultaneous criticism of their limitations. For example, throughout the three works which have been examined, the investigation is confined to the small and inevitably particularistic city-state. To some in the modern world, whose political theorizing must be in terms of vast nation-states with millions of persons sharing the citizenship, the observations of these ancient Greek philosophers seem useless because of their limited scope or scale. Other critics have been dissatisfied because all these ancient "ideal" states have been delineated statically, without adequate attention to the dynamics of political phenomena or to the development of states. Many of us perhaps tend to take this argument too seriously, imbued as we are with the legitimate and illegitimate implications and extensions of the evolutionary hypothesis. Also some see unfortunate primitivistic or unduly archaizing tendencies in these early Utopian documents. They would point to such notions as the inalienability of land or the theory that the individual citizen should pass through the various stages of soldier, office-holder and priest in his career as a member of a state. Still others justifiably resent the doctrine of the *Laws* and the *Politics* that the mechanic or laborer or farmer or artisan cannot be citizens because their "vulgar" activity does not permit the leisure to practise virtue. Similarly the criticism is often made that these states are predicated upon a slave economy and therefore can have nothing of value in them to repay a careful study in the twentieth century. It must be added here, however, that, though these last two strictures apply in some measure to the states of the *Laws* and the *Politics*, Plato in his *Republic* never contemplates either a slave economy or restriction of citizenship.

Whatever may be the relative merits of these various criticisms (and some, of course, are more fundamental than others), they may be properly regarded as more or less on the periphery of the deepest issues of political theory. Even the more serious, that is, those dealing with slavery and the limitation of citizenship, are not strictly essential, since the former merely reflects the particular economic structure prevailing in that period of Greek history, while the latter derives from the social and conventional thought of the time. Or to put it another way, what Plato and Aristotle say concerning the relation of the individual and the state *is* strictly essential and is relevant to all the basic contexts of political theory, irrespective of particular economic or social frames of reference. Hence it is far more important for us to consider the doctrine, in some sense shared by both philosophers, of the priority of the state over the individual.

One cannot dismiss lightly the accusation that Plato and Aristotle foster the totalitarian idea of "statism" by holding this view. In answering the charge we must not forget that proponents of statism have singled out this doctrine as a sanction for their theories, but in so doing have wrenched it violently from its context in Plato and Aristotle. As a matter of fact, Aristotle asserts the priority of the state on the ground that the whole is necessarily prior to the part and that the single individual does not possess self-sufficiency. In addition he maintains that such a self-sufficient individual needing nothing from society must be either a beast or a god. The priority of the state, thus understood, is obviously far from being an adequate sanction for statism. Though in the *Laws* Plato once says in substance that an individual, his estate and his family belong to the state, still the totalitarian overtones of this remark are more than offset by his steady insistence that the individual's goodness and well-being are the intimate concern of the state; and, of course, he defines goodness and well-being in terms of a metaphysical and religious idealism. Furthermore, he always maintains that the state must prevent any individual or group from pursuing personal interest or advantage to the detriment of the general happiness of the whole.

Plato can be defended against the accusation that his thought is the remote ancestor of statism by citing the frequently neglected passage in the *Republic* known as the "Parable of the Metals." In substance the myth tells how all men are born from the earth and hence are *brothers*. God has fashioned those who are to rule by mingling gold in their generation; in the auxiliaries he mingles silver and in the farmers and artisans iron and brass. In general, the parable continues, the children of the various types will be like their parents, but sometimes this will not happen. If a silver son is born to golden parents, the son must be assigned to the class of silver men and if a golden son is an offspring of brass and iron parents, he shall be raised up and honored among those of the golden class. The myth clearly signifies that Plato's state is not one of absolutely rigid castes, as many critics would have it, but rather one in which the principle of equality of opportunity is given genuine recognition. In his opinion the state must at all times make sure that those best qualified to rule actually do rule and that no one be prevented by accident of birth or economic status from fulfilling his high obligation, if he has the requisite abilities. Hence this myth, like the Myth of Er, gives evidence of Plato's unqualified interest in the individual. There is therefore every ground to assert that Plato would have found intolerable any statism oppressive to the individual. One needs no other proof for this conclusion than Plato's unrelenting account of the horror and misery of tyranny in the eighth and ninth books of the *Republic*.

Perhaps Aristotle thought that Plato had not given sufficient scope to the individual, since in the second book of the *Politics* he criticizes the state of the *Republic* as too unified through its extensive communism. This is not the place to argue that he partially misconceives Plato's doctrine, but it is important to note Aristotle's interest in the individual and individual freedom. His own conception of unity in the state is clearly revealed when he says, "The state ... is a plurality [*plethos*], which should be united and made into a community by education" (1263b26). And further, as in the case of Plato, Aristotle's view of the individual's value emerges in his detestation of real tyranny, as is so evident when he writes, "This tyranny is just that arbitrary power of an individual which is responsible to no one, and governs all alike, whether equals or betters, with a view to its own advantage, not to that of its subjects, and therefore against their will. No freeman, if he can escape from it, will endure such a government" (1295a19).

The Platonic and Aristotelian tradition, with its insistence that politics and ethics are fundamentally fused and that the problems of each inevitably involve the problems of the other, maintained itself in substance until the development of Christianity and the rise of Christian institutions. C. E. M. Joad has convincingly argued that, as a result largely of the pressure of Christianity, the two disciplines of ethics and politics split and each carried on its own separate existence more or less independently.[6] The Church naturally assumed control of morality and the state confined itself to man's political life. Certainly in a later day the separate pursuit of politics received considerable impetus from such writings as Machiavelli's *Prince*. Joad further contends that the tradition of the virtual autonomy of political theory lasted until the twentieth cenury, when Nazism and Communism in their political philosophies again assumed the fusion of ethics and politics. In his opinion this contemporary fusion is perverted in the extreme, though, of course, he would insist that it need not be perverted.

If Joad's thesis is sound and if a present-day philosopher believes, like Plato and Aristotle, that ethics and politics are ultimately one, then such a philosopher is faced with a most difficult problem, particularly if he is a proponent of democracy. Rigorous systematic analysis reveals to him, on the one hand, that ethics and politics are not distinct and, on the other, he sees their fusion breeding political enormities. Extreme statisms cannot be otherwise appraised, if they are viewed in the perspective of the dominant strains and highest wisdom of the Western European tradition. To the de-

[6] *Guide to the Philosophy of Morals and Politics* (New York, 1938).

fender of democracy it alone of all political systems seems to render possible the recognition of the basic unity of ethics and politics and *at the same time* it alone seems to provide means whereby a perverted fusion may be avoided.

Such a philosopher or contemporary political theorist, committed to the democratic view, can do no better than turn to the works of Plato and Aristotle. In them he can find most of the recurrent problems of politics minutely analyzed and always in terms of their ethical context or of the "good life." He need not be disturbed because Plato and Aristotle criticize what they call "democracy." Any careful study of their works and of their historical milieu reveals that the "democracy" to which they are unfriendly is the political system found in Athens during the late fifth and fourth centuries. Then it had indeed become corrupted and then "democratic" freedom really meant anarchy. Such was not the case when the Athenian democracy was at its best in the years immediately following the Persian Wars. However this may be, the twentieth century theorist can and must use the political writings of Plato and Aristotle as models for effective thinking on the true nature and structure of democracy. Surely democracy more than any other form of government is committed to the fundamental doctrine of the dignity of man. On this ground it grants him freedom, but it is a controlled freedom, for no man can exercise it in such a way as to impair the freedom of his fellows. The same point can be expressed in another way. Democracy in a very real sense is a mean between the opposing extremes of tyranny and anarchy; and one can argue effectively that when both Plato and Aristotle express their preference for the "mean" state they are casting their decision for democracy in its very essence. Both are clearly committed to the principle of individual human dignity, to the principle of controlled freedom and to the hatred of tyranny.

The largest and most difficult aspect of the problem yet remains. One can readily see that the fusion of ethics and politics makes the state a specific force for the moral betterment of man. It *must* assume the exercise of a high degree of moral superintendence over its citizens. But human experience seems to cry out the literal impossibility of improving men morally by the application of external force. Hence some philosophers, who have felt strongly that the state somehow has a moral duty toward its citizens, have approached the problem negatively. They have urged, for example, that the state should provide "hindrances to the hindrances" which stand in the way of the moral amelioration of the citizen. But one might reasonably urge that the state's moral function, thus negatively defined, is not sufficient and that some more constructive means must be discovered. If then the exertion of external force upon an individual is ultimately fruitless for providing genuine moral development, then the only other distinct and legitimate means for providing such a force must come from within the individual himself. In other words, only if an individual imposes upon himself a moral control, does there seem to be any hope that he will achieve a significant degree of moral maturity. If this contention be accepted as a premise, then it is possible to define the state's moral function as the positive and active provision of all available means for the development of individual moral responsibility among its citizens.

Plato and Aristotle have both been criticized frequently, because they hold in varying degrees of explicitness that the state, in making men good, can legitimately employ external force; and in many respects such criticism is sound. Nevertheless their unwavering insistence that men are and must be morally responsible and that education is the only means to produce this end shows how fundamentally they have pointed the way toward the only solution to the problem available in a democracy. Democracy assumes the dignity and the worth of the individual and, if our argument be at all compelling, an individual must be morally responsible if he is to possess any dignity worth the name. Hence, if education can make for the development of moral responsibility, the education of its citizens becomes the primary obligation of a democratic state.

Statism or, if one wishes to become more specific, Nazism and Communism have long been aware of the central importance of education. But their education is an education of dogma, dogma in the worst sense, which is imposed by force and which does not have to submit to the criteria of truth which men have painfully struggled through the ages to construct. In distinction to the education of dogma, in democracy there must be the education of free inquiry and a democratic state must positively institute and foster such an education. All propositions and interpretations, whether they be scientific, aesthetic, religious, philosophical or historical, must be *freely* scrutinized: first, in order to discover error and, second, in order to carry on the dynamic process of improving their validity—a process which for finite man must be never-ending. Only out of such an education of free inquiry can emerge those truths and norms of value which a man must comprehend to the limit of his ability if he is to be morally controlled or, what is in the end the same, if he is to be genuinely free. Only such an education is appropriate to the doctrine of the dignity of the individual which democracy holds and only such an education will inevitably entitle a man to assume the duties and privileges of democratic citizenship.

Long ago Plato and Aristotle held this view in its essence. Surely their own contributions to the thought of our Western European culture derived from investigations carried on unfalteringly in the spirit of free inquiry. These investigations led Plato to a metaphysical and religious idealism; and it is in these transcendental terms that he moulded his political theory. Hence education for him means not the communication of man-made dogma, whose scale is confined to narrow spatial and temporal limits, but rather an invitation to explore freely the infinite mysteries of all reality and to derive therefrom principles by which to live. Though Aristotle constructed a different metaphysical frame, yet his quest too is always for the first principles which will accord with the nature of reality as he sees it. Thus his educational and political theories become functions of these principles. Consequently, if the positions of Plato and Aristotle support the basic beliefs of democracy, they become indispensable allies to those thinkers who wish to clarify and substantiate the high claims of democracy. Therefore, in every age the political writings of Plato and Aristotle, because of their metaphysical scope, their analytical depth and their extensive empirical foundation, will be unfailing guides for men as they investigate the theory and practice of government.

XIV. EPILOGUE

BY ALLAN CHESTER JOHNSON

THE Greeks of the classical period regarded the city-state (*polis*) as the highest form of political organization. According to Aristotle its evolution was a natural phenomenon. Man, endowed by nature with political instincts, unites in family groups; the families give rise to villages; "and when several villages are united in a single community, perfect and large enough to be nearly or quite self-sufficing, the state comes into existence, originating in the bare needs of life and continuing in existence for the sake of the good life."

While Aristotle held that justice was the bond which united citizens in the state, he did not attempt to define the "bare needs of life" which led to union. In primitive society these needs may be many. Fustel de Coulanges believes that religious motives, particularly ancestor worship, united people in a common cult. Heichelheim holds that the economic concept of interest on capital is the common denominator in the development of ancient cities. The need for security undoubtedly led people of kindred stock to unite voluntarily in a common policy of defence. Personal ambition probably inspired powerful leaders to extend their domination over their neighbors. Sometimes individual settlements or fortified posts expanded naturally because of their convenient location as anchorages, markets or trading centers and the necessity for law or some sanction for law led to the organization of the state in order to preserve the integrity of their commercial relations. The first colonial settlements probably evolved in some such way, but the later colonies may have sprung into existence fully armed with laws and constitutions already formulated by their founder or mother-city. When several villages united in a single community, the union might be physical in that the individual settlements were abandoned for a fortified center, as was the case when Arcadian Megalopolis was founded in the fourth century. Sometimes the villages continued their corporate existence, but shared a common citizenship and common cult in some center, such as Athens. In the Hellenistic period the synoecism of villages and even of cities was effected by royal authority, but these foundations were no longer independent states.

Not only the reasons for the rise of individual cities, but also the date of their first appearance are hidden in the mists of antiquity. The concept of the city-state was unknown to the Homeric Achaeans and is only faintly adumbrated in the *Odyssey* and by Hesiod. According to Athenian tradition the synoecism of Attica was effected by Theseus about the beginning of the first millennium, but in classical times we hear of a Tricomia, a Tetracomia and a Tetrapolis, while the Mesogaea and Epacria appear to have been religious amphictyonies. It also seems clear that Eleusis did not become a part of Athens until about the end of the eighth century. Whatever Theseus may have contributed to the synoecism of Attic villages, it is evident that the process was not the result of a single act but came as a gradual development. At what point in this evolution Athens may be called a city-state is uncertain. Ehrenberg places the rise of the polis about the beginning of the eighth century. Probably the movement began on the coast of Asia Minor and spread thence to the Greek mainland. The eastern coast was dotted with city-states, but inland and remote districts, especially in the north and west, retained their village or tribal organizations for many centuries. It is even questioned whether Sparta should be regarded as a true polis.

Little is known of the Dark Age which followed the Dorian invasions. The destruction of the Achaean culture was so thorough that the invaders learned little from their predecessors and their own advancement in the arts of civilization was extremely slow. If the polis came into being in the eighth century, the development of some political consciousness may be postulated. Private ownership of land seemingly was widespread and already there was a sharp division between rich and poor. For the majority farming was on the subsistence level and in many districts the population had reached the maximum which could be supported from the land. About this time an era of widespread colonization set in, during which Greek settlements were founded over all the shores of the Euxine and Mediterranean except where blocked by Phoenicians and Etruscans. These colonies were in no sense dependencies of the mother country and the bond between them, save for blood relationship and religious ties, was often of the slightest. The colonial movement not only reduced the overcrowded condition of the homeland, but also served to open up trade and commerce between various parts of the Greek world as well as between Greek and barbarian. About the beginning of the sixth century active colonization came to an end, probably because there was a lessening of pressure from increasing population.

On the Greek mainland neither Sparta nor Athens had shared in this wave of colonial expansion. Sparta had, to be sure, sent a colony consisting of political malcontents and inferiors to Tarentum, but her need for land was satisfied by the conquest of Messenia. This victory led to unexpected results. In order to maintain her security at home and to preserve her prestige abroad, Sparta was forced to adopt a rigid military and social system whereby she deliberately isolated herself from all economic and intellectual intercourse with the world about her. Security was won at the cost of the amenities of life and her polity tended to become more or less static. With a small but highly disciplined citizen army she was still able to exert considerable political influence abroad. However, her peculiar internal situation did not permit aggressive warfare far from home. After her failure to conquer Tegea about the middle of the sixth century, her foreign policy was directed towards security for herself and for her Dorian neighbors. With these Sparta concluded treaties of alliance, thus constituting the so-called Peloponnesian League in which she was the dominant member. There seems to be no clear evidence that this League ever developed the formal organization or constitution characteristic of those in later times, though there is no question that its members met on occasion to discuss matters of common interest.

Athens followed a different policy and with far different results. Little is known of her history during the first four centuries of the first millennium, but she had evidently remained in a backwater, while other states had forged ahead. She had not joined in the colonial movement, possibly because her territory was large and the pressure of over-population may have been less. In the sixth century the reforms of Solon and the legislation of Peisistratus checked the growth of great estates and converted Attica into a land of small farmers. These were encouraged to shift from subsistence farming to

EPILOGUE

specialization in cash crops, especially wine and oil, while industry was fostered in the city. These changes came at a time when Persia was beginning to threaten the security of the Asiatic Greeks and Athens fell heir to much of their trade, especially in the Euxine, whence cheap corn could be imported to supply the needs of her citizens. The invention of coined money had increased enormously the possibilities of local and international trade and in the sixth century these began to be realized.

At the same time intellectual horizons were widening. The shackles of old taboos and old beliefs were broken and there arose in the Athenian people an active curiosity concerning the world in which they lived. Their emergence from economic and intellectual isolation to play an important part in this strange new world was a challenge which they quickly accepted. The farmer, the artisan and the trader looked far beyond the slopes of Parnes and Hymettus to markets in distant lands and for the first time international relations became a matter of vital interest. With the development of democratic institutions and the extension of political responsibility in ever-widening circles, the Athenians responded to their new duties with surprising facility.

To these stimuli the Persian War brought the challenge of a great mission—a challenge superbly met, though at heavy cost. Attica was ravaged and Athens destroyed, but in the ruins were buried outworn practices and archaic traditions. Thermopylae and Plataea simply served to confirm Sparta in her former militaristic policy and she retired from further participation in the war, content with her hegemony in the Peloponnese. Marathon and Salamis opened new horizons to the Athenians and the value of sea power was deeply impressed upon their consciousness. By liberating the Greeks of Asia from Persian rule the Athenians became the acknowledged champions of Hellenism against barbarism. To the generation following Salamis the consciousness of these services to the Hellenic world was the inspiration leading to the splendid intellectual and artistic accomplishments which justified their proud claim to be the school of Hellas.

The Persian War had demonstrated that the individual city-state could not by itself withstand attack from a great power and some form of union was necessary. Athens took the lead in constituting the so-called Delian League, a union apparently based on treaties of alliance and held together by the threat of a common danger. When this danger ceased to exist, there was the likelihood that particularism would reassert itself, especially since the alliance involved the payment of an annual tax for the support of the armed forces. But when the Persian menace actually disappeared, the Delian League was not allowed to dissolve. Athens, always the dominant member and the chief naval power, transformed it into an empire with her former allies reduced to political and economic subservience, though still retaining their local institutions. Tribute to the common fund was now openly converted to the sole use of the sovereign power. Thus Athens took the step in political evolution from a polis to an imperial state. Uniform coinage and uniform laws tended to promote trade and stability in commercial transactions. But the exploitation of subjects for the benefit of the sovereign state blunted the dynamic force of Athenian idealism and the growing lust for power ultimately led to acts of economic injustice and inhuman cruelty. The growth of Athenian imperialism began to excite fear and jealousy and, when the city-states under the leadership of Sparta took up the challenge of the new order, issue was joined in the Peloponnesian War. Particularism won and the Athenian Empire was resolved into its component parts.

In the fourth century the Persians reasserted their dominion over the Greeks of Asia Minor; in the north the kingdom of Macedonia was taking shape as a great power with whose ambitions Greece had ultimately to reckon; in the west the imperialistic states of Rome and Carthage began to close in on Magna Graecia. Against these forces the individual city-state was powerless. After the fall of the Athenian Empire and the miserable failure of Sparta to provide competent leadership, parochialism once more determined the policies of the older and leading cities of Greece. Isocrates preached Panhellenism, but his academic counsel carried little weight. The Utopias of Plato and Aristotle glorified the particularism of the old order, which they sought to preserve as a static society, with no apparent realization of the forces gathering for its destruction. To be sure, they advocated the greatest good to the greatest number, but unfortunately their greatest number was limited to citizens of untainted blood[1] and to an aristocracy of the few supported by serfs or slaves.

The vision of a true cosmopolis came from the Stoics Zeno and Iambulus of a later age. Meanwhile the city-state remained a political fetich both in theory and in practice, perhaps, as Toynbee suggests, the surest symptom of its decline. While it is true that various unions were attempted, they were local and short-lived. The Congress of Greek cities at Corinth under the leadership of Philip carried out the Panhellenic ideal of Isocrates, but it lacked spontaneity and was inevitably dominated by the personality of the Macedonian king.

The new order created in the eastern Mediterranean by the conquests of Alexander the Great dealt a severe blow to the city as an independent polity. Although he restored their democratic forms to the old Greek cities within his empire and organized his new foundations on similar lines, their autonomy and freedom were held on sufferance and rarely, if ever, by treaty. Though his allies in the Corinthian League were *de jure* sovereign powers, *de facto* they were so far overshadowed by the commander in chief of their forces that they differed in no way from their Ionian neighbors. Whatever might have been the status of the cities in his future empire, it is clear that their former independence of action could not be tolerated and it is probable that they would have continued merely as administrative units with more or less limited powers of self-government. In abandoning definitely the theory of racial superiority Alexander took a great step forward in the concept of a world-state. But his kingdom with its divine ruler was a frank adoption of oriental political theory and interposed a definite check to further political evolution of the Greek polis. Henceforth the cities had no voice in the determination of imperial policies and their destiny was merged in that of the sovereign state.

The early death of Alexander brought about a collapse of his empire. Since none of the Successors could establish an hegemony over the others, they reverted to a sort of particularistic nationalism. Many of the Greek cities regained a precarious freedom in which

---

[1] Plato makes this plain in his *Laws*, but does not discuss the problem in the *Republic*, probably taking it for granted with his Athenian audience.

they clung to past political tradition with stubborn tenacity. But in the new world order they could no longer be self-sufficient. Economic forces had been unleashed with which social and political reforms had failed to keep in step. The gap between rich and poor had steadily widened and with the growth of great estates manned by slave labor the landless class had increased. Class strife had unhappily never been wholly absent in the history of the Greek cities, but what had once been sporadic now became chronic and hastened their decline. At the same time other cities, especially in Achaea and Aetolia, united in leagues, which, though constituted on a sounder and more enduring basis, were still limited to comparatively small areas and still unable to combine with one another for the common good. City, league and kingdom engaged in fratricidal strife, which exhausted their resources and left them an easy prey to the advancing might of Rome. The Caesars were the political heirs of Alexander and under the guiding genius of Rome were laid the foundations of a world empire destined to destroy the last vestiges of the political sovereignty of the Greek city-state.

In the history of political institutions the city-states usually emerged from a primitive social order and preserved their political integrity so long as they maintained a reasonable balance of power with their fellows and were not menaced by any powerful combination of forces outside their immediate environment. Their territorial limitations made possible the development of intense political and intellectual activity, but the same conditions tended to develop parochialism and to keep the city as a political organism in a state of arrested development. In spite of common bonds of race, religion and language the Greeks were unable to devise a satisfactory formula for the evolution of a united nation. Alliances and hegemonies were ephemeral. Athenian imperialism was a parasitic growth which destroyed itself. Leagues created by compulsion usually perished with the founder. Voluntary association of free states in a political union, with common citizenship and common rights in framing and directing sovereign policies, was unquestionably the natural stage in political evolution from the sovereignty of individual cities. Leagues of this kind came too late in Greek history to be effective and even these were hampered by particularism and rivalries which prevented any genuine Panhellenic movement. Whether such a movement could have laid the foundations of an enduring state is a moot question. From Greek political experience this much is clear: no state can endure if it is based on principles of self-sufficiency, racial arrogance, glorified militarism and ruthless exploitation whether of serf or of slave or of subject people.

Bibliography

BIBLIOGRAPHY

The three maps, which are from Vols. V and VII of the *Cambridge Ancient History*, are reproduced in this volume by the courteous permission of the Cambridge University Press secured through the Macmillan Company.

CHAPTER I

Buck, C. D., *Introduction to the Study of the Greek Dialects* (2nd ed.; Boston, 1928), pp. 1-14
Evans, A. J., *The Palace of Minos* (6 vols.: London, 1921-35)
Glotz, G., *The Aegean Civilization* (London, 1925)
Jardé, A., *The Formation of the Greek People* (London, 1926)
Myres, J. L., *The Political Ideas of the Greeks* (New York, 1927)
Nilsson, M. P., *Homer and Mycenae* (London, 1933)
Prentice, W. K., *The Ancient Greeks* (Princeton, 1940), pp. 3-71
Teggart, F. J., *The Processes of History* (New Haven, 1918)
Whibley, L., *A Companion to Greek Studies* (4th ed.; Cambridge, 1931)

CHAPTER II

Aristotle, *Politica*
———, *Res Publica Atheniensium*
Herodotus, *Historiae*
Homer, *Ilias*
———, *Odyssea*
Pausanias, *Graeciae Descriptio*
Plutarch, *Vitae Parallelae*: Solon
Thucydides, *Historiae*

Adcock, F. E., "The Growth of the Greek City-State" in *The Cambridge Ancient History*, vol. III (Cambridge, 1925), pp. 687-701
Barker, E., *Greek Political Theory: Plato and His Predecessors* (2nd ed.; London, 1925)
Beloch, K. J., *Griechische Geschichte*, vol. I, pt. 2 (2nd ed.; Strassburg, 1913)
Bonner, R. J., *Aspects of Athenian Democracy* (Berkeley, 1933)
Francotte, H., *La polis grecque* (Paderborn, 1907)
Freeman, K., *The Work and Life of Solon* (Milford, 1926)
Gardner, E. A. and Cary, M., "Early Athens" in *The Cambridge Ancient History*, vol. III (Cambridge, 1925), pp. 571-97

226   THE GREEK POLITICAL EXPERIENCE

Gilbert, G., *The Constitutional Antiquities of Sparta and Athens* (New York, 1895), pp. 95-118
Glotz, G., *The Greek City and Its Institutions* (New York, 1930)
Greenidge, A. H. J., *A Handbook of Greek Constitutional History* (New York, 1896)
Halliday, W. R., *The Growth of the City State* (Liverpool, 1923)
Jacoby, F., *Das Marmor Parium* (Berlin, 1904)
Kenyon, F. G., *Aristotle on the Constitution of Athens* (2nd ed.; London, 1891), Introduction and Notes
Linforth, I. M., *Solon the Athenian* (Berkeley, 1919)
Myres, J. L., *The Political Ideals of the Greeks* (New York, 1927)
Nilsson, M. P., *Homer and Mycenae* (London, 1933), pp. 212-247
Rupprecht, E., *Die Schrift vom Staate der Athener* (Leipzig, 1939)
Sandys, J. E., *Aristotle's Constitution of Athens* (2nd ed.; London, 1912), Introduction and Notes
Seltman, C. T., *Athens: Its History and Coinage before the Persian Invasion* (Cambridge, 1924)
Seymour, T. D., *Life in the Homeric Age* (New York, 1907), pp. 78-116
Vlachos, N. P., *Hellas and Hellenism* (Boston, 1936), pp. 68-127
Wilamowitz-Möllendorff, U. von, *Aristoteles und Athen* (Berlin, 1893)
Zimmern, A. E., "Political Thought" in *The Legacy of Greece* (Oxford, 1922), pp. 321-52
―――, *The Greek Commonwealth* (5th ed.; Oxford, 1931)

CHAPTER III

Barker, E., *The Political Thought of Plato and Aristotle* (New York, 1906)
Bonner, R. J., *Aspects of Athenian Democracy* (Berkeley, 1933)
Calhoun, G. M., *The Business Life of Ancient Athens* (Chicago, 1926)
Cohen, R., *Athènes, une démocratie, de sa naissance à sa mort* (Paris, 1936)
Glotz, G., *The Greek City and Its Institutions* (New York, 1930)
Gomme, A. W., *The Population of Athens in the Fifth and Fourth Centuries B.C.* (Oxford, 1933)
Greenidge, A. H. J., *A Handbook of Greek Constitutional History* (New York, 1896)
Zimmern, A. E., *The Greek Commonwealth* (5th ed.; Oxford, 1931)

CHAPTER IV

Thucydides, *Historiae*

―――

The Cambridge Ancient History: vol. V, *Athens, 478-401 B.C.* (Cambridge, 1927)
Highby, L. I., *The Erythrae Decree* (Leipzig, 1936)

BIBLIOGRAPHY 227

Larsen, J. A. O., "The Constitution and Original Purpose of the Delian League" in *Harvard Studies in Classical Philology*, vol. LI (1940), pp. 175-213
Meritt, B. D., "Athens and Carthage" in *Harvard Studies in Classical Philology*, vol. XLIX (1940), pp. 247-53
Meritt, B. D. and West, A. B., *The Athenian Assessment of 425 B.C.* (Ann Arbor, 1934)
Meritt, B. D., Wade-Gery, H. T. and McGregor, M. F., *The Athenian Tribute Lists*, vol. I (Cambridge, 1939)
Nesselhauf, H., *Untersuchungen zur Geschichte der delisch-attischen Symmachie* (Leipzig, 1933)
Oliver, J. H., "The Athenian Decree concerning Miletus in 450/49 B.C." in *Transactions and Proceedings of the American Philological Association*, vol. LXVI (1935), pp. 177-98
Segré, M., "La legge ateniese sull' unificazione della moneta" in *Clara Rhodos*, vol. IX (1938), pp. 151-78
Tod, M. N., *A Selection of Greek Historical Inscriptions to the End of the Fifth Century B.C.* (Oxford, 1933)
Wade-Gery, H. T., "The Peace of Kallias" in *Harvard Studies in Classical Philology*, supp. vol. I (1940), pp. 121-54

CHAPTER V

Aristotle, *Politica*, II, 9
Plutarch, *Vitae Parallelae*: Agesilaus, Agis, Aratus, Cleomenes, Philopoemen, Lycurgus, Lysander
———, *Apophthegmata Laconica*
———, *Instituta Laconica*
Xenophon, *Res Publica Lacedaemoniorum*

Busolt, G., *Die Lakedaimonier und ihre Bundesgenossen* (Leipzig, 1878)
Cary, M., "The Ascendancy of Sparta" in *The Cambridge Ancient History*, vol. VI (Cambridge, 1927), pp. 25-54
Dickins, G., "The Growth of Spartan Policy" in *Journal of Hellenic Studies*, vol. XXXII (1912), pp. 1-26
Ehrenberg, V., "Spartiaten und Lakedaimonier" in *Hermes*, vol. LIX (1924), pp. 23-72
Ferguson, W. S., *Greek Imperialism* (Boston, 1913), pp. 79-115
———, "Sparta and the Peloponnese" in *The Cambridge Ancient History*, vol. V (Cambridge, 1927), pp. 254-81
Kahrstedt, U., *Griechisches Staatsrecht*: vol. I, *Sparta und seine Symmachie* (Göttingen, 1922)

Meier, T., *Das Wesen der spartanischen Staatsordnung* (Leipzig, 1939)
Neumann, K. J., "Die Entstehung des spartiatischen Staates in der lykurgischen Verfassung" in *Historische Zeitschrift*, vol. XCVI (1906), pp. 1-80
Nilsson, M. P., "Die Grundlagen des spartanischen Lebens" in *Klio*, vol. XII (1912), pp. 308-40
Ollier, F., *Le mirage spartiate* (Paris, 1933)
Pöhlmann, R. von, *Geschichte der sozialen Frage und des Sozialismus in der antiken Welt*, vol. I (3rd ed.; München, 1925), pp. 46-114, 347-92
Tarn, W. W., "The Greek Leagues and Macedonia" in *The Cambridge Ancient History*, vol. VII (Cambridge, 1928), pp. 732-68
Toynbee, A. J., *A Study of History*, vol. III (London, 1934), pp. 50-79
Wade-Gery, H. T., "The Growth of the Dorian States" in *The Cambridge Ancient History*, vol. III (Cambridge, 1925), pp. 527-69

CHAPTER VI

Barker, E., *The Political Thought of Plato and Aristotle* (New York, 1906)
———, *Greek Political Theory: Plato and His Predecessors* (2nd ed.; London, 1925)
Busolt, G., *Griechische Staatskunde* (2 vols.: München, 1920-26)
Cornelius, F., *Die Tyrannis in Athen* (München, 1929)
Highbarger, E. L., *The History and Civilization of Ancient Megara* (Baltimore, 1927)
Jaeger, W., *Paideia* (Oxford, 1939)
Nilsson, M. P., *The Age of the Early Greek Tyrants* (Belfast, 1936)
Nordin, R., "Aisymnetie und Tyrannis" in *Klio*, vol. V (1905), pp. 392-409
Plass, H. G., *Die Tyrannis in ihren beiden Perioden bei den alten Griechen* (2 pts.: Leipzig, 1859)
Robinson, C. A., Jr., "Greek Tyranny" in *American Historical Review*, vol. XLII (1936), pp. 68-71
Skalet, C. H., *Ancient Sicyon with a Prosopographia Sicyonia* (Baltimore, 1928)
Ure, P. N., *The Origin of Tyranny* (Cambridge, 1922)
Westlake, H. D., *Thessaly in the Fourth Century B.C.* (London, 1935)
Zeller, E., "Über den Begriff der Tyrannis bei den Griechen" in *Sitzungsberichte der königlich preussischen Akademie der Wissenschaften zu Berlin, Jahrgang 1887* (Berlin, 1887), pp. 1137-46

CHAPTER VII

Aymard, A., *Les assemblées de la confédération achaienne* (Bordeaux, 1938)
———, *Les premiers rapports de Rome et de la confédération achaienne* (Bordeaux, 1938)
Ferguson, W. S., *Greek Imperialism* (Boston, 1913)
Ferrabino, A., *Il problema dell' unità nazionale nella Grecia antica*: vol. I, *Arato di Sicione e l'idea nazionale* (Firenze, 1921)

BIBLIOGRAPHY

Flacelière, R., *Les Aitoliens à Delphes* (Paris, 1937)
Frank, T., *Roman Imperialism* (2nd ed.; New York, 1925)
Freeman, E. A., *History of Federal Government in Greece and Italy* (2nd ed.; New York, 1893)
Glotz, G., *The Greek City and Its Institutions* (New York, 1930)
Glover, T. R., *Democracy in the Ancient World* (Cambridge, 1927)
Marshall, F. H., *The Second Athenian Confederacy* (Cambridge, 1905)
Tarn, W. W., *Hellenistic Civilisation* (2nd ed.; London, 1930)
Tod, M. N., *International Arbitration amongst the Greeks* (Oxford, 1913)
West, A. B., *The History of the Chalcidic League* (Madison, 1919)
Wilhelm, A., *Attische Urkunden*, vol. I (Wien, 1911)

CHAPTER VIII

Arrian, *Anabasis Alexandri*
————, *Indica*, VIII
Plutarch, *Vitae Parallelae*: Alexander
Q. Curtius Rufus, *Historiae Alexandri Magni Macedonis*

Berve, H., *Das Alexanderreich auf prosopographischer Grundlage* (München, 1926)
————, "Die Verschmelzungspolitik Alexanders des Grossen" in *Klio*, vol. XXXII (1938), pp. 135-68
Birt, T., *Alexander der Grosse und das Weltgriechentum* (Leipzig, 1924)
Ehrenberg, V., *Alexander and the Greeks* (Oxford, 1938)
Endres, H., "Krateros, Perdikkas und die letzten Pläne Alexanders" in *Rheinisches Museum für Philologie*, vol. LXXII (1917-18), pp. 437-45
Ferguson, W. S., *Greek Imperialism* (Boston, 1913), pp. 116-148
Glotz, G., Roussel, P. and Cohen, R., *Alexandre et le démembrement de son empire* (Paris, 1938)
Jouguet, P., *L'impérialisme macédonien et l'hellénisation de l'orient* (Paris, 1926)
Kolbe, W., *Die Weltreichsidee Alexanders des Grossen* (Freiburg i. B., 1936)
Kornemann, E., "Die letzten Ziele der Politik Alexanders des Grossen" in *Klio*, vol. XVI (1920), pp. 209-38
Meyer, E., "Alexander der Grosse und die absolute Monarchie" in his *Kleine Schriften*, vol. I (2nd ed.; Halle, 1924), pp. 265-314
Tarn, W. W., "Alexander's ὑπομνήματα and the 'World-Kingdom'" in *Journal of Hellenic Studies*, vol. XLI (1927), pp. 1-17
————, "Alexander: The Conquest of Persia"; "Alexander: The Conquest of the Far East"; "Greece: 335 to 321 B.C."; "The Heritage of Alexander" in *The Cambridge Ancient History*, vol. VI (Cambridge, 1927), pp. 352-504

———, "Alexander's Plans" in *Journal of Hellenic Studies*, vol. LIX (1939), pp. 124-35
Wilcken, U., *Alexander der Grosse* (Leipzig, 1931)
———, "Die letzten Pläne Alexanders des Grossen" in *Sitzungsberichte der preussischen Akademie der Wissenschaften (Philosophisch-historische Klasse), Jahrgang 1937* (Berlin, 1937), pp. 192-207

CHAPTER IX

Aymard, A., *Les assemblées de la confédération achaienne* (Bordeaux, 1938)
Beloch, K. J., *Griechische Geschichte*, vol. IV, pts. 1 and 2 (2nd ed.; Berlin, 1925-27)
The Cambridge Ancient History: vol. VI, *Macedon, 401-301 B.C.*; vol. VII, *The Hellenistic Monarchies and the Rise of Rome*; vol. VIII, *Rome and the Mediterranean, 218-133 B.C.* (Cambridge, 1927-30)
Ferguson, W. S., *Hellenistic Athens* (London, 1911)
Flacelière, R., *Les Aitoliens à Delphes* (Paris, 1937)
Freeman, E. A., *History of Federal Government in Greece and Italy* (2nd ed.; New York, 1893)
Glotz, G., Roussel, P. and Cohen, R., *Alexandre et le démembrement de son empire* (Paris, 1938)
Holleaux, M., *Rome, la Grèce et les monarchies hellénistiques au troisième siècle avant J-C.* (Paris, 1921)
Jouguet, P., *Macedonian Imperialism and the Hellenization of the East* (New York, 1928)
Kaerst, J., *Geschichte des Hellenismus*, vol. II (2nd ed.; Leipzig, 1926)
König, W., *Der Bund der Nesioten* (Halle, 1910)
Newell, E. T., *The Coinages of Demetrius Poliorcetes* (London, 1927)
Niese, B., *Geschichte der griechischen und makedonischen Staaten*, vols. I-III (Gotha, 1893-1903)
Tarn, W. W., *Antigonos Gonatas* (Oxford, 1913)
———, *Hellenistic Civilisation* (2nd ed.; London, 1930)
Zancan, P., *Il monarcato ellenistico nei suoi elementi federativi* (Padova, 1934)

CHAPTER X

Bevan, E., *A History of Egypt under the Ptolemaic Dynasty* (London, 1927)
Heichelheim, F. M., *Wirtschaftsgeschichte des Altertums* (2 vols.: Leiden, 1938)
Hunt, A. S. and Edgar, C. C., *Select Papyri*: vol. I, *Private Affairs*; vol. II, *Official Documents* (London, 1932-34)
Préaux, C., *L'économie royale des Lagides* (Bruxelles, 1939)
Rostovtzeff, M., "The Foundations of Social and Economic Life in Egypt in Hellenistic Times" in *Journal of Egyptian Archaeology*, vol. VI (1920), pp. 161-78

BIBLIOGRAPHY

———, "Ptolemaic Egypt" in *The Cambridge Ancient History*, vol. VIII (Cambridge, 1928), pp. 109-54
———, "The Hellenistic World and Its Economic Development" in *American Historical Review*, vol. XLI (1936), pp. 231-52
Tarn, W. W., *Hellenistic Civilisation* (2nd ed.; London, 1930)
Westermann, W. L., "The Greek Exploitation of Egypt" in *Political Science Quarterly*, vol. XL (1925), pp. 517-39
———, "The Ptolemies and the Welfare of Their Subjects" in *American Historical Review*, vol. XLIII (1938), pp. 270-87

CHAPTER XI

Bikerman, E., *Institutions des Séleucides* (Paris, 1938)
———, "La cité grecque dans les monarchies hellénistiques" in *Revue de philologie, de littérature et d'histoire anciennes*, vol. LXV (1939), pp. 335-49
Ferguson, W. S., *Greek Imperialism* (Boston, 1913), pp. 183-214
———, "The Leading Ideas of the New Period" in *The Cambridge Ancient History*, vol. VII (Cambridge, 1928), pp. 1-40
Goodenough, E. R., "The Political Philosophy of Hellenistic Kingship" in *Yale Classical Studies*, vol. I (1928), pp. 55-102
———, *The Politics of Philo Judaeus* (New Haven, 1938), pp. 86-120
Jones, A. H. M., *The Greek City from Alexander to Justinian* (Oxford, 1940)
Rostovtzeff, M., "Syria and the East" in *The Cambridge Ancient History*, vol. VII (Cambridge, 1928), pp. 155-96
Seyrig, H., "Les rois séleucides et la concession de l'asylie" in *Syria*, vol. XX (1939) pp. 35-39
Tarn, W. W., *The Greeks in Bactria and India* (Cambridge, 1938)
Toynbee, A. J., *A Study of History*, vol. I (London, 1934), pp. 5-6; vol. IV (London, 1939), pp. 303-20

CHAPTER XII

Abbott, F. F., and Johnson, A. C., *Municipal Administration in the Roman Empire* (Princeton, 1926), pp. 39-55, 69-83, 152-61
Bikerman (Bickermann), E., "Bellum Antiochicum" in *Hermes*, vol. LXVII (1932), pp. 47-76
———, "Rom und Lampsacus" in *Philologus*, vol. LXXXVII (1932), pp. 277-99
———, "Alexandre le Grand et les villes d'Asie" in *Revue des études grecques*, vol. XLVII (1934), pp. 346-74
———, "Notes sur Polybe: Le statut des villes d'Asie après la paix d'Apamée" in *Revue des études grecques*, vol. L (1937), pp. 217-39
———, *Institutions des Séleucides* (Paris, 1938), pp. 106-210
———, "La cité grecque dans les monarchies hellénistiques" in *Revue de philologie, de littérature et d'histoire anciennes*, vol. LXV (1939), pp. 335-49

Cardinali, G., *Il regno di Pergamo* (Roma, 1906), pp. 78-102, 205-43
Corradi, G., "L'Asia Minore e le isole dell'Egeo sotti i primi Seleucidi" in *Rivista di filologia e di istruzione classica*, vol. XLVIII (1920), pp. 161-91 and vol. L (1922), pp. 20-37
Ghione, P., "I communi del regno di Pergamo" in *Memorie della reale accademia delle scienze di Torino (Classe di scienze morali, storiche e filologiche)*, vol. LV (1905), pp. 67-149
Heuss, A., *Stadt und Herrscher des Hellenismus in ihrer staats- und völkerrechtlichen Beziehungen* (Leipzig, 1937)
———, "Antigonos Monophthalmos und die griechische Städte" in *Hermes*, vol. LXXIII (1938), pp. 133-94
Jones, A. H. M., "Civitates Liberae et Immunes in the East" in *Anatolian Studies Presented to W. H. Buckler* (Manchester, 1939), pp. 103-17
———, *The Greek City from Alexander to Justinian* (Oxford, 1940), pp. 1-26, 95-128, 157-69
Kaerst, J., *Geschichte des Hellenismus*, vol. II (2nd ed.; Leipzig, 1926), pp. 348-61
Magie, D., "Rome and the City-States of Western Asia Minor from 200 to 133 B.C." in *Anatolian Studies Presented to W. H. Buckler* (Manchester, 1939), pp. 161-85
Meritt, B. D., Wade-Gery, H. T. and McGregor, M. F., *The Athenian Tribute Lists*, vol. I (Cambridge, 1939), pp. 463-566
Sanctis, G. de, "Eumene II e le città greche d'Asia" in *Rivista di filologia e di istruzione classica*, vol. LIII (1925), pp. 68-78
Täubler, E., *Imperium Romanum*: vol. I, *Die Staatsverträge und Vertragsverhältnisse* (Leipzig, 1913)
Welles, C. B., *Royal Correspondence in the Hellenistic Period* (New Haven, 1934)
Zancan, P., *Il monarcato ellenistico nei suoi elementi federativi* (Padova, 1934)

CHAPTER XIII

Barker, E., *The Political Thought of Plato and Aristotle* (New York, 1906)
———, *Greek Political Theory: Plato and His Predecessors* (2nd ed.; London, 1925)
Bosanquet, B., *The Philosophical Theory of the State* (3rd ed.; London, 1920)
Jaeger, W., *Aristotle: Fundamentals of the History of His Development* (Oxford, 1934), esp. pp. 228-92
Nettleship, R. L., *Lectures on the Republic of Plato* (2nd ed.; London, 1925)
Newman, W. L., *The Politics of Aristotle* (4 vols.: Oxford, 1887-1902)
Piat, C., *Aristote* (Paris, 1912), esp. pp. 287-370
Pöhlmann, R. von, *Geschichte der sozialen Frage und des Sozialismus in der antiken Welt* (2 vols.: 3rd ed.; München, 1925)
Ritter, C., *The Essence of Plato's Philosophy* (New York, 1933)

BIBLIOGRAPHY 233

Robin, L., *Platon* (Paris, 1935)
Ross, W. D., *Aristotle* (2nd ed.; London, 1930), esp. pp. 187-269
Taylor, A. E., *Plato: The Man and His Work* (3rd ed.; New York, 1929)

CHAPTER XIV

The Cambridge Ancient History: vol. III, *The Assyrian Empire*; vol. IV, *The Persian Empire and the West*; vol. V, *Athens, 478-401 B.C.*; vol. VI, *Macedon, 401-301 B.C.*; vol. VII, *The Hellenistic Monarchies and the Rise of Rome* (Cambridge, 1925-28)
Ehrenberg, V., *Die griechische und der hellenistische Staat* (Leipzig, 1932)
———, *Alexander and the Greeks* (Oxford, 1938)
Fustel de Coulanges, N. D., *The Ancient City* (12th ed.; Boston, 192-)
Glotz, G., *The Greek City and Its Institutions* (New York, 1930)
Heichelheim, F. M., *Wirtschaftsgeschichte des Altertums* (2 vols.: Leiden, 1938)
Jones, A. H. M., *The Greek City from Alexander to Justinian* (Oxford, 1940)
Tarn, W. W., *Hellenistic Civilisation* (2nd ed.; London, 1930)
Toynbee, A. J., *A Study of History* (6 vols.: London, 1934-39)

Index

INDEX

BY HOLMES V. M. DENNIS, III

A

absolute power, 123, 171
absolute ruler, 163
absolutism, 164, 165
Academy, 190
Acamantis, 54
Acarnania, 106, 136
Acarnanians, 136, 138, 143
Acastus, 22, 23
accountants, 156
accounts, 156
Achaea, 77, 95, 102, 106, 220
Achaean League, *see* Leagues
Achaeans, 7, 76, 77, 138, 139, 140, 141, 142, 144, 215
Achaeus, 181
Achilles, 122
Acragas, 88
acreage tax, 152
Acrocorinth, 128, 135, 138, 139
acropoleis, 15
Acropolis, 19, 20, 25, 31, 52, 54, 55, 58, 60
Actium, 161
"Activity," 203
Ada, 115
Adeimantus, 187, 194
Adriatic, 136, 137, 140, 141
Aegina, 95
Aegium, 105
Aegospotami, 60
Aemilius Paullus, 145
Aeolic-Ionic epics, 23
Aeolis, 181
Aeschylus, 78
Aetolia, 18, 102, 106, 141, 143, 220
Aetolian League, *see* Leagues
Aetolians, 76, 94, 106, 131, 132, 136, 139, 140, 141, 142, 143, 144
Africa, 7, 153
Agamemnon, 16, 17
Agathocles, 129
Age of Pericles, 30
agenda, 40, 66
Agids, 19, 65
Agis IV, 74-76, 104

Agora, 20, 22, 27, 28
agricultural science, 157
agriculture, 9, 69, 150, 159, 160
Alcibiades, 47, 54
Alcman, 62
Alcmeon, 23
Alcmeonids, 25, 32
Alexander, 75, 101, 109-124, 125, 130, 147, 148, 162, 163, 164, 167, 169, 173, 174, 175, 177, 179, 180, 185, 190, 191, 219, 220
Alexander, son of Craterus, 134
Alexander, son of Pyrrhus, 136
Alexander the Younger, 126
Alexandria, 117, 147, 151, 152, 155, 157, 160
Alexandria Troas, 176, 181
aliens, *see* foreigners
alliances, 220
allies, 116, 126, 139
"Allotted Land," 151
allotments, 67-69, 150
American excavations, *see* excavations
Ammon, 120
amnesties, 159
Amphictyonic League, *see* Leagues
Amphictyonies (religious), 215
Amphipolis, 57
Amyclae, 64
Amyntas, 113
Anabasis Alexandri, 122 note 11
Anacharsis, 35
Anacreon, 88
anarchy, 14, 211
ancestor worship, 214
Andocides, 91
Andriscus, 145
Andros, 134
"Anger," 204
"Animate Law," 166
Antalcidas, 110, 173, 174
Anthela, 94
antidosis, 44
Antigone, 57
Antigonids, 125-146
Antigonus I Monophthalmus, 125, 126, 127, 128, 145, 175, 176, 177, 178, 179, 185

INDEX

Antigonus II Gonatas, 129, 130, 131, 132, 133, 134, 135, 136
Antigonus III Doson, 75, 106, 137, 138, 139, 140, 142
Antiochus I Soter, 132, 177, 178, 180, 183
Antiochus III (The Great), 142, 143, 144, 161, 181, 182
Antipater, 116, 120
Antony, 161
Aoüs, 140
apella, see Assembly
Aphrodisias (in Caria), 185
Aphytis, 54
apokletoi, 103
Apollo, 50, 167
Apollonius, 149, 150
Apology, see Plato
apotheosis, 122
Appian, 167
Arabia, 123, 148
Arachosia, 117
Aratus, 136, 137, 138, 141
Aratus of Sicyon, 103, 104, 106, 135
Arcadia, 7, 8
Archilochus, 78
archon basileus, 22 note 1
archons, 18, 22-24, 26, 27, 29, 31, 33, 34, 38, 42
archonship, see archons
Areopagus, see Council of the Areopagus
Areus of Sparta, 131
Argeads, 126
Argolid, 15, 20
Argos, 18, 95, 132, 133
Aristaechmus, 25
Aristides, 50, 56
aristocracies, 91
aristocracy, 14, 18, 22, 23, 24, 61, 71, 80, 91, 96, 116, 201, 219
Aristocratic Council, see Council
Aristodemus, 133
Aristodemus of Cumae, 86
Aristogeiton, 31, 91
Aristomachus, 133
Aristophanes, 42, 78
Aristotle, 16, 18, 19, 21, 23, 24, 25, 26, 27, 28, 30, 31, 32, 33, 34, 35, 37, 47, 48, 54, 64 note 7, 69, 79, 80, 81, 82, 84, 85, 86, 87, 88, 90, 91, 99, 110, 111, 112, 116, 117, 120, 165, 166, 187-213, 214, 218
army, 45, 64
Arnold, Matthew, 11
Arrian, 114, 115, 116, 122, 147

Arsinoë, 131, 167
Artaxerxes II, 173
artisans, 27, 28, 201, 207
Asia, 106, 111, 115, 122, 129, 205
Asia (Roman province), 183, 186
Asia Minor, 5, 7, 8, 50, 127, 129, 130, 132, 142, 162, 173-186
Asianic Greeks, 130, 173, 183, 217, 218
Asiatic empire, 125
Asiatic Greeks, see Asianic Greeks
assassination, 89
Assembly
  Achaean League, 104
  Aetolian League, 102, 103, 108
  Athenian (*ekklesia*), 17, 21, 23, 24, 26, 28, 30, 33, 36, 37, 38, 39, 40, 41, 45, 47, 48, 51, 53, 54, 56, 59, 99
  Chalcidian League, 98
  Corinthian League, 100, 101
  Late Helladic, 17
  Peloponnesian League, 95, 96
  Sparta (*apella*), 65, 66, 68
  Termessus, 184
assessment of tribute, 56
assessments, 44
Assos, 190
astronomy, 195
Astyages, 82
Astypalaea, 183
asylum, 158, 159, 169-171
Athamanians, 143
Athena, 52, 53, 55
Athenagoras, 47
Athenian Confederacy, see Leagues
Athenian constitution, 19-35, 36
Athenian Council, see Council
"Athenian Stranger," 198
Athenian tradition, 215
Athens, 15, 17, 19, 20, 21, 22, 23, 24, 29, 30, 31, 32, 46, 50-60, 62, 69 note 9, 72, 73, 82, 85, 87, 88, 89, 91, 93, 95, 96, 99, 113, 126, 128, 133, 135, 137, 139, 143, 173, 179, 186, 190, 191, 198, 216, 217, 218
Atintania, 140
Attalus, 141, 143, 181, 182
Attica, 7, 15, 19, 20, 21, 22, 32, 34, 36, 37, 44, 45, 69, 216, 217
audit (of accounts), 38
autarchic state, 110
autochthony, 4
autocracy, 14

INDEX

autonomy, 93, 96, 97, 99, 102, 110, 115, 125, 126, 127, 130, 174, 175, 176, 179, 185, 219
Aymard, A., 105 note 4

B

Babylonia, 125, 126
Bactria, 114
balance of power, 116
banking, 154
barbarian invasion, *see* invasions
barbarians, 109, 111, 112, 121, 123, 146
barbarism, 217
Barker, Sir Ernest, 192
basileus, 14, 15, 16, 20, 22, 78
Beas, 122
"Beauty," 203
beehive tombs, 15, 16
Beloch, J., 31, 33, 34
"Benefactor," 165, 166, 171
benevolent paternalism, 123
bicameral parliament, 37
Bikerman, E., 135 note 1
Black Sea, *see* Euxine
Board of Ten Generals, 31, 34
bodyguard, 30, 85, 117
Boeotarch, 97
Boeotia, 8, 20, 85, 96, 97, 106
Boeotian League, *see* Leagues
Boeotians, 138
Bosporus, 183
boule, 33, 37, 39
bouleuterion, 28
Brea, 57
brewing, 154
bribery, 42, 73
Bronze Age, 14-23, 30
brotherhood of man, 109, 162, 209
building program, 30, 43, 88, 89, 117, 155, 158
bureaucracy, 156, 157, 159, 161, 167
burial practices, 6

C

Caesar, *see* Julius Caesar
Caesars, 220
calendar, 27
Callias, 52, 53, 55
Callimachus, 33
Callisthenes, 120
Calynda, 180
Campbell, L., 80 note 1
canals, 149, 155, 158
capitalism, 69
Caracalla, 123
caravan routes, 148
caravan trade, 158
Caria, 54, 115, 180, 181, 183
Carpathia, 8
Carthage, 59, 60, 157, 218
Carthaginians, 60, 84, 140
Cary, M., 105 note 4
Carystus, 51
cash crops, 217
cash payment, 51
Cassander, 125, 126, 127, 128, 175
Cassius Dio, *see* Dio Cassius
castes, 209
Castor, 20
"Catalogue of Ships," 20
cattle, 152
cattle-raiding, 19
Caunus, 178
"Cave," 195
Cecrops, 20
Celtic invasion, *see* invasions
Celts, 131
censorship, 199
central government, 151
centralized control, 151
Ceramicus, 22
Chaeron, 77
Chaeronea, 99, 190
Chalcedon, 183
Chalcidice, 8, 98
Chalcidian League, *see* Leagues
Chalcis, 101, 133, 191
Charops, 23
chauvinism, 4
Chersonese, 57, 81, 88
"Chief Accountant," 156
chieftains, 14, 61, 118
Chios, 58, 138, 174, 179
Chorasinians, 123
choruses, 43
Chremonidean War, 133, 134
Chremonides, 133
Christianity, 210
chronographers, 20, 21
Chryses, 17
Church (the), 210
Cibyra, 183
Cicero, 81

INDEX

Cilicia, 116, 125, 180
Cimon, 51
citizens, 64, 67
citizenship: 28, 44, 67, 110, 111, 112, 120, 123, 196, 207, 208, 213; common, 94, 98, 102, 105, 107, 111, 112, 119, 214
City Dionysia, 88
city-state, 36-49, 93, 100, 107, 110, 163, 164, 165, 178, 214, 215, 219, 220; *see also polis*
class struggles, 71, 83 note 3, 84, 93, 220
Clearchus, 89, 120
Cleisthenes, 32, 33, 37, 41
Cleisthenes of Sicyon, 88, 89
Cleitus, 113, 114
Cleombrotus, 74
Cleomenes, 31, 75, 76, 106, 137, 138
Cleomenes of Naucratis, 147, 148
Cleomenic War, 138
Cleon, 47, 82
Cleonymus, 57
Cleopatra, 160, 161
climate, 9, 49
Clinias, 54, 57
Cnidus, 183
coalition, 95
coalition government, 29
code of laws, 25, 27
Codrus, 18, 20, 22
coinage: 13, 53, 71, 117, 148, 151, 154, 156, 217; copper, 159; depreciation, 159; federal, 98, 103, 104, 218; monetary decree, 53, 54; monetary standard, 27; silver, 159; Spartan, 70, 73
collections, 156, 157
college of archons, 22
colonies, 99, 163
colonists, 43, 150, 155
colonization, 7, 110, 214, 215, 216
Colophon, 62, 175
commerce, 30, 70, 72, 83, 98, 148, 155, 157, 216
commercial interests, 48
"Common Interest," 202
common meals, 86, 203
common range, 153
Commonwealth of the Macedonians, 138
communism, 104, 194, 196, 209, 210, 212
commutation, 152, 184
"Companions," 113, 117
Concerning Revenues, 48
confiscation, 74, 84, 87, 90, 101
Congress of Greek cities, 219

Conooura, 64
"Contemplation," 203
co-regency, 19
"Consent," 188
conservatism, 65
constitutional monarchy, 101
Constitution of Athens (*Constitution of the Athenians*): anonymous, 47; Aristotle, 19, 27, 203
contributions, 50, 51, 96, 173, 179, 180
control of labor, 160
Corinth, 82, 84, 85, 86, 89, 95, 101, 106, 107, 131, 132, 133, 134, 135, 136, 137, 176, 219
Corinthian League, *see* Leagues
Coronea, 54
corporations, 118
Cos, 53, 54, 134, 174, 178, 181
cosmopolis, 219
Council
 Achaean League, 104, 105
 Aetolian League, 103
 Amphictyonic, 94
 Athenian: Aristocratic Council, 22; Council of the Areopagus, 17, 23, 24, 26, 28, 29, 33, 37, 38, 41; Council of Elders, 22; Council of 500, 32, 37, 39, 53, 54, 99; Council of 400, 28, 32; Council of 401, 26
 Boeotian League, 97
 Hellenic League of Philip II, 127
 Late Helladic Council of Elders, 17
 Spartan (*gerousia*), 17, 65, 66, 67, 75
Courts: federal, 101, 103; law, 28, 29, 36, 41, 42, 57, 67
Crannon, 36
Craterus, 133
Cratylus, 190
"Creator," 165, 166
Creon, 25
Crete, 5, 6, 8, 15
Crito, see Plato
Croesus, 172
Cronus, 31, 198
crown lands, 130
culture: Achaean, 215; Minoan, 5-6; Mycenaean, 6, 20
Cumae, 86
currency, *see* coinage
Cyclades, 7, 8, 135, 147
Cyclopean walls, 15, 20
Cylon, 25, 85
Cyme, 54

Cynoscephalae, 106, 144
Cyprus, 7, 127, 147
Cyrene, 147, 160
Cypselids, 88, 89
Cypselus, 91
Cythera, 8

D

Damasias, 29
Dardanians, 136, 137, 143
Darius, 113, 114, 117, 118, 122
Dark Age, 215
De Alexandri Magni Fortuna aut Virtute, 112 note 6, 121 notes 8 and 9
debt, 25, 26, 27, 28, 74, 75, 83, 101, 106
deforestation, 9
deification, 120-122, 165
delegates, 100
Delian League, *see* Leagues
Delos, 50, 52
Delphi, 94, 96, 102, 106
Delphic Amphictyony, *see* Leagues
Delphic Oracle, 31, 71
Delta, 149
demagogues, 39, 40, 59
Demaratus the Spartan, 9
demarchs, 32
demes, 32, 45
Demeter Pylaea, 94
Demetrias, 131, 133
Demetrius of Phalerum, 126
Demetrius of Pharos, 140, 141
Demetrius I Poliorcetes, 101 note 2, 125, 127, 128, 129, 130, 131, 134, 138, 176
Demetrius II, 136, 137, 139
Demetrius, son of Philip, 144
demiourgoi, 105
democracy, 12, 14, 17, 21, 26, 27, 28, 29, 32, 33, 34, 35, 36-49, 54, 57, 58, 61, 71, 80, 84, 89, 96, 103, 173, 174, 190, 193, 196, 198, 202, 206, 210, 211, 212, 213, 217, 219
democratic ideal, 47
Demosthenes, 35, 56, 99
"Desire," 204
despotism, *see* tyranny
determinism, 9
dialectic, 195, 200
dialects (Greek), 6-8
dictators, 89
dictatorship, *see* tyranny
Didyma, 120

dikaiosyne, 193
dikasts, 41, 42, 43
dikes, 149, 155, 158
dike tax, 152
Dio Cassius, 86
Diodorus, 109 note 2
Dionysius the Elder, 84, 86, 87, 88, 89
Dionysius II, 190, 197
Dionysus, 88
"Divided Line," 195
divine ruler, 219
division of labor, 187, 193
Doctrine of Ideas, 191
dogma, 212, 213
dominant culture, 123
dominant race, 123
Dorian invasion, *see* invasions
Dorians, 5, 7, 61, 64
Doson, *see* Antigonus III
Draco, 25, 26, 27, 41
drainage works, 150
drama, 30, 43
dry docks, 117
Dymanes, 64
dynaton, 204

E

Early Helladic, *see* Helladic
economic conditions, 29
economic control, 57
Edson, C. F., Jr., 126 note 1
education: 86, 89, 194-195, 199, 204, 206, 212, 213; Spartan, 67, 72
Egypt, 5, 19, 29, 75, 106, 118, 125, 127, 131, 132, 133, 134, 135, 142, 143, 167, 177, 180, 181
Ehrenberg, V., 215
ekklesia, see Assembly
Eleusis, 18, 20, 215
Elis, 139, 141
emancipation, 74
emigration, 83 note 3
empire, *see* imperialism
Endres, H., 109 note 2
entrepreneurs, 153
environment, 8-9
Epaminondas, 99
Ephesus, 181
Ephialtes, 54
ephorate, 66, 67, 75
ephors, 64, 66, 68, 70, 75
Epirotes, 138, 144

INDEX

Epirus, 18, 106, 136, 137
eponymous ephors, see ephors
equality, 38, 40, 46, 47, 48
equality of the sexes, 197
Er, see Myth of Er
Eratosthenes, 112, 121
Erechtheus, 18
Eretria, 130, 133
Erythrae, 120, 175, 177, 179
Ethica Nicomachea, 188 note 1, 192, 203, 206
ethics, 192, 196, 210, 211
ethnology, 4-8
ethnos, 93, 102
ethos, 204
Etruscan language, 5 note 2
Etruscans, 215
Euboea, 7, 51, 133, 134, 191
Euboeans, 138
Eubulus, 39
Euergetes I, see Ptolemy III
Euergetes II, see Ptolemy VIII
Eumenes of Pergamum, 144, 145
Eunomia, 63, 64, 66
eupatrids, see nobles
Euphrates, 122
Euphron of Sicyon, 84, 87
Europe (natives of), 111, 205
Eurotas, 61
Eurypontids, 19, 65
Eusebius, 20
eutaxia, 203
Euxine, 7, 8, 88, 183, 215, 217
evolution, 207
ex-archons, 24, 41
excavations, 22
exemptions, 156
experimental planting, 152
exploitation, 149, 153, 158, 218, 221
exploration, 117, 123
exports, 9, 148, 152, 154, 155, 158
expropriation, 160
"Evil," 187, 188

F

factory (Egypt one great), 157
family, 201
family groups, 214
famine, 147
farmers, 29, 70
farming, 49, 215
farming of taxes, 156

farmland, 62
Fascist Italy, 160
fatherhood of God, 109, 121
Fayûm, 150, 151
federal army, 97
federal idea, 95
federal unions, 93-108, 135
festivals, 30, 43, 45, 94, 97, 103
"Fetters of Greece," 133
feudal lord, 118
"Fifty Tribes," 34
finance, 31, 39, 40, 47, 55, 86, 103, 116, 154, 156
fines, 42
First Illyrian War, 137
First Macedonian War, 141
fisheries, 153
Flamininus, 106, 144
fleet, see sea power
"Force," 188
foreign affairs, 9, 36, 39, 40, 93, 95, 104, 107, 110, 112, 128, 216
foreigners, 32, 64, 67, 70, 71, 74
foreign policy, see foreign affairs
fortified posts, 214
"Four Tribes," 23, 26, 28, 32, 34
Fowler, H. N., 80 note 1
franchise, 48
fraternity, 46
free cities, 115, 142
freedom, 12, 219
freedom of association, 89
freedom of the seas, 55
free industry, 154
Fustel de Coulanges, N. D., 214

G

Galatian fund, 177, 179
games, 30
garrisons, 134, 139, 180, 181, 186
Gaugamela, 116, 122
Gaul, 7
Gauls, 102, 140
Gaza, 125, 126
generals: 26, 31, 33, 38, 39, 40, 41, 125; Spartan, 73
geography, 8
Geometric Age, 16
geometry, 195
German excavations, see excavations
gerousia, see Council

INDEX

gerousiasts, 66
"Gift Estates," 151, 152, 155
"Gifts," 155
Glaucon, 187
god-king, 123
God Manifest, 165
gold, 153
"Golden Mean," 35
Gonatas, *see* Antigonus II
"The Good," 195
"The Good Life," 211
Gorgias (Plato), 199
Gortyn, 62
government: 188; forms of, 14
governors, 116
governors (Spartan), *see* harmosts
Graeco-Macedonian troops, 162
grain, 9, 40, 130, 150, 151, 152, 157, 158, 180
grain market, 147
granaries (state), 151, 152
Granicus, 173
graphe paranomon, 41
great estates, 29, 61, 69 note 9, 150, 216, 220
Great King of Persia, 113, 114
Great Panathenaea, 57
Greek cities: essentially independent, 3, 114, 163; of Asia Minor, 115
Greek History (study and use of), 10-12
Greek liberty, 143
Greek political theory, 110
Greek settlements, 215
"Guardians," 194, 199
Gyges, 78
gymnasia, 86
gymnastic, 194

H

Halicarnassus, 178, 179, 180, 181
Halys, 122
Hannibal, 60, 140, 141, 142
Hannibalic War, 142
"Happiness," 204
harbors, 117, 125
Harmodius, 31, 91
"Harmony," 195
harmosts, 72, 73
Hebraism, 11
Herrenvolk, 72
hegemon, 100, 101, 107, 112, 118
hegemony, 52, 72 note 10, 73, 75, 98, 99, 128, 138, 220

Heichelheim, F. M., 214
Helladic: Early, 14, 19; Middle, 15, 20; Late, 15-22
"The Hellenes," 100
Hellenic League of Leagues, *see* Leagues
Hellenic race, 111
Hellenism, 11, 93, 217
Hellenization, 117, 162
hellenotamiai, 52, 55, 56, 57
Hellespont, 8, 50, 88
helots, 61, 62, 63, 64, 67, 68, 69, 70, 72, 74, 76, 77
Heracleia on the Euxine, 183
Heracles, 122
Heraea, 139
herding, 70
hereditary kings, 14
hereditary monarchy, 161
Hermodorus, 82
Herodotus, 9, 19, 25, 78, 82, 86, 91, 172
Heroic Age, 16
Herondas, 78
Hesiod, 215
Hieron of Syracuse, 86, 88, 89, 91
Hieronymus of Cardia, 129
Himilco, 60
Hipparchus, 26, 31, 33, 87 note 4, 88
Hippias, 31
Hippias the 'Sophist, 78
Hippomenes, 24
Homeric epics, 7, 15, 16, 18, 20, 21, 23
homicide, 27
homoioi, 65
homonoia, 121, 122
hostages, 170
hunting rights, 153
huntsmen (royal), 153
Hylleis, 64
Hymettus, 217
Hyperboulus, 40
hypomeiones, 68, 72 note 10

I

Iambulus, 219
idealism, 192, 209, 213
Ideal State, 79-80, 187-213
"Idea of the Good," 195
"Ideas," 191, 195, 197
ideology, 112
Iliad, 17, 18, 20
Ilium, 181

INDEX

Illyria, 140, 141, 142
Illyrians, 136, 137, 140, 143
"Imitation," 191
immigration, 157
impeachment, 40
imperialism, 36, 39, 43, 44, 50-60, 73, 82, 93, 98, 99, 108, 116, 161, 218, 219, 220
import quotas, 155
imports, 9, 40, 148, 154, 155
independent cities of Asia Minor, 173-186
India, 115, 116, 122, 123
"Individual," 188, 193, 212, 213
individualism, 48
Indo-Europeans, 6
Indus, 142
industrialists, 63
industrial production, 110
industry, 43, 48, 62, 70, 72, 83, 150, 155, 156, 158, 159, 160, 217
integration, 115
interest, 150
"Interest on Capital," 214
international co-operation, 96
inundation, 149, 151
invasions: barbarian, 131, 139; Celtic, 132; Dorian, 18, 20, 22, 61 note 1, 215; early, 6; Persian, 50, 96
Ion, 18
Ionia, 176, 181
Ipsus, 126, 128, 129, 130
Iran, 116, 162
irrigation, 9, 149, 151, 157
Isagoras, 32
Islanders, 15
Isocrates, 4, 91, 99, 110, 111, 112, 113, 121, 122, 218, 219
isolationism, 70, 71, 216
isopolity, 102, 112
Issus, 114
Isthmian Festival, 182
Isthmian Games, 106, 144
Italy, 7, 62, 140, 141, 143, 145, 160
Ithome, *see* Mt. Ithome

J

Jaeger, Werner, 202
Jews, 161
Joad, C. F. M., 210
Joppa, 125
Jowett, B., 58, 80 note 1, 188 note 1
Julius Caesar, 160, 184
Jupiter Capitolinus, 183

Jurors, *see* dikasts
"Justice," 193, 202, 205, 214

K

Kenyon, F. G., 25, 26
king-god, 121
King of the Macedonians, 118, 139
kings: 14-23, 79, 90, 118, 127; list of legendary, 20; Spartan, 64, 66
kingship, 201
kingship, *see* monarchy
kleros, 67
"Knowledge," 195
kolakretai, 17
Kolbe, W., 109 note 2, 117
Kornemann, E., 109 note 2
krypteia, *see* secret police

L

Lacedaemonians, 62 note 2, 68, 69 note 9
Laconia, 61, 70, 73, 76, 77, 85, 104
Laconian schools, 62
Lade, 143
Laïus, 78
Lake Trasimene, 140
Lampsacus, 176, 181, 182, 183
land, 24, 43, 160
landed proprietors, 63
landless class, 220
landowning aristocracies, 83
Larsen, J. A. O., 95 note 1, 101 note 2
Late Helladic, *see* Helladic
latifundia, 69 note 9
Laurium, 48
"Law," 205, 206
Laws (Plato), 188 note 1, 192, 197, 198, 199, 200, 201, 204, 205, 207, 208, 219 note 1
League for War against Persia, *see* Leagues
League of the Islanders, *see* Leagues
Leagues
  Achaean, 76, 102-108, 135-138, 186
  Aetolian, 94, 102-108, 135-139, 180
  Amphictyonic, 94
  Athenian Confederacy, 112; Second Athenian Confederacy, 44, 72 note 10; Second Athenian League, 99
  Boeotian, 72 note 10, 97, 138
  Chalcidian, 98
  Corinthian, 94, 100, 101, 106, 107, 120, 219

INDEX

Delian, 50-60, 218
Delphic Amphictyony, 94
Hellenic, 50, 75, 96, 127, 128, 129, 130, 134, 138, 139, 141, 144
Hellenic League of Leagues, 106, 138
League of Demetrius, 139
League of the Islanders, 125, 128, 131, 134
League for War against Persia, 53, 112
Peloponnesian, 94-96, 107, 216
religious, 94
Thessalian, 94
Leagues of: Acarnanians, Achaeans, Boeotians, Epirotes, Euboeans, Locrians, Macedonians, Phocians, Thessalians, 138
leased monopoly, 154
Lebanon, 147
Lebensraum, 62
Lebedos, 130, 176, 179
legality, 80
leisure, 203
Leonidas, 71, 74, 75
Lesbos, 8, 58, 62, 180, 183
Leuctra, 68, 74
levy, *see* contributions
lexicographers, 57
"Liberator," 177
liberty, 46, 47, 174, 175, 176, 199
library, 89, 157
Libya, 122
Limnae, 64
lion-hunts, 153
Lissus, 137, 141
liturgies, 43, 44
"Living Law," 121
Livingstone, R. W., 11 note 3
Locrians, 138
logic, 191
logos, 200, 204, 207
"Lot," *see* sortition
luxury products, 148, 155
Lyceum, 191
Lycurgus, 39, 63, 64, 71, 73, 74, 77
Lydia, 116
Lygdamus, 84
Lysander, 120
Lysimachia, 131
Lysimachus, 125, 127, 128, 129, 131, 176

M

Macedonia (*or* Macedon), 7, 18, 46, 98, 99, 100, 102, 106, 112, 114, 115, 116, 125, 127, 129, 130, 131, 132, 133, 134, 136, 137, 138, 139, 140, 141, 142, 144, 145, 175, 182, 183, 218
Macedonian army, 113, 115, 117, 129
Macedonian phalanx, 117
Macedonians, 111, 114, 116, 117, 118, 119, 120, 121, 129, 138, 161, 172
Machiavelli, 210
Magie, David, 143 note 3
magistracies, 26, 29, 38, 104
magistrates: 38, 39, 41, 42, 48, 57, 174; Spartan, 66, 67, 74
Magna Graecia, 85, 218
Magnesia-on-Maeander, 183, 186
Mallus, 115
"Manager of Economic Affairs," 156
manufacturing, 69, 153, 154
manumission, 70, 76
Marathon, 33, 36, 46, 217
Mason, A. T., 199 note 5
masses, 83, 84
mathematics, 195
"The Mean," 198, 204, 205, 206, 207, 211
measures, 53, 104
Medon, 22, 23
Medontids, 22, 23, 24
Megacles, 25
Megalopolis, 132, 133, 214
Megara, 95, 133
Melos, 59
"Melting Pot," 6, 117
Menedemus of Eretria, 130
Menidi, 20
"Men of the Coast," 29, 32
"Men of the Hills," 29, 30, 32
"Men of the Plain," 29, 32
mercenaries, 75, 76, 84, 87, 116, 118, 121, 132, 161
Merv, 117
Mesoa, 64
Meson, 204
Mesopotamia, 158, 162
Messene, 141
Messenia, 62, 139, 141, 216
Messenian Rebellion, 65
metaphysic, 189
Methymna (in Lesbos), 183
metoecs, 75
Middle Ages (Greek), 7
middle classes, 48
Middle Helladic, *see* Helladic
Midea, 17
Miletus, 86, 175, 176, 178, 180, 183, 186
militarism, 70, 217, 221

military despotism, 62
military dictators, 83 note 3
military policy, 39
military service, 197
Miltiades, 81
mines, 145, 148, 153
Minoan language, 5
Minoans, 5-6, 15
Minos, 5
Minyans, 15, 20
Mithridates (King of Pontus), 183
mixed marriages, 115
monarchy: 14-23, 34, 61, 71, 79, 80, 81, 82, 98, 99, 101, 112, 119, 198; Spartan 65
monarchy (theory of), 162-172
monetary decree, *see* coinage
money, *see* coinage
monopoly, 71, 147, 154, 155
monotheism, 197
mother-city, 214
Mt. Ithome, 141
Mummius, 107
municipalities, 101
music, 194
mutiny, 117, 119
Mycale, 50
Mycenae, 6, 15, 17, 20
Mycenaean Age, 16, 20
Mycenaean tomb, 20
Myndus, 178, 181
Myth of Er, 196, 209
Mytilene, 41, 59, 174, 183

N

Nabis, 76, 77, 144
nation, 188
national groups, 116
national industry, 155
nationalism, 3-4, 131
native rulers, 119
natives, 118
natural resources, 9
naukraries, 28, 34
naval bases, 125, 147
naval power, *see* sea power
navy, *see* sea power
Naxos, 51, 84, 181
Nazi Germany, 160
Nazism, 210, 212
Neolithic Age, 5, 19
Nepos, 81

Nicaea (widow of Alexander), 132, 134
Nicias, 59
Nicocles, 135
Nicolaus of Damascus, 91
Nicomachean Ethics, see Ethica Nicomachea
Nietzsche, 4 note 1
Nile, 149
Nilsson, M. P., 16
Nisaea, 133
nobles, 17, 18, 19, 23, 24, 25, 29, 30, 35, 74, 83, 87
Nocturnal Council, 200
nomes, 149, 150, 151, 156
nomos, 200
nomothete, 63
"Nordic Man," 4 note 1
nous, 200, 202, 204
nouveaux riches, 83

O

Octavian, 160
Odyssey, 17, 18, 20, 215
Oedipus the King, 78, 82
oekumene, 122
oil (olive), 154, 157, 158, 217
oligarchies, 125, 173
oligarchy, 14, 18, 22, 23, 24, 25, 31, 32, 35, 43, 46, 48, 61, 71, 80, 82, 84, 96, 97, 138, 196, 201, 206
olive trees, 152
Olympia, 96
Olympian Games, 25, 89
Olympus, 8, 16
Olynthus, 98
Opis, 115, 119
orators, 38, 39
orchards, 150, 152
Orchomenus, 139
oriental political theory, 219
Orthagoras, 85
Orthagorids, 89
ostracism, 21, 33, 34, 40, 56, 91
ousia, 195
over-rajah, 118
overseers, 57
overseers (Spartan), *see* ephors

P

Paeonia, 135
Pagasaean Gulf, 131

INDEX

247

palaces, 15, 16, 20
palaestrae, 86
Pamphyloi, 64
Panathenaic Festival, 88
Panathenaic year, 56
Panegyricus (Isocrates), 111
Panhellenic congress, 55
Panhellenic festivals, 128
Panhellenic ideal, 219
Panhellenic union, 100, 107
Panhellenism, 10, 111, 119, 127, 218, 220
Panionian festivals, 50
papyrus, 154, 155, 157
"Parable of the Metals," 209
Parian Marble, 20, 21, 23
Parium, 176
Parmenio, 113, 114, 115, 122
Parnes, 217
parochialism, 218, 220
Parthenon, 55
particularism, 8, 10, 93, 100, 130, 190, 207, 218, 220
particularistic nationalism, 219
party strife, 26, 29, 32, 93
pasture land, 153
patriarchy, 61
patronage of art, 89
patronomoi, 75
Paullus, *see* Aemilius Paullus
Pausanias, 14, 16, 21, 25, 35
Peace of Antalcidas, 110
Peace of Callias, 52, 53
Peace of 449, 54
Peace of Nicias, 59
Peace of Phoenice, 142, 143
Peisistratids, 87, 88
Peisistratus, 21, 25, 30, 31, 32, 33, 34, 84, 85, 87, 88, 90, 91, 216
Pelasgian language, 5 note 2
Pelasgians, 5
Peloponnese, 8, 23, 61, 73, 75, 76, 95, 96, 102, 104, 106, 132, 133, 134, 135, 136, 137, 138, 141
Peloponnesian League, *see* Leagues
Peloponnesian system, 135
Peloponnesian War, 36, 39, 44, 46, 51, 57, 59, 72, 96, 98, 218
Pelusium, 155
Pergamum, 143, 144, 181, 182
Periander, 86
Pericles, 30, 32, 33, 38, 40, 43, 45, 46, 47, 54, 55, 56, 57, 58, 59, 82, 96, 199

perioecs, 61, 62, 63, 64, 67, 68, 69, 70, 72, 74
Perseus, 106, 145, 183, 184
Persia, 52, 60, 72 note 10, 99, 111, 113, 116, 119, 121, 122, 198, 217
Persian invasions, *see* invasions
Persian nobility, 116
Persians, 46, 55, 114, 115, 116, 117, 119, 121, 147, 167, 172, 173, 174, 175, 179, 218
Persian War, 217
Peucestas, 117
Phaedo, see Plato
Pharaoh, 118
Pharaohs (the), 148, 149
Pheidon of Argos, 80
"Phenomena," 191, 195
Pherae, 85
Phila, 132
Philadelphus, *see* Ptolemy II
Philhellenism, 129
Philip II, 94, 99, 100, 101, 112, 113, 114, 121, 122, 132, 190, 219
Philip V, 76, 106, 139, 140, 141, 142, 143, 144, 145, 182
Philopator, *see* Ptolemy IV
Philopoemen, 106
philosophe sans le savoir, 189
Philotas, 113, 114
Phocians, 138
Phocis, 106
Phoenice (in Epirus), 137
Phoenicia, 52, 116, 125, 147
Phoenicians, 148, 215
phoros, see tribute
Phthia (Epirote princess), 136
Phylarchus, 74
phylo-basileis, 23
physis, 204
Pillars of Heracles, 122
Pindar, 86, 88, 89
piracy, 19, 137
Piraeus, 58, 128, 133, 135
pirates, 125, 157, 169, 170
Pisidia, 183
Pitana, 64
planned economy, 147-161
Plarasa (in Caria), 185
Plataea, 50, 68, 217
Plato: 23, 47, 48, 74, 79, 80, 91, 99, 110, 111, 112, 165, 187-213, 218, 219 note 1; *Apology*, 12; *Crito*, 12; *Phaedo*, 190. *See also Gorgias, Laws, Politicus, Republic*
plethos, 209

Pleuratus, 141, 143
Plutarch, 35, 51, 54, 69 note 9, 112 note 6, 121
plutocracy, 14
poleis, 173
Polemarch, 18, 22 note 1, 23, 33
poletai, 31
police, 156
Poliorcetes, *see* Demetrius I
polis, 110, 111, 112, 119, 174, 176, 185, 193, 214, 215; *see also* city-state
politeia, see polity
Politica (Aristotle), *see Politics*
political exiles, 120
political instincts, 214
political patchwork, 119
"Politics," 192, 195, 196, 210, 211
politics, 14, 34
Politics (Aristotle), 19, 28, 80, 90, 91, 188 note 1, 192, 200, 202, 203, 204, 205, 207, 208, 209
Politicus (Plato), 79, 91, 201
polity, 80, 201, 206, 207
poll tax, 155
Polybius, 46, 81, 105 note 4, 107, 172
Polycrates of Samos, 86, 88
Polymnestus, 62
Pontus, 123, 157, 183
Popular Assembly, *see* Assembly
Post-Helladic Period, 18
poverty, 111
"Power," 188
Prentice, W. K., 83 note 3
prepon, 204
price-fixing, 147, 154, 160
Priene, 176, 179, 181, 183
priesthood, 161
priests, 147, 150, 156, 158, 159
primus inter pares, 16
primitive society, 214
primogeniture, 67
Prince (Machiavelli), 210
private ownership, 150, 152, 215
private property, 160, 194 196, 197
private traders, 154
privileged minority, 48
profit, 153, 154
proletariat, 48
propaganda, 62
"Property Income," 160
property qualifications, 26, 27, 36, 45, 48, 105
Propontis, 8, 173

prostration, 120
protectorate: Athenian, 88; Macedonian, 135 note 1; Roman, 140
Proto-Geometric Period, 18, 22
Prytaneis, 23, 37
Prytaneum, 91
Ptolemaeus, 131
Ptolemaic Egypt, 147-161
Ptolemies, 172
Ptolemy I Soter (son of Lagus), 125, 127 128, 129, 131, 147, 148, 167
Ptolemy II Philadelphus, 131, 133, 134, 148, 150, 152, 157, 158, 161, 167, 177, 178, 180
Ptolemy III Euergetes I, 138, 158, 161, 181
Ptolemy IV Philopator, 142, 161
Ptolemy V Epiphanes, 143
Ptolemy VIII Euergetes II, 159, 161
Ptolemy Ceraunus, 131
public baths, 154
public health officer, 156
public opinion, 39
public ownership of land, 74
public threshing floors, 151
public works, *see* building program
Punjab, 118
puppet government, 84
Pydna, 106, 145
Pyrrhus, 129, 131, 132, 136
Pythagoreans, 165
Pythian Games, 89

Q

quarries, 148, 153

R

racial arrogance, 221
racial purity, 9
racial superiority, 219
Raphia, 142
rationing (of consumers' goods), 160
raw materials, 158
realism, 192
"Reality," 191, 195, 213
real property, 160
"Reason," 195, 202
rebellion, 62, 70
reclamation, 149, 150, 157
reconsideration, 41
reforms, 25, 26, 29, 32, 64, 74-76

INDEX

refugees, 40
regimentation, 73
registration (of transfers of property), 154
religion: Minoan, 5; Athenian, 45
rents, 150, 151, 152, 153, 156, 158
reports, 156
representation, 37, 97, 100
representative government, 100, 103, 107
representatives, 95
Republic (Cicero), 81
Republic (Plato), 91, 187, 192, 193, 194, 196, 197, 199, 200, 208, 209, 219 note 1
requisition, 151
resident aliens, 32, 36, 44, 48, 197
Revenue Laws (Apollonius), 149, 154
Revolt of Naxos, 51
Revolt of the Athenian Allies, 60
revolution, 18, 27, 41, 71, 74, 76, 83, 85, 106
Rhodes, 8, 125, 127, 143, 183, 186
Rhodians, 182
"Right," 198
right of appeal, 28
"Rights of Man," 63
roads, 15
Roma (deified), 182
Roman domination, 146
Roman Empire, 107, 123
Roman politicians, 160
Romans, 76, 77, 142, 164
Rome, 99, 106, 107, 108, 136, 137, 140, 141, 143, 144, 145, 146, 157, 158, 159, 161, 172, 182, 183, 184, 185, 186, 218, 220
Rose, H. J., 112 note 5
Ross, W. D., 188 note 1
Roxana, 114, 125, 126
royal court, 161
"Royal Cultivators," 150
royal domain, 19
royal estates, 180
"Royal Herdsmen," 152
"Royal Land," 150, 151, 152
Royal Stoa (at Athens), 27
"Rulers," 194-195
ruling races, 116

S

"Sacred Land," 150, 151, 152
Saint Joan, 187
Salamis, 34, 46, 50, 217
Salamis (in Cyprus), 127
sales tax, 154

Samos, 7, 8, 57, 86, 174, 178, 181, 183
Sardis, 62
satraps, 114, 116, 147
"Savior," 165, 166, 171
"Savior Gods," 167
Scepsis, 176
Scerdilaidas, 141
Schliemann, H., 6
School of Hellas, 217
scientific institute, 157
Scythian tribes, 123
sea power: 5, 58, 125, 134, 148, 157, 217, 218; Athenian, 28, 45, 51, 57, 59; Carthaginian, 140, 141; Egyptian, 177, 179; Persian, 50
secession, 104
Second Athenian Confederacy, *see* Leagues
Second Athenian League, *see* Leagues
secret ballot, 42
secret police, 70, 86, 89
sectionalism, *see* particularism
seed-loan, 150
seisachtheia, 27
Seleucid Empire, 158
Seleucids, 132, 158, 162-172, 181, 183, 185, 186
Seleucus I Nicator, 125, 126, 127, 129, 131, 162, 167, 176, 177
Seleucus II Callinicus, 178, 179, 181
self-sufficiency, 71, 148, 152, 158, 160, 203, 221
Sellasia, 75, 138, 139, 170
Senate (Roman), 143, 144, 145, 182, 183, 184
separatism, 77
sequestration (of the crop), 151, 156
serfdom, 61, 83
serfs, 25, 62, 63, 67, 69, 77, 219
Seventh Epistle, 190
shaft graves, 15
Shaw, G. B., 187
shipboards, *see* naukraries
shipbuilding, 161
shipyards, 125
Shorey, P., 188 note 1
Sicilian Expedition, 37
Sicily, 7, 59, 60, 85, 157
Sicyon, 84, 135
Sigeum, 88
silver, 153, 158
silvermines, 34, 48
Simonides, 88
Siphnos, 54

250

INDEX

slave economy, 208
slave labor, 48, 220
slavery, 24, 25, 26, 48, 72, 83, 196, 197, 201, 208
slaves, 32, 36, 44, 48, 63, 154, 219
Smyrna, 54, 178, 179, 181, 182
socialism, 61-77
social revolution, 74, 76, 101, 107, 138
Social War, 139, 141
"Society," 188
Socrates, 12, 13, 42, 47, 79, 82, 187, 190, 194
Sogdiana, 114
Soli, 115, 180
Solon, 25, 26, 27-29, 32, 33, 34, 35, 41, 172, 216
Sophocles, 57, 78, 82
Sophron, 134
sortition, 27, 33, 37, 38, 41, 42, 44, 47
"Soul," 193, 199
Soviet Russia, 160
Sparta, 17, 18, 19, 46, 50, 55, 58, 61-77, 95, 96, 97, 98, 100, 104, 106, 107, 132, 133, 134, 137, 138, 139, 141, 144, 190, 215, 216, 217, 218
Spartans, 113
Spartiatai, 72 note 10
spies, 70
Sporades, 7, 8
Stageira, 190
Stalin, 160
standardization, 70
stasis, 71, 74
"State," 188, 193
state land (Spartan), 68
state monopolies, 154
state (origin), 214
static society, 218
"Statism," 208, 209, 210, 212
status quo, 126
stereometry, 195
stewards, *see hellenotamiai*
Stoa Poikile, 21
Stoics, 219
Stoicism, 131
storage, 150, 151
Strabo, 112 note 6, 121 note 8
Strait of Mermeris, 173
Strassburg Papyrus, 56
strategia, 38, 54, 116
strikes, 159
subject cities, 115
subsidies, 39, 43, 49

subsistence farming, 216
subventions, 150, 157
"Successors," 126, 129, 162, 219
successor states, 164
super-tyrant, 81
surplus population, 110
surprise vote, 41
surveying tax, 152
Sweden, 34
synedrion, 127, 128, 139
symmachy, 95, 111, 139
symmoria, 44
sympolity, 98, 102, 104, 112
synkletos, 104, 105 note 4
Synod, 99
synodos (Achaean), 105
synoecism (of Attica), 215
synoecisms, 130
synthesis, 119
Syracuse, 47, 60, 84, 86, 190
Syria, 116, 132, 142, 143, 147, 158, 162, 172
Syrian Wars, 167
syssitia, 68
"System" of tyrants, 135

T

Tabae, 183
Tarentum, 62, 141, 216
tariff, 154
Tarn, W. W., 103 note 3, 105 note 4, 109 notes 1 and 2, 113, 115, 120, 121
Tarquinius Superbus, 86
taxation, *see* taxes
taxes: 44, 88, 130, 145, 147, 150, 151, 152, 153, 154, 155, 156, 157, 158, 160, 186; direct, 87; income, 44; license, 153; on slaves, 154; property, 44; remission of, 159; special, 156; trades, 154
tax farmers: 156, 157, 158, 159; Roman, 184
Taylor, A. E., 188 note 1
Tegea, 216
teleology, 192, 203
Telesinus, 33
temple-robbery, 87
tenant farmers, 24
"Ten Tribes," 31, 32
tenure of office, 38
Teos, 130, 176, 179
Termessus (in Pisidia), 184, 185
Terpander, 62
Teuta, 137, 140

INDEX

textiles, 154, 157
thalassocracy, 125
Thaletas, 62
theater, 43
Theater of Dionysus, 45
Thebans, 74, 113
Thebes, 15, 97, 101, 190
"The Lacedaemonians and Their Allies," *see* Peloponnesian League
Themistocles, 34, 46
"The Old Oligarch," 47
"Theocracy," 197
"Theodicy," 197
Thermopylae, 71, 74, 217
Thermum, 103
Theron of Acragas, 88, 89
Thersites, 17
Theseus, 20, 21, 25, 215
thesmothetes (or *thesmothetai*), 24, 38
Thessalian League, *see* Leagues
Thessalians, 138
Thessaly, 8, 23, 85, 102, 106, 132, 135, 137
thetes, *see* artisans
"The Thirty," 82
tholos tombs, *see* beehive tombs
Thompson, H., 28
Thoricus, 20
Thrace, 7, 8, 50, 125, 143, 144, 190
Thrasybulus, 86
Thucydides, 14, 16, 19, 21, 25, 36, 40, 46, 47, 51, 58, 79, 82, 88
Thucydides, son of Milesias, 56
Tigris, 117
timber, 127, 147, 152, 161
timocracy, 14, 196
Timophanes of Corinth, 84
tin, 153
Tiryns, 15, 17
tode ti, 191
to ta hautou prattein, 194
totalitarianism, 160, 192, 193, 208
Toynbee, A. J., 4 note 1, 219
trade, 19, 43, 49, 62, 70, 71, 73, 110, 117, 148, 152, 154, 158, 159, 216, 217, 218
traders, 63
"Trades," 197
trading centers, 214
transient population, 118
transportation, 150, 151, 152
Trasimene, *see* Lake Trasimene
treason, 113

treasurers, 27
Treasurers of Athena, 55, 56
Treasurers of the Other Gods, 55
treasury, 26, 52
Treasury of Atreus, 16
tribal group, 94
tribal organizations, 215
tribes: Athenian, 23, 28, 31, 32, 33, 38; Spartan, 64, 66
tribute, 39, 43, 51, 53, 54, 57, 73, 96, 128, 177, 179, 180, 182, 186, 218
tribute quota-lists, 52, 53, 54, 56
trittyes, 28, 32
Troad, 175, 178, 181
Troy, 20, 111
"Truth," 195
Turkestan, 116
tyrannicides, *see* Harmodius and Aristogeiton
tyrannies, 173
tyrannis, 30, 82
tyrannos, 30, 78, 82
tyranny, 14, 25, 30, 31, 33, 34, 40, 61, 76, 78-92, 80, 102, 134, 135, 196, 201, 209, 210, 211
tyrants, 82, 104, 115, 134, 135
Tyre, 122, 125
Tyrians, 113
Tyrtaeus, 62

U

ultimatum, 143
union of Attic towns, 21-22
"Universals," 191
Ure, P. N., 85
usurpation, 82
usurper, 79, 81, 89
Utopia, *see* Ideal State
Utopias, 218

V

vagrancy, 111
Ventris, N. G. F., 5 note 2
villages, 214
vines, 9, 152
vineyards, 150, 152
"Vision," 195
Vita Alexandri, 121 note 10
voluntary association, 220

W

wages, 160
Ways and Means, 48
weights, 53, 104
Wilcken, U., 109 note 2
wine, 158, 217
women (Spartan), 69
world domination, 59
world empire, 220
World State, 109-124
world unity, 123
written law, 41
writing, 6

X

xenelasia, 70
Xenophon, 48, 65, 69 note 9, 71, 79, 82, 85, 91
Xerxes, 34, 116

Z

Zeno, 130, 219
Zeus, 16, 105, 120
Zimmern, A. E., 16, 34